LAURENCE KELLY, author of *Lermontov: tragedy in the Caucasus* and recently a biography of Alexander Griboyedov, is the editor of the Traveller's Companion series. Born in Brussels and educated at New College, Oxford, where he read history, he joined the Life Guards in 1950 and served in the Foreign Office. The son of a former British ambassador to Russia, he has been a regular visitor to St Petersburg for many years.

Praise for *St Petersburg: A Travellers' Companion*

'An indispensable anthology of writing about the city from earliest days to the Revolution.'   *Harpers & Queen*

'Enthralling reading . . . a well-balanced selection that affords marvellous glimpses of its grandeur and its grimness, its magnificence and its horrors. For the contemporary tourist it will add much-needed substance and flavour to the bare factual bones all too often served up by modern Intourist guides.'
                    Elisabeth de Stroumillo, *Daily Telegraph*

'With this guide or "topographical anthology" in his pocket, the modern traveller may relive some of the great events of history in the places where they actually occurred . . . Even for those who may never visit Leningrad, this book will be a source of enjoyment and interest.'   Denis J. B. Shaw, *British Book News*

'A rich gallimaufry of impressions of the Tsarist city from early days to the eve of revolution.'   *The Tablet*

'An indispensable guide to the heart of Russian history and culture.'   John Rae, *Universe*

'Future visitors will be grateful to Mr Kelly. He has provided them with a sort of anthology, or bedside book, which seems to me just what is needed to supplement and bring alive the conventional and necessary guide book – a conversational tour of the centuries with glances down all sorts of human byways it would take months to discover in the ordinary way, all contained in a manageable paperback of 300 p
                    Ed

'Altogether this is a most evocative b
a (fortunately) vanished past.'
                    John M

Other titles in the Traveller's Companion series
(Series Editor Laurence Kelly)

A TRAVELLER'S COMPANION TO
ST PETERSBURG

SELECTED AND INTRODUCED BY

Laurence Kelly

ROBINSON
London

Constable & Robinson Ltd
3 The Lanchesters
162 Fulham Palace Road
London W6 9ER
www.constablerobinson.com

First published in the UK as *St Petersburg: A Travellers' Companion*
by Constable and Co. Ltd, 1981

This revised edition published by Robinson,
an imprint of Constable & Robinson Ltd, 2003

A copy of the British Library Cataloguing in
Publication data is available from the British Library

ISBN 1-84119-707-6

Printed and bound in the EU

10 9 8 7 6 5 4 3 2 1

For my children,
in the hope that they will visit
the place described here and find the *genius loci*

Contents

THE BRONZE HORSEMAN, AND THE DECEMBRIST REVOLT ON SENATE SQUARE (THEN CALLED ST ISAAC'S SQUARE)

THE ADMIRALTY

THE NEVA

THE SUMMER GARDEN

THE YUSUPOV PALACE ON THE MOIKA CANAL

THE MARIINSKY THEATRE AND THEATRE STREET

THE APPROACHES TO ST PETERSBURG
FOUR PALACES IN THE COUNTRY

PETERHOF

TSARSKOYE SELO AND THE LYCÉE

LIFE, CUSTOMS AND MORALS
IN ST PETERSBURG

Illustrations

The Bronze Horseman – Falconet's sculpture of Peter the Great (1782) on Senate Square, by K. P. Beggrow. *(Courtesy of the Ashmolean Museum, Oxford)*, p. 19

Monplaisir: the summer-house of Peter the Great and Catherine the Great at Peterhof, by J. Meyer, engraved by Dazziaro. *(Courtesy of the Ashmolean Museum, Oxford)*, p. 185

Two o'clock on the Nevsky Prospekt': *c.* 1830, artist unknown. *(Courtesy of the State Literary Museum, Moscow)*, p. 243

Plate sections

The Bronze Horseman and Evgeny, from Alexander Pushkin's poem by A. Benois, 1905. *(Courtesy of the 'Pushkin' State Museum of Representational Art, Moscow)*

'The Czar Peter the Great founds the city of Petersburg' by P. A. Novelli, *c.* 1797. *(Courtesy of the Ashmolean Museum, Oxford)*

The Winter Palace, by K. P. Beggrow, *c.* 1822. *(Courtesy of the State Russian Museum, Leningrad)*

The Great Fire of 1837 at the Winter Palace, by F. Wolff. *(Courtesy of the Ashmolean Museum, Oxford)*

Cavalry charge on the Champ de Mars, St Petersburg. Illustration from *La Sainte Russie*, by Comte Paul Vassili

The Emperor Paul I drilling his soldiers before the Mikhailovsky Castle, by A. Benois. *(Courtesy of the Ashmolean Museum, Oxford)*

The Great Flood of 1824: engraving by an unknown artist from *Pushkin's St Petersburg*, by A. M. Gordin.

Nicholas I takes command of his troops, facing the 'Decembrists' on Senate Square, 1825, by C. Collmann. *(Courtesy of Novosti Press Agency, London)*

The poet Alexander Pushkin speaking to the hero of his poem, *Eugene Onegin*, from the frontispiece of the first edition, 1833, by E. Notbeck. *(Courtesy of the State Literary Museum, Moscow)*

Alexander I attends the *Te Deum* at the Kazan Cathedral for the deliverance of his people in 1812, by I. Ivanov. *(Courtesy of the Ashmolean Museum, Oxford)*

The Fortress of St Peter and St Paul, with the Rostral Column in the foreground, by I. Ivanov. *(Courtesy of the Ashmolean Museum, Oxford)*

The Marriage-Fair in the Summer Garden, from *Les Mystères de la Russie*, by F. Lacroix, 1845. *(Courtesy of the Ashmolean Museum, Oxford)*

Constables punish prostitutes by making them sweep the Nevsky Prospekt, from *Les Mystères de la Russie*, by F. Lacroix, 1845. *(Courtesy of the Ashmolean Museum, Oxford)*

The mock-execution of Fyodor Dostoyevsky on the Semyonovsky Square, 1849. *(Courtesy of the Museum of St Peter and St Paul and of the History of Leningrad, Leningrad)*

The Assassination of the Tsar Alexander II on the Ekaterininsky Embankment, 1881, artist unknown. *(Courtesy of the Novosti Press Agency, London)*

The 'Institute for the Education of Well-Born Young Ladies' by the Smolny Monastery, by I. Ivanov, 1815. *(Courtesy of the State Hermitage Museum, Leningrad)*

The Palace of Paul I at Pavlovsk, by G. Lory, 1805. *(Courtesy of the State Hermitage Museum, Leningrad)*

The Palace of Peterhof, by M. I. Makhayev, c. 1756–1760. *(Courtesy of the Ashmolean Museum, Oxford)*

Catherine II's entry into St Petersburg, accompanied by the Orlov brothers, after the coup which made her Empress of all the Russias, by P. A. Novelli, c. 1797. *(Courtesy of the 'Pushkin' State Museum of Representational Art, Moscow)*

Catherine the Great walking her greyhound in the gardens of Tsarskoye Selo, by V. Borovikovsky. *(Courtesy of the Novosti Press Agency, London)*

The Wedding-feast of Peter the Great's dwarfs, 1710, in Prince Menshikov's house, by R. F. Zubov. *(Courtesy of the 'Pushkin' State Museum of Representational Art, Moscow)*

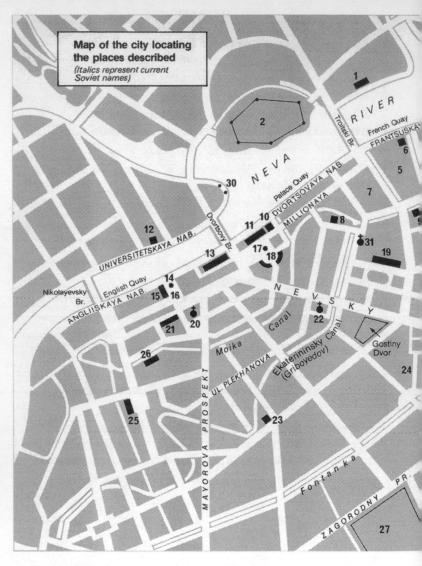

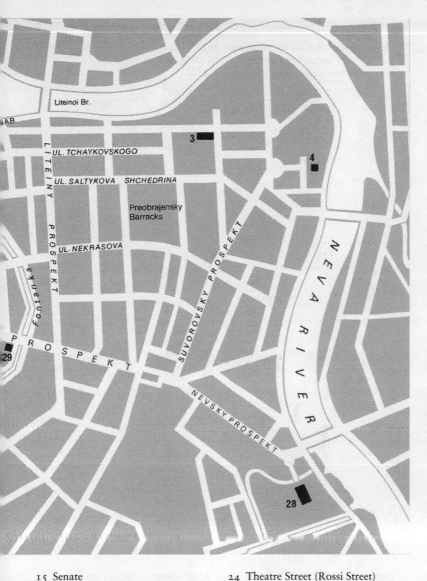

Acknowledgements

I wish to thank most warmly for excellent suggestions as to contents or presentation the following: George Vasiltchikov, Kyril Zinoviev, George Galitzine, Philip Longworth, Thomas Pakenham, and my wife Linda; my mother, Marie Noële Kelly, for a number of helpful translations from French texts; Maria Ellis and Shila Ladak for their help in a thousand ways apart from the chores of typing; my editor at Constable & Company, Mrs P. Fay, whose suggestions were all adopted with pleasure; Patrick Leeson, who drew the map; and Serenissima, whose lecture tour in 1978 gave me the idea of this book.

I also wish to make acknowledgement to the following for extracts used from their editions, translations, or where copyright permission was needed:

P. Descargues and Thames & Hudson for *The Hermitage*; Hutchinson Publishing Group for *An Ambassador's Memoirs 1914–1917* by Maurice Paléologue, translated by Edith Bone; Granada Publishing and Elek Books for *Charles Cameron* by Isobel Rae, for *Rebel on the Bridge* by Glyn Barratt and for *Dostoyevsky: his life and work* by Ronald Hingley; David

Higham Associates and Sir Sacheverell Sitwell for *Valse des Fleurs*; University of Massachusetts Press and Helen Saltz Jacobson who edited and translated Alexander Nikitenko's *The Diary of a Russian Censor* (1975); Faber & Faber and Christopher Marsden for *Palmyra of the North*; A. D. Peters and Robert Byron for *First Russia, then Tibet*; Cambridge University Press and Clarence Brown for *Mandelstam*; Routledge and Kegan Paul and V. Nabokov for *Eugene Onegin: A novel in Verse by Aleksandr Pushkin*, translated from the Russian with a *Commentary* (in four volumes); *The Listener* for William Gerhardie's *Memories of St Petersburg*; The Marquess of Londonderry and H. Montgomery Hyde for *The Russian Journals of Martha and Catherine Wilmot 1803–1808*; John Murray (Publishers) and W. A. L. Seaman and J. R. Sewell for *The Russian Journal of Lady Londonderry 1836–37*; John Calder and Kyril Fitzlyon for *The Memoirs of Princess Dashkov*; Mrs David Magarshack for translations made by her late husband from Gogol's *Nevsky Avenue*, Goncharov's *Oblomov*, Tolstoy's *Anna Karenina*, and from his own life of Pushkin; Stanford University Press and Anatole Mazour for *The First Russian Revolution 1825*; Sir Charles Johnston, who published his own translation of Pushkin's *Eugene Onegin*; Progress Publishers, Moscow and Irina Zheleznova for *The Bronze Horseman* by Pushkin, and *The Captain's Daughter*, also by Pushkin (anonymous translation); Penguin Books and Paul Foot for *Hadji Murad* by Tolstoy; Edward Arnold and James H. Bater for *St Petersburg: Industrialisation and Change*; Constable & Co. and Philip Longworth for *The Three Empresses*; Robert Maguire, John Malmstad and Harvester Press for *Petersburg* by Andrei Bely; and Frank Cass & Co. for *A Tour of Russia, Siberia and the Crimea, 1792–1794*, by John Parkinson, edited by William Collier.

All the extracts have been reprinted as they originally appeared, which accounts for apparent discrepancies.

My thanks also go to the following persons who either obtained for me pictures or made pertinent suggestions, and to the Keepers and Institutes which they represent:

Madame I. S. Tchistova, and the Soviet Academy of Sciences

(Pushkin House), Leningrad; Madame L. N. Belova, and The Peter and Paul Fortress Museum, ('Commandant's House'), belonging to the Museum of the History of Leningrad; Mr A. Polyakov, *Inotdel*, and Madame Komelova, of the State Hermitage Museum, Leningrad; Madame V. Akopdjanova, and The State Literary Museum, Moscow; Mr J. K. Gordon, Cultural Attaché, British Embassy, Moscow; Mr C. Mallaby, Foreign & Commonwealth Office; HE Sir C. Keeble, HBM Ambassador, Moscow; Monsieur N. Wyrubov, Paris; Prince and Princess N. Lobanov Rostovsky, London; Professor I. Zilbershtein, Moscow; Miss Noelle Brown, The Ashmolean Museum, Oxford; Mrs Larissa Haskell; Madame N. Borisovskaya and Madame N. I. Aleksandrovna of the Department of Prints, State Museum of Representational Arts ('Pushkin'), Moscow; Mrs S. Alford, and the Novosti Press Agency, London, Mr M. Higgins and the staff of the London Library.

L.K.
1981

Introduction

The Grand Tours of Lords Burlington and Bristol replaced by 'packages' of Lord Thomson; the claims of groups given priority over those of the individual; the search for the rare, interesting, and beautiful compressed within a fortnight's holiday, time being now of the essence in a world where charter jets have to be sardine-filled to capacity, hotels cost-effectively pre-booked, and guides programmed on a semi-industrial basis: how the estate of the tourist has fallen since the eighteenth century!

In East Europe and the Soviet Union, where the claims of the 'collective' and the masses are exalted, the practice of travel by group has been fine tuned by Intourist and its equivalents. A tribute should be paid to these loyally industrious Soviet shepherds and shepherdesses manoeuvring their unpredictable (and often monoglot) Western flock through trial after trial, reconciling the rule book with the whims of these undisciplined, often tiresome, consumers. In a society where the State should see to all, the Western tourist would indeed be in grave difficulties without the help of his shepherds. Not speaking the language, unable to read any notices, stranded for transport, competing as an individual against the group, a Kon-Tiki helpless in the wake of those flotillas of Intourist buses, how could the lone tourist extract any pleasure from a few days spent battling for survival outside the System? Wisdom surely dictates a temporary surrender to the latter with grace. There is a moral for tourists in the story of those ambassadors of King Alexander II of Kakhetia, south of the Caucasus, sent to Moscow to Tsar Fyodor Ivanovitch in 1589–90, who, to their dismay, were confined to their quarters. When Russian envoys returned the compliment and visited Kakhetia, King Alexander pointedly remarked that they were free to go about his kingdom as they pleased, in stark contrast to the treatment of the Kakhetians. 'No,' replied the smooth-tongued envoys, 'our great Sovereign did not keep your ambassadors locked up. They were free to ride wherever they wanted, but they had to be accompanied by attendants for their own safety.'[1] Intourist, legatees of this long tradition in Russia, which requires foreigners to be insulated against little local difficulties, perhaps deserves our understanding. 'Security' has different meanings for host and guest.

In this battle where thesis is propounded by the Intourist shepherd, and anti-thesis querulously and often pointlessly requested by the tourist-sheep, victory usually lies with the home-team, after all on their ground. But there is one flaw to the whole package. Information may be readily available about palaces, Kremlins, cathedrals, museums, monuments and churches, all the five-star attractions so magnificently restored or maintained, now that tourism has been accepted as a major economic activity generating a massive contribution to the foreign currency reserves of the State. But what information? Factual, doubtless, but what kind of facts? The facts available on the spot, or predigested in guidebooks, are usually quantitative in character: so many tons of marble, so many kilos of malachite, bronze, copper in this artefact of culture, or that statue; the lectures on icons, possibly

---

[1] *Russian Embassies to the Georgian Kings 1589–1605*, ed. W. E. D. Allen, Cambridge University Press, 1970.

objective, are technical in subject matter: problems of dating, varnish, oils, of high or low lights, the School of Pskov versus that of Suzdal, a vocabulary of the art-historian perhaps not too interested in the ideas or spiritual content of Rublev, more in his technique. Similarly, how often are portraits analysed as only of interest in terms of brush-work, light and shade, artistic pedigree, in fact any technicality, and not in terms of the relevance historically of the sitter? And as for the palaces, 'ways of life of the former landed classes', a catalogue of architectural styles and the idiosyncrasies of plasterwork and pillars, are pale substitutes for the raw stuff of history that was made within their walls by individuals.

The Muse of history, as far as mass tourism, its shepherds and its sheep are concerned, sleeps. There is a risk that sixty years of teaching in post-Revolutionary schools has forever dimmed the chances of a presentation focusing on history as it took place, whether in the Kremlin, Hermitage, or in the fastnesses of the Caucasus. I recall (on a lecture tour in 1978) reading extracts of Catherine the Great's *Memoirs* (to a group of English travellers), recounting how she took power, using the house of Monplaisir at Peterhof as her spring-board. These memorable pages describe incredible, reckless play for the highest stakes. My shepherdess, extremely well-educated, told me with sorrow she had never been able to get a copy of this, a key source-book to the history of St Petersburg and Russia. And so it is with most other memoirs and similar source material. The tourist, however much he has dipped into a competent biography of Alexander I or Nicholas I, could hardly, for practical reasons alone, crowd into his luggage the relevant eye witness accounts directly connected with their reigns: a description, for instance, of the Decembrist revolt of 1825, unforgettably associated with the Senate Square; or that given by John Reed so vividly of the 'storming' of the Winter Palace, in his *Ten Days that Shook the World*, conveying the hectic chaos of those first hours when the world of Nicholas II and Kerensky collapsed before that of Lenin. The factual, quantitative recital of mildly boring 'cultural' information, whether about art, architecture, or even general history, cannot take the place of the voices of the makers of history, or of their observant contemporaries, and by extension of the liveliest authority on the period (often out of print). It is intriguing that of the great series of Murray's handbooks, the one dealing with France in the second half of the nineteenth century recommended to its readers homework in the following terms: 'There are three authors whose works should be perused before entering France: Caesar for its ancient history, Froissart in his Chronicles for its feudal history, and Arthur Young for the picture of France before the Great Revolution.' A similar recommendation could be made for Russia.

There are indeed some anthologies that have resurrected Russia's history, customs and manners in this spirit. Cross's *Russia Under Western Eyes 1517–1825* and Francesca Wilson's *Muscovy: Russia Through Foreign Eyes 1553–1900* are excellent, and are evocatively illustrated. But they suffer from important *lacunae* as far as the tourist is concerned. These extracts are not related specifically to topography or places which the tourist would be likely to visit, and by definition Russian contributions, whether from history or literature, are excluded. A seductive case, too, can be made out for invoking the help of the Muses of poetry and letters, as well as that of history, to bring to life key aspects in history where they happened: Tolstoy's *Hadji Murad*, his account of the sack of Moscow in *War and Peace*, Lermontov's *Tale for Children* on the romantic vision of the city, Pushkin on the flood of 1824: why should such material be neglected? Between the Scylla of a limited cubic capacity of one's suitcase, and the Charybdis of guidebooks (and indeed guides) telling the traveller facts that fail to recreate the key events of history, there would seem to be a need for a new Traveller's Companion, a topographical anthology.

No sooner, however, has this desirable aim been stated, than its severe limitations appear. What if there is no appropriate document? No chronicler? No Pushkin nor Lermontov nor Tolstoy, whose poetry or prose is to immortalize the event or place? The reader must decide whether the art of selection, applied to the available material, has justified this book. It should save him hours in the private or public library, an attack of backache were he to lug around a heavy suitcase full of the appropriate source-books and, it is hoped, it will yield him the lively pleasure of recapturing the past as vividly as our elders could hand it down to us; truth, varnished or not, closer to the event or place than a guidebook or guide can usually provide. Manners and morals are as entertaining and illuminating, in some contexts, as historical events themselves. And literature has been also quarried for that indefinable, the spirit of place.

No single section, dealing with a specific place to be visited, should take the reader more than fifty minutes to read, say, on the preceding evening. More would be too demanding in the context of a Soviet package. The material has been arranged, as far as is possible, chronologically by place. There are doubtless as many sins of omission as of commission. For example, it may be pointed out that whilst an exciting number of major historical events in the history of the city have been described – the seizure of power by Elizabeth and Catherine, thanks to the Guards; the murder of Paul I; the suppression of the Decembrists – and placed in the context of the buildings and squares where these dramatic events happened, other equally dramatic moments, not only of Petersburg's history but of Russia's, are missing: Peter's interrogation and torture, unto death, of his own son Alexis in 1718 in the Fortress of St Peter and St Paul; his waterborne announcement to the burghers of the Peace of Nystad in 1721 which 'opened the window' on to the Baltic and Europe; the first night of Gogol's *The Government Inspector*, encouraged so unexpectedly by Nicholas I; Father Gapon on 'Bloody Sunday' in 1905 seeing the workers in the Palace Square being shot down. There is only one excuse: this is an anthology and not an exhaustive history.

It would have been satisfying to have included in this anthology standard guidebook information. Practical considerations of space excluded this. Furthermore, a good guidebook needs frequent updating. There seems to be no alternative but to travel with two books: one of the excellent guides currently available (Nagel, Louis, Cross, etc.) and a second one, left to the reader's imagination!

* * *

'Petersburg is Russian but it is not Russia' – Nicholas I, quoted by the Marquis de Custine.[1]

The stupendous phenomenon of the creation of Petersburg, (so called after St Peter and not Peter the Great) tends to be taken for granted by the visitor of the 1980s. One hundred and eighty years ago, the spirit of the Founder still moved one Western traveller to refer to 'these prodigious piles of stones, these temples and palaces, these canals, these bridges, . . . the work of our times, of our generation',[2] and to remind us, in the ornate prose of the 1800s, that 'on the marshy shores of the gulf of Finland, under an inhospitable sky, buried in fogs and snow, stood a miserable village, inhabited by fishermen, gaining their scanty sustenance from the produce of the sea. At a command of a prince this rude and savage spot, abandoned by nature, and deserted by mankind, is converted into a receptacle of the arts, the residence of his majesty, the cradle of the nurture of his civilizing nation. Human powers and human industry extort from nature what she had refused to bestow, noxious swamps now swell into beneficient canals, the rocks of the adjacent wildernesses are piled into stately monuments and gorgeous palaces; ships from the remotest countries visit the untried seas, the colony of the frozen north becomes the seat of luxury, the source of light, the mart of commerce for the world-like Russian empire; and – the period of one human life was sufficient for accomplishing this miraculous production.'

This enduring myth of Peter the Colossus has inspired both historical precedent and literary genius in Russia, and

[1] *Russia, abridged from the French, of the Marquis de Custine,* 1954.
[2] *Picture of Petersburg* by H. Storch, 1801.

was brought to life for all time in Pushkin's ballad, *The Bronze Horseman* (Falconet's famous statue of Peter the Great, dominating the Neva). The following anecdote (quoted by the French Ambassador before the 1914–18 War, Maurice Paléologue) casts a searching light on to one aspect of the paradoxes of Peter, destroyer or creator, reformer or revolutionary, 'essentially Russian' or 'Westernizer':

Returning from a call at the end of the English Quay, I saw the Chamberlain, Nicholas Besak, staggering through the thawing mud in a fierce and cutting north wind. I offered him a lift in my car. . . .

When we reached the Holy Synod Square, crowned by the monument of Peter I, Falconet's masterpiece, I once more expressed my admiration of the majestic effigy of the tsar legislator, who seems to be directing the very course of the Neva from the vantage point of a prancing horse. Besak raised his hat.

'I greet the greatest revolutionary of modern times,' he said.

'Peter I a revolutionary? I always thought he was a fierce, impetuous and rabid reformer, without scruples or mercy, but possessed to a very high degree of creative genius and the instinct for order and authority.'

'No, all Peter Alexeievitch liked was destroying things. That is why he was so essentially Russian. In his savage despotism he undermined and overturned the whole fabric. For nearly thirty years he was in revolt against his people; he attacked all our national traditions and customs; he turned everything upside down, even our holy orthodox Church. You call him a reformer. But a true reformer allows for the past, recognises the limits of the possible and impossible, is cautious with his changes and paves the way for the future. He was quite different. He destroyed for the sheer delight of destroying, and took a cynical pleasure in breaking down the resistance of others, outraging for conscience, and killing their most natural and legitimate feelings. . . . When our present day anarchists dream of blowing up the social edifice on the pretext of reconstructing it *en bloc*, they are unconsciously drawing their inspiration from Peter the Great. Like him, they have a fanatical hatred of the past; like him, they imagine they can change the whole soul of a nation by ukases and penalties. Once more, I say that Peter Alexeievitch is the true ancestor and precursor of our revolutionaries.'

In sharp contrast to this view of Peter – almost heretical in identifying the Tsar with the 'Asiatic', Tartar, nihilism of Russian history – is the familiar image of Peter as the Western Enlightener, the opener of windows, the standard-bearer of young Russia's imperialism. No more fervent disciple of this school existed than Russia's greatest polemicist of the nineteenth century, Alexander Herzen, who described 'the movement inaugurated by Peter, the whole gist of which lay in the secularization of the Tsardom and the diffusion of European culture'.[1] Herzen even claimed that Petrine Russia 'was from the first more *national* than the period of the Muscovite Tsars'. Peter was a Russian Frederick II or Joseph II, a typically eighteenth-century Caesar, imposing his 'Petersburg culture terrorism' upon the Slavophils, Schismatics, Old Believers, clergy, patriots and dissidents of all kinds.

It was Nicholas I who, during his long reign from 1825 to 1855, reverted to becoming the 'representative and leader' of the Old Russian party, of the values of autocracy, nationalism and orthodoxy, of a pre-Petrine 'ponderous Byzantine ritual formality', obsessed by customs of 'unalterable precedence' or 'rigid proprieties' and 'dignified formalities'. Patriotism was imposed by the knout (a particularly savage – even lethal – form of flogging) and the police; and it was easy for Nicholas to cow those subjects, for 'Peter's upheaval made us into the worst that men can be made into – enlightened slaves'[2] who were to people Petersburg's palaces and *prospekts*. Education, such as that inculcated at Pushkin's Lycée, was perverted, and 'lay in instilling the religion of blind obedience, leading to power as its reward'.[3] So the

---

[1] *My Past and Thoughts*, vol. 4, by Alexander Herzen.
[2] Ibid.
[3] Ibid.

legacy of Muscovite Russia was inherited by Peter's successor only in the nineteenth century.

In his compelling analysis of Russia of the mid-1840s, the Marquis de Custine,[1] to a degree, agreed with Herzen:

> Petersburg, a city built rather against Sweden than for Russia, ought to be nothing more than a seaport, a Russian Dantzic. Instead of this, Peter the First made it a box, from which his chained boyars might contemplate, with envy, the stage on which is enacted the civilisation of Europe; a civilisation which, in forcing them to copy, he forbade them to emulate!
>
> Peter the Great, in all his works, acted without any regard to humanity, time or nature.
>
> All his ideas, with the faults of character of which they were the consequence, have spread and multiplied under the reigns that followed.

But de Custine did not condemn Nicholas' nationalism out of hand:

> Nicholas is the first who has endeavoured to stem the torrent, by recalling the Russians to themselves: an enterprise that the world will admire when it shall have recognised the firmness of spirit with which it has been conceived. After such reigns as those of Catherine and Paul, to make the Russia left by the Emperor Alexander a real Russian empire; to speak Russian, to think as a Russian, to avow himself a Russian – and this, while presiding over a court of nobles who are the heirs of the favourites of the 'Semiramis of the North' – is an act of true courage. Whatever may be the result of the plan, it does honour to him who devised it.

What desperately worried de Custine were the uses to which the 'real Russian Empire' would put its newfound powers. After Nicholas' death, 'Russia dashed once more upon the path traced out by Peter', a phrase vividly echoing the clattering hooves of the Bronze Horseman. But there were, at

[1] Op. cit.

least so Herzen believed, limits to the Superman: the Petrine Revolution was not just 'the consequence of personal will and the caprice of genius'; rather it came 'in response to the instinctive demands of Russia to develop its powers'.[1]

Very different views exist, therefore, of the Petrine achievement and legacy, and no historical anthology of Petersburg would be truthful without recognizing them.

And the Bronze Horseman, possessive, menacing,[2] provides yet another major theme in Petersburg's history and literature: that of the tyrant indifferently viewing the struggles, sacrifices and annihilation of the individual, such as the crazed clerk Evgeny, or Dostoyevsky's Raskolnikov, or Gogol's Akaky of *The Overcoat*. Symbols of the underdog, shaking their fists powerlessly at the Idol, are the millions of poor labourers, soldiers, serfs, prostitutes, down-at-heel pen pushers and lowly bureaucrats, all that slave-labour upon whose bones the city was erected. As in a Dürer etching of Beauty holding hands with Death, so there lurks behind the pretty yellow and green façades of the palaces, a vast charnel-house.

It was these wretches who had to endure the deadly cold (or worse still, the Neva) in their cellars, the miasmas, fogs and other caprices of nature, in other words, every kind of climatic oppression; and there was another, even more insidious oppression to be endured, this time man-made: the chafing corset of Peter the Great's Table of Ranks. For Peter the Great 'could devise nothing better in his profoundly deep yet narrow penetration than to divide the herd, that is to say the people, into classes. Thus it is that Russia had become a Regiment of sixty million strong; and this is the *Tchinn*, the mightiest achievement of Peter.'[3]

As a consequence of this regimentation, the whole capital,

---

[1] Herzen, op. cit.

[2] The lines from Pushkin are clear enough: 'Terrible was he in the surrounding gloom! What thought was in his brow! What strength was hidden in him! And in this steed what fire! Where are you galloping, proud horse, and where do your hoofs fall? O mighty master of fate! Was it not thus, aloft on the very edge of the abyss, that you reined up Russia with your iron curb?'

[3] Custine, op cit.

this garrison universe, was consumed with the 'fever' of ambition, of promotion, the race for stars and ribbands, titles and ranks. It was said that Petersburg would be a desert without the Court. There was only one force exempt from this fever, that of cruel, indifferent Nature herself. Alexander I is made to exclaim, in *The Bronze Horseman*, as he mournfully sees the Neva flood of 1824 swirl about the caryatids of the Winter Palace: 'Tsars cannot master the divine elements'.

But the argument applied only to those fortunate few galloping across the Millionaya or the Nevsky to keep rewarding appointments with fate. What of the impotent, servile rest? What of the Petersburg population which doubled between 1850 and 1890, piled pell-mell into a frantic industrialization? Out of these apparently mute masses – standing silently around the Decembrist mutineers of 1825 – were to come the characters of Russia's great novels of the nineteenth century. The alienated, disaffected, unhappy, isolated, rootless nomads of the city now seem familiar to us. But their pedigree is not 'Western'; it is Petersburgian. Their lives were a search for relief from the kicks of the Horseman, the corset of the Petrine system of ranks, the Muscovite disciplines of a Nicholas I. The search, as we know from Gogol, Lermontov, Dostoyevsky, Blok, and others, took these frenzied, solitary, trapped denizens of this 'most fantastic' city (the phrase is Dostoyevsky's) into a world of illusions and dreams, of the half-truths of schizophrenia and, in the end, of madness. 'Progress', in our sense, meant nothing to them. The soul of Russia, of the 'Eternal Maiden', had remained, so the Slavophils asserted, in Moscow and in the country; Petersburg was but an administrative shell. as Gogol put it, 'Moscow is necessary to Russia; Petersburg needs Russia.' Murder and suicide stalked these frustrated Lizas and Hermanns. The city's beautiful canals were convenient coffins. Pushkin had foretold all this in his dedication for *The Bronze Horseman*: '*Pechalen budet moy rasskas*' – Sad will be my tale.

The more the city's symmetrical gridiron sought to brand itself into their flesh, the more they would seek to escape it.

The Founder in the 1710s certainly had not worried about this aspect of his creation; nor did his successors. For in their grand plan of huge squares and enormous *prospekts*, in conspiracy with the very width of the Neva, humanity is dwarfed and 'there is in this city the pathos of space'. Even the golden spires of the cathedrals, fortresses and of the Admiralty shrink to a needle thinness lost in the winter skies.

For fleeting moments, the masses might take some kind of revenge on the Founder and his legatees, only to be shot down (as in 1905) or to triumph for a few hours (as in 1917) by investing the empty shells of power of an abandoned Winter Palace. Indeed, the 'crawling, howling myriapod' of humanity (in Andrei Bely's striking phrase) would have had only one ironic consolation for all their humiliations, to see power transferred back from 'Western' Petersburg to 'Asiatic' Moscow. The 'Dowager Empress' would take her revenge.

It is to Russian literature that due recognition must be given for its deft unravelling of the skeins and bandages protecting the mummified soul of past Petersburg. Allowing for the crushing weight of a half Tartar, half Byzantine despotism, of a line of mainly German rulers, where else indeed would Petersburg find its living soul except through the liberating powers of literature? We Western visitors, have, of course, no trouble in assimilating the Western aspects of Petersburg's life: it is Russianized aspects of our own culture and civilization that are visually on show in the palaces, pictures and architecture; but to the impalpable, intuitive, irrational *Russian* Petersburg, literature is the best passport.

The subject is not an easy one. Even the Russian himself, confused by siren voices of 'progress' heard at his Western window, has suffered from a crisis of values and identity, though ultimately his patriotic loyalties reverted to powerful atavisms of steppe and forest, to a Mother Russia where the Bronze Horseman would find no place. For Gogol, the splendours of Petersburg's façades were deceptions; nothing could be what it seemed to be; the straighter the *prospekt*, the madder its denizens. In Andrei Bely's *Petersburg* (finished before 1914), an extraordinary description of these Petrine paradoxes is to be found, where these myths are brought to culmination.

Secondary themes, it is hoped, also enliven this anthology. After all, most visitors to Petersburg before 1917, or even acute observers living there, were not obsessed with questions of reform or revolution, of Western civilization and Eastern despotism, and were content enough to chronicle the pleasures of four frivolous Empresses, or those of the Court, aristocracy, and of the merchant class (one-third German, let it not be forgotten). Indeed, the formal festivities of the *ancien régime* (such as the Blessing of the Waters) deserve an honourable mention.

The anthology stops with the 1917 Revolution. To have done justice to Leningrad's massive expansion since then, and heroic defence in World War II, would require a book at least a third as long again, which must remain a desirable project for the future.

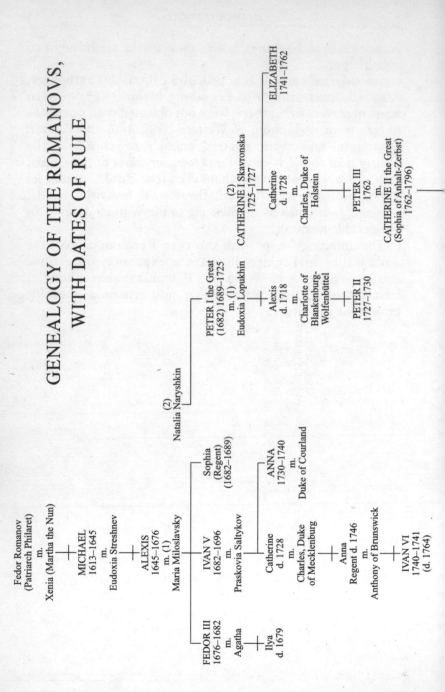

GENEALOGY OF THE ROMANOVS,
WITH DATES OF RULE

Fedor Romanov
(Patriarch Philaret)
m.
Xenia (Martha the Nun)

MICHAEL
1613–1645
m.
Eudoxia Streshnev

ALEXIS
1645–1676
m. (1)
Maria Miloslavsky

(2)
Natalia Naryshkin

FEDOR III
1676–1682
m.
Agatha

Ilya
d. 1679

IVAN V
1682–1696
m.
Praskovia Saltykov

Sophia
(Regent)
(1682–1689)

PETER I the Great
(1682) 1689–1725
m. (1)
Eudoxia Lopukhin

Catherine
d. 1728
m.
Charles, Duke
of Mecklenburg

ANNA
1730–1740
m.
Duke of Courland

Alexis
d. 1718
m.
Charlotte of
Blankenburg-
Wolfenbüttel

(2)
CATHERINE I Skavronska
1725–1727

Anna
Regent d. 1746
m.
Anthony of Brunswick

PETER II
1727–1730

Catherine
d. 1728
m.
Charles, Duke of
Holstein

ELIZABETH
1741–1762

IVAN VI
1740–1741
(d. 1764)

PETER III
1762
m.
CATHERINE II the Great
(Sophia of Anhalt-Zerbst) (1762–1796)

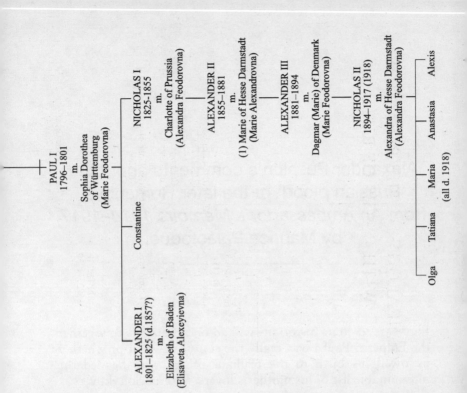

PAUL I
1796–1801
m.
Sophia Dorothea
of Württemburg
(Marie Feodorovna)

ALEXANDER I
1801–1825 (d.1857?)
m.
Elizabeth of Baden
(Elisaveta Alexeyievna)

Constantine

NICHOLAS I
1825–1855
m.
Charlotte of Prussia
(Alexandra Feodorovna)

ALEXANDER II
1855–1881
m.
(1) Marie of Hesse Darmstadt
(Marie Alexandrovna)

ALEXANDER III
1881–1894
m.
Dagmar (Marie) of Denmark
(Marie Feodorovna)

NICHOLAS II
1894–1917 (1918)
m.
Alexandra of Hesse Darmstadt
(Alexandra Feodorovna)

Olga   Tatiana   Maria   Anastasia   Alexis
(all d. 1918)

Alexander Pushkin's comments about the 'Russian blood' of the later Romanovs, from *An Ambassador's Memoirs 1914–1917* by Maurice Paléologue.

For years to come historians will go on arguing as to whether the Emperor Paul I was really the son of Peter III or whether he owed his birth to the brilliant officer who headed the interminable list of his mother's lovers, Sergius Soltykov.

If the latter is true the successors of Catherine the Great cannot be the true heirs of the Romanovs. But whatever may be the solution of this conjugal puzzle, a problem remains. Does the Tsar Nicholas II trace his descent from the same family as his people? Is he of the same race? In a word, what proportion of Russian blood has he in his veins?

A very minute proportion.

This is his descent:

1. The Tsar Alexis Michailovitch (1629–1676) marries Nathalie Narischkin (1655–1694);
2. Their son Peter the Great (1672–1725) marries the Livonian, Catherine Skavronsky (1682–1727);
3. Their daughter Anna Petrovna (1708–1728) marries Charles Frederick, Duke of Holstein-Gottorp (1700–1739);
4. Their son Peter III (1728–1762) marries Catherine, Princess of Anhalt-Zerbst (1729–1796);

5. Their son Paul I (1754–1801) marries Marie Feodorovna, Princess of Würtemberg (1759–1828);
6. Their son Nicholas I (1796–1855) succeeding his brother, Alexander I (1777–1825), marries Alexandra Feodorovna, Princess of Prussia (1798–1860);
7. Their son Alexander II (1818–1881) marries Marie Alexandrovna, Princess of Hesse Darmstadt (1824–1880);
8. Their son Alexander III (1848–1894) marries Marie Feodorovna, Princess of Denmark (1847–. . . .);
9. Their son Nicholas II (1868–. . . .) marries Alexandra Feodorovna, Princess of Hesse Darmstadt (1872–. . . .);
10. Their son Alexis (1904–. . . .) is the present Tsarevitch.

When Peter III was born the heirs of the Romanovs thus had only one-fourth Russian blood in their veins to three-fourths German.

At each successive stage the national element loses one-half of its coefficient, so that the proportion of Russian blood is reduced to $\frac{1}{16}$ in Nicholas I, $\frac{1}{32}$ in Alexander II, $\frac{1}{64}$ in Alexander III, $\frac{1}{128}$ in Nicholas II, and only $\frac{1}{256}$ in the Tsarevitch Alexis.

The poet Pushkin was fond of poking fun at the Teutonism of the modern Romanovs. To illustrate his sarcasms he one evening sent for several glasses, a bottle of red wine, and a decanter of water. He set out the glasses in a row and filled the first with wine up to the brim: 'That glass,' he said, 'is our glorious Peter the Great: it is pure Russian blood in all its vigour. Just look at the crimson glow!'

In the second glass he mixed wine and water in equal quantities. In the third he put one part wine and three parts water, and continued thus mixing each fresh glass in accordance with the same inverse progression.

At the sixth glass, which represented the Tsarevitch, the future Alexander III, the proportion of wine had already become so small ($\frac{1}{32}$) that the liquid was hardly tinged with it.

I have continued Pushkin's experiment down to the present Tsarevitch. The disproportion between the two liquids is so enormous ($\frac{1}{256}$) that the very presence of the wine is no longer perceptible.

ST PETERSBURG

Previous page:
The Bronze Horseman – Falconet's statue (1782) of Peter the Great, inscribed 'Petro Primo, Catharina Secunda'. By K.P. Beggrow

The Early Days

[1] The foundation of the city in 1703, from *Peter the Great* by K. Waliszewski.

The story of [Peter's] own foundation of the town has become legendary and epic. One popular description represents him as snatching a halbert from one of his soldiers, cutting two strips of turf, and laying them crosswise with the words, 'Here there shall be a town!' Foundation stones were evidently lacking, and sods had to take their place! Then, dropping the halbert, he seized a spade, and began the first embankment. . . . This occurred on the 16th of May 1703.

History adds, that the Swedish prisoners employed on the work died in thousands. The most indispensable tools were lacking. There were no wheelbarrows, and the earth was carried in the corners of men's clothing. A wooden fort was first built, on the island bearing the Finnish name of Ianni-Saari (Hare Island). This was the future citadel of St Peter and St Paul. Then came a wooden church, and the modest cottage which was to be Peter's first palace. Near these, the following year, there rose a Lutheran Church . . . and also a tavern, the famous inn of the Four Frigates, which did duty as a Town Hall for a long time before it became a place of diplomatic meeting. . . .

But, up to the time of the Battle of Poltava, Peter never thought of making St Petersburg his capital. It was enough for him to feel he had a fortress and a port. He was not sufficiently sure of his mastery over the neighbouring countries, not certain enough of being able to retain his conquest, to desire to make it the centre of his Government and his own permanent residence. This idea was not definitely accepted till after his great victory.[1] His final decision has been bitterly criticised, especially by foreign historians. . . . The great victory, we are told, diminished the strategic importance of St Petersburg, and almost entirely extinguished its value as a port; while its erection into the capital city of the Empire was never anything but madness. Peter, being now the indisputable master of the Baltic shores, had nothing to fear from any Swedish attack in the Gulf of Finland. Before any attempt in that direction, the Swedes were certain to try to recover Narva or Riga. If, in later years, they turned their eyes to St Petersburg, it was only because that town had acquired undue and unmerited political importance. It was easy of attack, and difficult to defend. There was no possibility of concentrating any large number of troops there, for the whole country, forty leagues round, was a barren desert. . . .

From the commercial point of view, St Petersburg, we are assured, did command a valuable system of river communication – but that commanded by Riga was far superior. The Livonian, Esthonian, and Courland ports of Riga, Libau, and Revel, all at an equal distance from St Petersburg and Moscow, and far less removed from the great German commercial centres, enjoyed a superior climate, and were, subsequent to the conquest of the above-mentioned Provinces, the natural points of contact between Russia and the West. . . .

Besides this, the Port of St Petersburg, during the lifetime of its founder, never was anything but a mere project. Peter's ships were moved from Kronslot to Kronstadt. Between St

[1] Tsar's letter to Apraxin (July 9, 1709), Cabinet No. i, Book 28. The victory was that of Poltava.

Petersburg and Kronstadt, the Neva was not, in those days, more than eight feet deep, and Manstein tells us that all ships built at Petersburg had to be dragged by means of machines fitted with cables to Kronstadt, where they received their guns. Once these had been taken on board, the vessels could not get up stream again. The Port of Kronstadt was closed by ice for six months out of the twelve, and lay in such a position that no sailing ship could leave it unless the wind blew from the east. There was so little salt in its water, that the ship timbers rotted in a very short time, and besides, there were no oaks in the surrounding forests, and all such timber had to be brought from Kasan. . . . On the other hand, and from the very outset, the commercial activity of St Petersburg was hampered by the fact that it was the Tsar's Capital. The presence of the Court made living dear, and the consequent expense of labour was a heavy drawback to the export trade, which, by its nature, called for a good deal of manual exertion. . . . The cost of transport, which amounted to between nine and ten kopecks a pood between Moscow and Archangel, five to six between Yaroslav and Archangel, and three or four between Vologda and Archangel, came to eighteen, twenty and thirty kopecks a pood in the case of merchandise sent from any of these places to St Petersburg. This accounts for the opposition of the foreign merchants at Archangel to the request that they should remove to St Petersburg. Peter settled the matter in characteristic fashion, by forbidding any trade in hemp, flax, leather, or corn, to pass through Archangel. . . . As a capital city, St Petersburg, we are told again, was ill-placed on the banks of Neva, not only for the reasons given, but for others, geographical, ethnical and climatic, which exist even in the present day, and which make its selection an outrage on common sense. Was it not, we are asked, a most extraordinary whim which induced a Russian to found the capital of his Slavonic Empire among the Finns, against the Swedes.[1] – to centralise the administration of a huge extent of country in its remotest corner, . . . and to force every one about him, officials, Court, and Diplomatic Corps, to inhabit one of the most inhospitable

[1] *Russia, abridged from the French, of the Marquis de Custine,* 1854.

spots, under one of the least clement skies, he could possibly have discovered? The whole place was a marsh – the Finnish word Neva means 'mud'. . . . There is no pasturage, no possibility of cultivation – fruit, vegetables, and even corn, are all brought from a distance. The ground is in a sort of intermediate condition between the sea and *terra firma*. Up to Catherine's reign inundations were chronic in their occurrence. On the 11th of September, 1706, Peter drew from his pocket the measure he always carried about him, and convinced himself that there were twenty-one inches of water above the floors of his cottage.

[2] The cost in human lives of building the city, and the need for autocracy, from *Mémoires pour Servir l'Histoire de l'Empire Russien sous le Règne de Pierre le Grand* by F. C. Weber.

This Resolution was no sooner taken, but Orders were forthwith issued, that next Spring a great number of Men, *Russians, Tartars, Cosacks, Calmucks, Finlandish* and *Ingrian* Peasants, should be at the Place to execute the Czar's Design. Accordingly in the beginning of May 1703, many thousands of Workmen, raised from all the Corners of the vast Russian Empire, some of them coming Journies of 200 to 300 German Miles, made a beginning of the Works on the new Fortress. There were neither sufficient Provisions to furnish them with the necessary Tools, as Pickaxes, Spades, Shovels, Wheelbarrows, Planks and the like, they even had not so much as Houses or Huts; notwithstanding which the Work went on with such Expedition, that it was surprising to see the Fortress raised within less than five Months time, though the Earth which is very scarce thereabouts, was for the greater part carried by the Labourers in the Skirts of their Clothes, and in Bags made of Rags and old Mats, the Use of Wheelbarrows being then unknown to them. It is computed that there perished on this Occasion very nigh one hundred thousand Souls, for in those Places made desolate by the War, no Provision could be had even for ready Money, and as the usual Supplies carried by the Lake Ladoga were frequently retarded by contrary Winds, those People often were in the utmost Misery.

At the same time that they were going on with the Fortress, the City also by degrees began to be built, and to this End Numbers of People both of the Nobility and the trading Part of the Nation were ordered to come from Russia to settle at Petersbourg and to build Houses there, all which was executed with such Forwardness, that in a short time the Place swarmed with Inhabitants. . . .

By order of the Czar in the month of November (of 1716), one hundred noble families arrived in St Petersburg. They complained because due to this change, they were losing two-thirds of their incomes and were obliged to build and pay cash for their stores. On their own estates, they lived cheaply.

Equally miserable were the peasants, transplanted to St Petersburg. But whatever the troubles which they endured, both grandees and the poor accepted their sufferings with unbelievable patience. The common people talked of life as a burden of which they wanted to be freed. When sick, they lie on the floor hardly concerned whether they will recover or die of their illness. They won't even take medicine. One day, a Lutheran Minister told me how he had questioned some simple peasants as to their beliefs about their salvation. They answered *they did not know if they would ever reach heaven* and that they thought Paradise was only for the Czar and the leading Boyars.

[3] The progress of the city 1704–1712, from *Palmyra of the North* by Christopher Marsden.

After four or five years, the Petrograd Side had begun to resemble a town. At the end of 1704, there had been fifteen major houses; in 1709 there were a hundred and fifty. . . . Then, in June 1709, came the victory of Poltava – the final triumph over the Swedes. 'Now indeed', wrote Peter on the evening after the battle, 'we can lay the foundation of Sankt Piterburkh'. It is from 1709 onwards that the history of Petersburg becomes real and tangible.

Activity was increased to fever pitch. Encampments, larger

than the city itself, swelled to absorb the incoming labour. The work went on winter and summer, day and night, in the face of every obstacle. The privations and set-backs which the workers endured were appalling. Disastrous floods constantly overwhelmed the low-lying islands, and in 1705 the whole city was several feet deep in water. As late as 1721 the Neva was still not controlled; in that year all the streets of St Petersburg were navigable and Peter was nearly drowned in the Nevsky Prospekt. Fire, too – an almost weekly occurrence – played its sinister part. . . . Wolves roamed the streets after dark: even in 1715 a woman was devoured in broad daylight not far from Menshikov's house. There was as yet little at St Petersburg to attract the people of Moscow.

But in 1710 all the members of the Imperial family moved to the new city, together with all government institutions still remaining in Moscow. The same year a ukase was issued demanding forty thousand workmen a year, together with their essential tools, to be sent from the provinces: . . . Then [Peter] forbade the erection, owing to the shortage of masons, of any stone buildings in any part of the empire outside St Petersburg . . . while every boat or cart entering the city had to bring a certain quantity of unhewn stones, as stone was sadly lacking in these marshy wastes. . . . The city was populated by force. All officials, nobles and landowners possessing not less than thirty families of peasant serfs were obliged to settle in St Petersburg and build houses for themselves, of stone, brick, pise or wood according to their means: those who owned five hundred peasants had to raise a stone house of two stories, while the poorer ones often found themselves obliged to club together to build one. . . .

The haste with which these dwellings must have been put up is reflected later on in the dilapidated state of the city under Peter's successors; they often did not even stand up to the first winters after their erection and rich banquets in the new houses were spoiled by cracking walls, gaping floors and leaky roofs. They were built with groans and curses both from the wretched labourers and the unwilling occupants, who still saw only evil in every idea and action of the heretical tsar. Nevertheless, in 1712 Peter announced that Sankt Piterburkh was to be the Imperial capital.

The chief square of the original city was Troitskaya (Trinity) Square near the fortress, where Peter's first house stood. Here, in 1710, was built the wooden Church of the Trinity and here also an enterprising German had opened an Osteria, subsequently called the Triumphal Osteria of the Four Frigates, where Peter used to refresh himself with his favourite beverage of vodka and cayenne pepper. The names of the streets which radiated from the neighbourhood of this square give an idea of the different classes of people who lived there – Dvorianskaya (from *dvoriani*, nobles), Pushkarskaya (*pushkari*, gun-makers), Ruzheinaya (*ruzheiniki*, rifle-makers), Monetnaya (minters).

But already building had been progressing elsewhere than on the two original islands – on the adjacent Isle of Buffaloes, afterwards called Vasilievsky Ostrov, also on the northern bank of the Neva; and on the left bank of the river, opposite Vasilievsky Ostrov, where the Admiralty had been built. There was of course no bridge, not even a pontoon, linking the islands. The twenty boats, manned by ignorant peasants, which were used as ferries were a severe menace to the population. ... As the Neva, at the time of the first ice and again when it breaks, is almost untraversable, the northern islands were virtually cut off from the rest of Russia. Many important buildings, to be sure, were to appear on Vasilievsky Ostrov in Peter's reign and afterwards, as we shall see; but the subsequent history of the city is that of a withdrawal to the mainland – and in the first place to the environs of the Admiralty.

The original Admiralty, founded in 1705, bore little relation to the impressive erection that stands on the site today. It was a simple shipyard. ... Already, from the centre of the line of shops which ran parallel to the river, gazing out over the woods and swamps down the future line of the Nevsky Prospekt to the site of the Alexander Nevsky monastery three miles away, rose a wooden tower with a tall, thin spire; surmounted by a wind-vane in the form of a ship. After 1711 the Admiralty was fortified with stone, and six bastions arose behind a moat.

Around the Admiralty, where at first few but the labourers in the shipyards dwelt, there arose a new settlement which went by the name of the German Suburb (many of the skilled naval workmen being of German nationality). In this district, in 1706, Giovanni Maria Fontana, an Italian who had come to Russia with Trezzini in 1703 as Master Builder of the Imperial Palaces and Fortifications, had designed and erected a palace for the all-powerful Prince Menshikov.

Outwards from the Admiralty spread other settlements – the Morskoy (Navy) to the west of the Moika canal; the Konyushenny (Stables) near the imperial stables east of the same canal; and the Liteiny (Foundry) some way farther east.

In 1710–11 Trezzini began to build for Peter himself a house on this bank of the river, but farther upstream, at the junction of the Neva and the Fontanka, another subsidiary arm which ran out on the south side opposite to the island on which the Peter and Paul fortress was now building. This, a sensible, solid house on two floors with big windows, is the so-called 'Summer Palace of Peter the Great' in the Summer Garden. Before it was quite completed in 1713, a new party of artists arrived in St Petersburg from Germany. At their head was a very celebrated man – the architect and sculptor Andreas Schlüter, Director of the Berlin Academy of Arts, who had to his credit, among other works, the great domed Royal Palace on the Spree in Berlin and a number of famous statues. Some seven years previously, Schlüter had fallen into disgrace owing to the collapse of the Mint Tower in Berlin which he was building, and although he had continued to work in Germany, Peter's agent, General Bruce, who was in Berlin hiring builders, carpenters and metalworkers, does not appear to have experienced any great difficulty in inducing Schlüter to sign even so renowned a name to a contract to go from the civilised grandeur of Berlin to the barbaric wastes of the Neva delta. . . . In his train went four other German architects; Gottfried Schädel of Hamburg, the Prussian Theodor Schwertfeger, Georg Johann Mattarnovy and Johann Christian Förster; also probably Schlüter's pupil, J. F. Braunstein. All these were destined to leave far more permanent impressions upon the young city than Schlüter himself.

For Schlüter, though not an old man – he was only a little over fifty – was sickly and becoming rather silly; he now thought about nothing but Perpetual Motion. Of the time he spent in St Petersburg, the only concrete traces are a number of mythological bas-reliefs let into the outside walls of Trezzini's 'Summer Palace' between the two rows of windows . . . he died in the spring of 1714, after barely a year in Russia.

Ten years, then, after the foundation of the city, and with some five hundred houses built, the active influences at work on its architecture are all Germanic: Trezzini and his pupils, Italian and Russian, working in the German-Dutch style of Baltic baroque, and the followers of Schlüter – Mattarnovy (who inherited Schlüter's plans and models), Schädel, Schwertfeger, Förster and Braunstein – in the equally Dutch-influenced North German manner.

[4] Peter the Great's displeasure at seeing the streets and canals at Wassili Ostrov (1718), from *Original Anecdotes of Peter the Great . . .*, by J. V. Stählin-Storckburg.

We are often surprised, when walking in Petersburgh, to see that the canals in the streets of Wassili Ostrov have neither the same direction nor the same proportions as the streets themselves. The following are the reasons that have been given me for this want of symmetry:

When Peter had chosen, among a great number of plans, that which was most favourable to his partiality for canals, he resolved to have it executed in Wassili Ostrov: he first surrounded the island with fortifications, and then ordered canals of communication to be opened in the middle of the streets, as we have said above, between the Great and Little Neva: but, unfortunately, he forgot to give directions concerning the width of the streets and of the canals, as well as the distance to be preserved between them; or else he depended on the intelligence of the persons appointed to superintend the works, convinced that they would at least take care to make the canals wide enough for two boats to pass abreast.

In the meantime, His Majesty set off for the army, and two years after, in 1716, travelled into Holland and France, after having given orders to carry on the works with all possible dispatch.

On his return to Petersburgh in 1718, he postponed every other care to pay them a visit. He saw in most of the streets, with much satisfaction, complete rows of houses, built either of wood or stone, and was particularly pleased with the beautiful palace of Prince Menchicoff, situated fronting the principal avenue: but his joy was soon overcast when he perceived the pitiful dimensions of both streets and canals. He was struck dumb with astonishment; but his gestures plainly showed how much his contempt and indignation were excited by so egregious a blunder.

Fearing, however, that he had been deceived in the dimensions of those of Amsterdam, which he had given as a model, he went immediately to the house of Mr Wilde, the Dutch resident, and asked him if he knew the breadth of the canals of that city. Mr Wilde presented a plan of it to the Czar, who took out his compasses, and having measured the length and breadth of the canals, wrote down their dimensions on his tablets. He then begged the Resident to go with him and see the works that had been finished during his absence. On measuring the first canals he met with, he found that their breadth, and that of the streets added together, were not equal to the width of one of the canals of Amsterdam. In a transport of rage he cried out, 'The Devil take the undertaking – all is spoiled', and retired to his palace.

The Emperor long remembered the unpleasant feelings of which this blunder had been the cause, and frequently cast an angry look on Prince Menchicoff, who had been charged with the inspection of the works. From time to time His Majesty went to Wassili Ostrov, and having examined for whole hours the streets and canals that were begun, returned sorrowfully without uttering a word.

When Mons. le Blond, a famous architect of Paris, whom he had taken into his service, arrived at Petersburgh, Peter took him to Wassili Ostrov, and after walking over the whole island with the plan in his hand, said to him, 'Well, Mons. le Blond, what is to be done to carry my plan into execution?' – 'Raze, Sir, raze,' answered Le Blond, elevating his shoulders; 'there is no other remedy than to demolish all that has been done, and to dig the canals anew.' – 'I thought so,' replied the Czar, and retired to his boat. – He employed Le Blond to construct some handsome edifices at Peterhoff and elsewhere, but never spoke to him again of Wassili Ostrov.

Source: Mr Swart, Dutch resident, successor to Mr Wilde, with whom he had lived at Petersburgh in quality of secretary.

[5] The further development of the city: the important role of the Masonry Commission, from *St Petersburg: Industrialisation and Change*, by James H. Bater.

It is said of Catherine II (1762–96) that when she came to St Petersburg it was of wood, when she left it was of stone.[1] The epigram contains more than a germ of truth. It was during the reign of this German born empress that St Petersburg came of age in the sense that it was no longer necessary to oblige the nobility to take up residence there; many now recognized the signs of a maturing civic society for themselves and flocked to the capital to take part in it. The combination of state and private enterprise brought building construction to an unprecedented pitch. By the 1760s the almost overbearing, baroque-like style of Rastrelli was already on the wane and the architects engaged by Catherine – men like J. Vallin de la Mothe, A. Rinaldi, C. Cameron and G. Quarenghi – ensured its demise. . . . While the volume and quality of building was impressive, it was the overall coordination of it which greatly enhanced the city's image. In this respect the Commission for the Masonry Construction of St Petersburg and Moscow played a central role.

Formed in 1760, the Commission had the heavy responsibility of seeing that planning objectives were realized.[2] Shortly after commencing operations, the Commission held an open competition in which two sets of design specifications for developing the city were invited. The first set entailed proposing a plan based on existing conditions in the city. The second was a competition for a design appropriate to the capital of the Russian Empire, in which existing conditions could be ignored to realize the desired aims – architectural definition

[1] Bashutskiy, *Panorama Peterburga*, p. 101.
[2] *Leningrad*, p. 177.

of the central area and a harmonious relationship with the suburbs. Out of this competition came many ideas subsequently adopted in the planned development of the city. . . . The first achievement was to complete the 'three-pronged' ensemble in Admiralteyskaya district by creating an open space in front of the Admiralty and Winter Palace. This entailed demolishing the existing St Isaac's Church. To carry out the entire plan necessitated a continuous line of buildings to the northeast along the Bol'shaya Neva from the Winter Palace, reconstruction of the Admiralty (fortuitously damaged by fire in 1783 but not rebuilt until early in the nineteenth century), the filling-in of the façade along the so-called English Quay to the southwest of the Admiralty and, of course, completion of the embankment of the Bol'shaya Neva in granite. To complement this part of the plan, further development began on the Strelka. The Academy of Arts building was started in 1764 and, following the destruction of the Kunstkammer by fire a few years later, a whole series of new buildings were planned, including the Academy of Science, the University, the Library, the Observatory, an Institute of Geography, as well as the Exchange. Not all these materialized but their number reflected the need to tie together the structures on the Strelka because the waterfront façade had become the element that would give visual unity to the central part of the city. . . . For the short time that the Commission was directly concerned with proposals for the capital, enormous changes were set in motion and the achievements were on a grand scale.[1] In less than forty years the talents of skilled architects too numerous to detail had transformed the city. . . . If there was not always agreement about the merits of what had been done, there was certainly consensus concerning the scale of the endeavours. Late in the century, W. Coxe noted:

> Succeeding sovereigns have continued to embellish Petersburg, but none more than the present empress, who may be called its second founder. Notwithstanding, however, all these

---

[1] After two decades the Commission's work turned to city planning throughout the Empire.

improvements, it bears every mark of an infant city, and, is still, 'only an immense outline, which will require future empresses and almost future ages to complete.' The views upon the banks of the Neva exhibit the most grand and lively scenes I ever beheld. . . .

The Winter Palace
and the Hermitage

[6] The Empress Anne returns from Moscow to St Petersburg in 1732 and commands Bartolomeo Rastrelli to build a stone palace, to become the Winter Palace; from *The Three Empresses* by P. Longworth.

Anne arrived in the city on 6 January 1732, attended a service of thanksgiving for her safe arrival, listened to a series of welcoming speeches, presided over a formal dinner, attended a fireworks display and finally a ball. The last two items alone cost 100,000 crowns but Anne was in a spending mood.

St Petersburg was as yet less than half the size of Moscow, and still consisted mainly of single-storey shacks. But more and more stone structures were rising up, government offices were worthily housed now in handsome buildings and Trezzini's great church of Saint Peter and Paul was almost finished, its graceful spire, awaiting its final sheath of gold, already dominating the city and the dreary marshes round about. In the middle of it all stood the Winter Palace. Rondeau's wife was not impressed with it – 'a great number of little rooms,' she wrote, 'and nothing remarkable either in architecture, painting, or furniture.' Anne, presumably, shared this opinion, for she took up residence next door in the palace that had once belonged to Count Apraxin, and sent for Bartolomeo Rastrelli, who had designed the triumphal arches which had welcomed her to St Petersburg, and various paraphernalia for the coronation masquerade. She commanded him to 'build a great stone Winter Palace' four storeys high not counting cellars and mezzanines. There was to be a great hall that was really great, a gallery, a theatre, grand formal staircases and a splendid chapel – all to be richly decorated with sculptures and with paintings.

[7] An indictment of Catherine the Great by Alexander Herzen, in his preface to *Memoirs of the Empress Catherine II written by Herself*.

In perusing these Memoirs, the reader is astonished to find one thing constantly lost sight of, even to the extent of not appearing anywhere – it is *Russia and the People*. And here is the characteristic trait of the epoch.

The Winter Palace, with its military and administrative machinery, was a world of its own. Like a ship floating on the surface of the ocean, it had no real connection with the inhabitants of the deep, beyond that of eating them. It was the *State for the State*. Organised on the German model, it imposed itself on the nation as a conqueror. In that monstrous barrack, in that enormous chancery, there reigned the cold rigidity of a camp. One set gave or transmitted orders, the rest obeyed in silence. There was but a single spot, within that dreary pile, in which human passions reappeared, agitated and stormy, and that spot was the domestic hearth; not that of the nation – but of the state. Behind that triple line of sentinels, in those heavily ornamented saloons, there fermented a feverish life, with its intrigues and its conflicts, its dramas, and its tragedies. It was there that the destinies of Russia were woven, in the gloom of the alcove, in the midst of orgies, *beyond* the reach of informers and of the police.

What interest, then, could the young German Princess take in that *magnum ignotum*, that people *unexpressed*, poor, semi-barbarous, which concealed itself in its villages, behind the snow, behind bad roads, and only appeared in the streets of St Petersburg like a foreign outcast, with its persecuted beard and prohibited dress – tolerated only through contempt.

It was only long afterwards that Catherine heard the Russian people seriously spoken of, when the Cossack Pougatcheff, at the head of an army of insurgent peasants, menaced Moscow.

When Pougatcheff was vanquished, the Winter Palace again forgot the people. And there is no telling when it would have been once more remembered, had it not itself put its masters in mind of its existence, by rising in mass in 1812, rejecting, on the one hand, the release from serfdom offered to it at the point of foreign bayonets, and, on the other, marching to death to save a country which gave it nothing but slavery, degradation, misery – and the oblivion of the Winter Palace.

This was the second *memento* of the Russian people. Let us hope that at the third it will be remembered a little longer.

London, November 15th, 1858.   A. Herzen.

[8] The French ambassador, the Comte de Ségur, hears his tragedy *Coriolanus* played in the Hermitage Theatre at Catherine the Great's command, from *Mémoires ou Souvenirs et Anecdotes, par M. le Comte de Ségur.*

The princess admitted me more and more often into her intimate company. She often asked me to dinner and nearly every day allowed me to watch with her a play taking place in her palace of the Hermitage. This 'Hermitage' did not really mean the same as its name. On arrival one was struck by the size of the rooms and the galleries, by the splendour of the furniture, of the great number of old masters, and especially by a winter garden where greenery, flowers and the song of birds appeared to create an Italian spring amidst the Polar ices.

In the admirably chosen library, one felt that the 'hermit' of this place had more of a taste for philosophical enlightenment than for monkish practices. A coin collection spanning all countries and centuries provided a course in living history.

At the far end of this palace one entered into an elegant theatre copied from the antique one at Vicenza: it was semi-circular. There were no boxes and its amphitheatre consisted of a series of stepped levels.

During the winter, but only once a fortnight, the Empress invited here the Diplomatic Corps. The rest of the time there were only about twelve spectators: generally the Grand Duke and Grand Duchess, Momonoff, her aide-de-camp, the Chamberlain, the Master of the Horse, Count Strogonoff, the Vice-Chancellor, Count Bezborodko, Prince Potemkin, Countess Skawronski, his niece, Mademoiselle Protasoff, Ambassador Cobentzel, the Prince de Ligne and myself.

At the orders of the Empress, a troupe of good French comedians had been procured from France. Those I saw offered us a galaxy of distinguished talents: noticeable were the celebrated actor Aufrène, some famous composers and virtuosi, first Paesiello, later Cimarosa, Sarti, the singer, Marchesi and Madame Todi, who one and all delighted – if not the Empress, whose ear remained insensitive to harmony, but Prince Potemkin and various enlightened amateurs.

Catherine II wanted a complete repertoire in our theatre: every evening she came to see a work by Molière or Regnard. Our poor actors were very troubled their first days to have to act in a large theatre brilliantly lit but practically empty where only a dozen people filled the void! The applause might be unanimous but could not provide very encouraging noises. It was a case of weighing the votes instead of counting them. On the vessel bringing me back from America, I had composed *A Tragedy: Coriolanus*. The Empress asked me to read it to her. She took such a favourable view of this work that she was determined to have it acted. Despite my remonstrances she forced my hand: all I obtained was that it should be played only before her immediate circle.

This was promised and my *Coriolanus* was acted two or three times in front of twelve spectators who would hardly turn into a hostile cabal. There was a unanimous 'bravo' and the author called for, but a wise man must not count on the promises of sovereigns. I was to be deceived, and in fact complete secrecy surrounded the comedy.

One fine Thursday I was asked to the Gala at the Hermitage before the whole Court and the Diplomatic Corps. I arrived; the Empress called me and made me sit below her, actually at her feet. The curtain rose, the actors appeared and to my astonishment I saw that it was my tragedy that they were declaiming. Never in my whole life was I so embarrassed; the actors played remarkably well and the public, imitative of the Empress, clapped loudly. My expression was most clumsy. I remained silent, motionless, my eyes lowered like a statue. The Empress who was behind and above me suddenly took my right hand in hers, my left hand in the other and forced me to applaud myself. At the end of the play, after this friendly joke, I had to nerve myself to accept numerous compliments from all those present whose gallant manners did not permit them to behave otherwise.

[9] Melchior Grimm, writing to Madame Geoffrin, gives his first impressions of the Russian Court, from *Melchior Grimm* by Edmond Scherer.

On the day after my arrival, at midday, I made my bow to Her Majesty [Catherine the Great] and kissed her hand with all the respect one owes to the august hand holding the reins of a great Empire and with the pleasure one has in bringing to one's lips the beautiful hand of a woman . . . The Empress showered me with kindnesses from the very first day. After some conversation, she ordered me to stay for dinner. Afterwards she smilingly said, 'I was very far from you, but hope it will not occur in the future.'

I had the honour to see her nearly every day, to dine two or three times with her, and above all, to converse as well for an hour and a half or two uninterruptedly with her in her study. There, one must settle oneself in to a comfortable armchair opposite the sofa of the Imperial Sovereign of all the Russians: one talks, one gossips of things serious, gay, grave, frivolous, often solemnly of gay subjects, or gaily of solemn ones. Then Her Majesty says goodnight.

Tonight we gossiped like two magpies. She is, I assure you, a charming woman who should have a Parisian home. Once or twice a week, the Empress dines in her Hermitage tacked on to the palace and leading into her apartments. Here is her treasure storehouse of pictures. Here too, on the first floor on the same level, you find a summer and a winter garden.

Equality is the rule as you enter the Hermitage; you leave your rank, hat and sword at the door. There is no hint of an Imperial Empress. In the dining rooms, there are two tables side by side laid for ten, waiting at table is done by machines. There is no need for footmen behind chairs, and the Provost of Police is distinctly at a disadvantage as he is unable to report to Her Majesty anything that is said at these dinners. You draw for your place out of hat and the Empress is often seated at a corner whilst Mr Grimm or another man of similar importance lords it in the middle.

[10] The formation of the Hermitage picture collection by Catherine the Great, from *The Hermitage* by Pierre Descargues.

[Catherine] entered into negotiations with the dealer Gotskowski. This gentleman also regularly supplied pictures to Frederick II of Prussia, who had done so much to further Catherine's marriage (which, incidentally, in no way inhibited her from calling him her mortal enemy once she was on the throne, nor yet from subsequently signing a Treaty of Alliance with him: she had, in fact, lost no time in mastering the rules of politics). Gotskowski was in debt and Catherine was delighted to strike a bargain with him and thus secure for herself in Berlin itself 225 pictures which should normally have gone to Sans Souci to delight the eyes of Frederick. Spite may, indeed, have been the mainspring of Catherine's love of art collecting. Gotskowski's collection was mixed but comprised several Rembrandts ('The Incredulity of St Thomas', 'Potiphar's Wife', 'Portrait of a Turk'), a 'Man with a Glove' by Frans Hals, the 'Market at Amsterdam' by B. van der Helst; two Goltzius: 'Adam and Eve' and 'The Baptism'; several portraits by Franz Pourbus the elder, etc. It was limited to Dutch and Flemish painting, as was indeed usual at this time: . . .

Satisfied with her first purchase, and determined to organise her collection on a serious basis. Catherine ordered her Ambassadors throughout Europe to keep her informed of interesting sales and estates for disposal. . . .

In 1765 her Ambassador in Paris, Dimitri Galitzin, a friend of the *Philosophes* and a habitué of the Salon of Madame Geoffrin, learned from the latter that Diderot was in need of cash and considering the sale of the library he had compiled for his work on the Encyclopaedia. Her Imperial Majesty immediately responded generously by making an offer higher than Diderot had asked and by appointing the writer librarian of his own books. Delighted to hear later that Diderot had included his own manuscripts in the sale, she paid him outright his salary for fifty years. Diderot thus found himself in possession of a fortune of 41,000 *livres*, and Catherine was in every sense celebrated in the world of the *Philosophes*. This, of course, made everybody happy. . . .

In 1766, Diderot had occasion to show his usefulness. Catherine had asked Galitzin to find her a sculptor to execute a statue of Peter the Great for St Petersburg. The price offered was 300,000 *livres*. Galitzin proposed the work in turn to Cousteau, to Louis-Claude Vassé and to Pajou. The first asked 450,000, the second 400,000 and the third 600,000 *livres*. Diderot then announced that Falconet offered to execute the memorial for 25,000 *livres* per annum and that he was prepared to devote eight years to its completion. This represented a considerable saving. In point of fact, Falconet's 'Peter the Great' took nearly twelve years to complete and was finally installed in 1782, in the absence of the sculptor, who, by this time, had quarrelled with the Tsarina. . . .

As long as he remained Ambassador in Paris, Galitzin was responsible for purchases for the imperial collection. It is no doubt to him that the acquisition, in 1766, of a magnificent Rembrandt is due: 'The Return of the Prodigal Son'. . . . When Galitzin departed from Paris for The Hague, Diderot undertook to supply Catherine with pictures, with the aid of Khotinski, the new Russian Chargé d'Affaires.

When in 1768 Diderot heard news of the death of the ex-secretary of Louis XV, Gaignat ('who', he wrote, 'had collected some wonderful works of literature almost without knowing how to read, and some wonderful works of art without being able to see any more in them than a blind man'), he wrote at once to Falconet and to General Betski, Intendant of the Imperial Buildings, to inform them of the forthcoming sale. Catherine replied that she had already heard about Gaignat's death and its repercussions in the art world from Galitzin, but doubted whether she could acquire anything as the Duc de Choiseul was certain to take it all. Diderot insisted that he had been told by an excellent informant (Rémy, the Duke's agent) that Monseigneur had no such intention. This was not accurate and Monseigneur in fact bought up almost everything. When the sale was held in December 1768, Diderot was, however, able to obtain four pictures: three Gerard Dou and one Murillo, to which he added a Jean-Baptiste Vanloo, for a total cost of 17,535 *livres*. . . .

The Empress had by this time already built her Hermitage, subsequently known as 'the Little Hermitage' to distinguish it from the Old Hermitage and the New Hermitage by which it was later to be flanked. Since it was, of course, useless to collect pictures without being able to exhibit them properly and since all the kings and nobles of Europe possessed their own galleries or cabinets, Catherine, who was in due course to have her own opera and ballet companies, her own orchestra and, for more private occasions, her own string quartet, had of course to have her own museum. Her plans were drawn up by the French architect Vallin de la Mothe (1729–1800) who had previously built for Elizabeth the Academy of Fine Arts and who, according to Sartoris, was spreading in Russia the style of Gabriel. The calm of his classical façades contrasted with Rastrelli's dancing baroque. . . . The walls were covered with pictures from top to bottom, in such quantity that it was necessary to invent a system of hinged panels making it possible to superimpose one picture on another and yet to see them easily. . . .

The credit for today's Hermitage is due not only to Catherine but also, indirectly, to aristocrats whose collections in whole or in part came to swell the treasures of the Hermitage after or even, in some cases, before the Revolution. Catherine's favourites must also be counted in the same category. To General Potemkin, the reigning favourite for fifteen years, we owe a 'Family portrait' by Corneille de Vos; 'Alexander and the family of Darius' by Mignard and two Reynolds, purchased for one hundred and five hundred *livres* respectively: 'Cupid untying the Girdle of Venus', a masterpiece of colour created by the artist on a theme which in the hands of any other painter might have been a mere piece of coquetry, and 'The Continence of Scipio'.

Catherine loved to inspire in those around her her own love of art. 'I am rendering a service to the Hermitage by undertaking to educate the taste of talented young men,' runs a revealing phrase apropos of her favourites. . . .

Following her example, her son the Grand Duke also took to collecting. 'The Grand Duke and the Grand Duchess', wrote Catherine, 'are stuffing their apartments full of all sorts of odds and ends of pictures and it gives me great pleasure to procure some for them. They actually have a hundred or so which would not disgrace the Hermitage.'

Even if Catherine cannot be said to have created a taste for art in St Petersburg, she did at least make it the fashion. It is doubtful if, without her example, the Boyars would ever have collected with such fervour. A certain feeling of rivalry certainly urged them to increase their purchases. The city now began to contain so many art collectors that several artists envisaged setting up their studios on the banks of the Neva and travelling dealers came to offer pictures and engravings. . . .

By the end of Catherine's reign three galleries were fully laid out: the Little Hermitage, finished in 1768 by Vallin de la Mothe, the Raphael *Loggie*, designed by Quarenghi and opened in 1788, and what is now called the Old Hermitage, built by Felten between 1775 and 1784 by extending the façade of the Winter Palace along the river bank. In order to visit them, it was necessary to seek the permission of General Betski who, in the course of a long stay in Paris, had conceived a great passion for the fine arts and who served Catherine as Intendant of Buildings. The sculptors and architects who worked for the Empress (particularly Falconet) often complained to her on this score: Betski, they said, sabotaged their efforts. Catherine, however, never forgot that he had been instrumental in putting her on the throne and always remained completely faithful to him. Betski's decision was thus final. In the galleries, accompanied by the Curator, one might see not only foreign visitors, and Russian collectors but also students from the Academy of Fine Arts, who came with their masters to copy the pictures of their choice.

[11] A conducted tour of the Hermitage for English and other distinguished visitors in 1792, from *A Tour of Russia, Siberia and the Crimea* by J. Parkinson.

Sunday, 25th November

The Empress [Catherine the Great] having graciously permitted all the foreigners in Petersburg to see the Hermitage – this morning, we repaired thither between the hours of ten and eleven. . . . We were not permitted to enter with swords or sticks; but they were required to be delivered up before we went in. Quarenghi joined us there and was of great service to us in pointing out what particularly deserved our attention. In so short a time, however, and in such a crowd, it was impossible to see such a profusion to any good purpose or with any satisfaction.

We first saw the Royal apartments, which occupy that side of the building which fronts towards the river, we then passed through the picture Galleries which [form] the three other sides of a square. Afterwards we went by Raphael's Gallery to the Cabinets of Medals, Mineralogy and what I must call for want of a better word 'bijouterie': and we concluded with the Theatre, which as well as Raphael's Gallery, copied after that at the Vatican, were the work of our friend Quarenghi. This last, he said, had given him immense trouble.

The Apartments as well as the Galleries are crowded with paintings, good and bad placed promiscuously together: composed on the whole I think of no less than ten collections. There are several valuable pieces in this number from the Italian School, but the finest are from the Dutch and Flemish. I shall only mention, the Adoration and the Bacchus by

Rubens, the Wounded Adonis by Vandyke, three pieces by
Teniers – two landscapes, and a third affair, the largest picture
he ever painted. At least if there is a duplicate of this or one
more as large that is all. Three or four admirable pieces by
Wouvermans. The prodigal returning by Rembrandt. The
pictures by Teniers are all hung up in one room, those by
Wouvermans in another, those by Vandyke in a third, those
by Nic. Poussin in a fourth, and those by Luca Giordano all
together in a particular part of the gallery. This is almost the
only order observable. In the galleries copies were making of
some pictures, particularly of Scipio's continence by Sir
Joshua Reynolds and of Guido's Doctors consulting on the
immaculate purity of the Virgin Mary (this is reckoned one
of the finest pictures Guido ever painted). Sir Watkin recognized here the Perseus and Andromeda by Mengs which
having been ordered by his father at Rome, was taken on its
way to England by a Spanish vessel and sold to the Empress.

At the back of the long room where the Empress usually
sits is a winter Garden composed of several little groves of
evergreen trees, encircled by gravel walks and inhabited by a
great variety of foreign birds. It is a curious circumstance that
the arrangement of this garden is altered every fortnight. In
point of size and beauty it is not to be compared with that at
the Horse Guards. The Empress, we were [told], takes no
delight in it and seldom goes into it, as one might conclude
indeed from the forlorn state, particularly of the gilding.

In one of the apartments we were shown the trap doors
through which her Majesty can have her dinners sent up
when she chuses to dine without any attendants. A portrait
of Zeuboff's brother, a young officer in the army, of the
French Princes and that of a favourite (who died, as Q
[uarenghi] expressed it *en sa place*, a very worthy young man,
qui convenoit parfaitement à l'Imperatrice) appear in the
Gallery. I was very much struck with a portrait of the Empress
in the uniform of the Guards and on horseback as she was
habited on the day she mounted the throne.

In one of the apartments we were particularly desired to
remark two models by Falconet, one of a female sitting, the
other of Pygmalion with the statue which he made before
him. They were greatly commended by Quarenghi. The Her-

cules of Sir Joshua Reynolds, which was ordered by the Empress, but for which it is doubtful whether she ever paid, is in the Cabinet of Medals. Quarenghi's opinion of Sir Joshua is that his excellence was confined to portraits, in which department he allows him all possible merit, as he does for his admirable discourses.

They manufacture larger mirrors at Petersburg than anywhere else in Europe. These apartments are embellished with a profusion of them and they often produce an agreeable effect. In the *Cabinet des Mineraux* etc. we saw several specimens of the Marbles in the neighbourhood of Petersburg, of which we were assured, both by Quarenghi and the Princess Dashkoff that there is a great variety, but almost totally unknown to the Russians themselves. In what I call the Toy Cabinet over each of the Cases there was a model of some ruin in Rome and Quarenghi told me that they have somewhere in the palace models like these of all the Roman Ruins. . . .

Monday, 26th November

About twelve we received a visit from Quarenghi. . . . Speaking of the Favourites, he told us that there had been fourteen *en titre*, that several had been dismissed for bad behaviour, especially for their infidelity. The Empress's hour of dining is one, after dinner she retires to the Hermitage where she passes about two hours with the favourite; as she is now old she varies her hours according to his inclination and finds it necessary to pay her court. His levée is attended every morning before the Empress's by all the People of the first Quality while he is dressing; during which time they all stand and he keeps his seat. His father himself pays court to the son. The Empress Elizabeth had her lovers but they were amongst her Ministers etc.

She is generous from ostentation. Her Valet de Chambre, the most honest man living and exceedingly attached, has never received anything above his wages.

[12] Catherine the Great's love letters to Prince Grigory Potemkin in the Winter Palace and Hermitage: problems

of communication; from *Lettres d'Amour de Catherine II à Potemkin*, edited by G. Oudard.

My little darling, good morning! As so often happens, I could not enter your apartments as the Palace is full of human cattle, wandering about in the passages. I greet you from afar and pray for your good health.

I am writing to you from the Hermitage where I have no page. Last night I suffered from colic. My little Gricha, it is difficult for me to come to you in the morning. From afar I bid you a written good morning and not *viva voce* as I used to at Tsarskoye Selo. The Neva is still covered with ice and people walk across it. Forbid Tolstoi to do this as he has children and serves me well. I won't have him drowning. What he said yesterday pleased me. '*Ce sont les sentiments d'un honnète homme et d'une âme remplie de candeur; cela ressemble à bon père.*' Enough talk about others, let's now talk about ourselves. Thanks to you I got up very happily, '*vous faites mon bonheur. Dieu donne que je paisse faire le vôtre.*' I was a little cross with you, but after punishing you, my anger melted away, and now I am well disposed towards you. This is how one must deal with you, my cossack of the Yaik.

Beloved soul, I feel such tenderness for you that if my heart could speak, my letter would be far too long and you do not like that. So, I am obliged to say farewell to my giaour, Muscovite, Cossack, darling, who in turn is sulky, handsome, the most intelligent, the bravest, the gayest! You well know that because you possess all these qualities which are those I like best, that I love you so much. I can't express my feelings. '*Mon coeur, mon esprit et ma vanité sont également et parfaitement contents de Votre Excellence parce que Votre Excellence est excellent, delicieux, très aimable, tres amusant, et, précisément, tout ce qu'il me faut. Et il faudrait, je crois, se donner au Diable pour pouvoir vous quitter.*'

Darling, I am going to bed and the door will be closed. If despite all you come and are unable to break through, I will shed bitter tears tomorrow. Therefore I ask you to stay in your rooms and to be assured, my little soul, that you cannot be loved more than you are.

Mon cher ami et Epoux – hearing you were unwell, I came out to see you but found in the corridors such a crowd of officers and servants, I had to turn back. Your illness upsets me greatly. I am told you are preparing yourself for death! My darling, you are not the only sick person in the world, there are invalids in the city whom not one Argus could heal. Darling soul, let me know if and when I can come and see you today?

Too much! Even at 9 p.m., I can't find you alone! I tried but there was a crowd walking about, coughing, making a noise. I came only to tell you I love you excessively.

[13] Catherine's social rules for herself and her guests at the Hermitage, from *Russia, abridged from the French of the Marquis de Custine.*

CODE OF THE EMPRESS CATHERINE

At the entrance of one hall, I found behind a green curtain the social rules of the Hermitage, for the use of those intimate friends admitted by the Czarina into her asylum of Imperial liberty.

I will transcribe, *verbatim*, this charter, granted to social intimacy by the caprice of the sovereign of the once enchanted place: it was copied for me in my presence: –

RULES TO BE OBSERVED ON ENTERING.

ARTICLE I.

On entering, the title and rank must be put off, as well as the hat and sword.

ARTICLE II.

Pretensions founded on the prerogatives of birth, pride, or other sentiments of a like nature, must also be left at the door.

ARTICLE III.

Be merry; nevertheless, *break nothing and spoil nothing.*

ARTICLE IV.

Sit, stand, walk, do whatever you please, without caring for any one.

ARTICLE V.

Speak with moderation, and not too often, in order to avoid being troublesome to others.

ARTICLE VI.

Argue without anger and without warmth.

ARTICLE VII.

Banish sighs and yawns, that you may not communicate *ennui*, or be a nuisance to any one.

ARTICLE VIII.

Innocent games, proposed by any members of the society, must be accepted by the others.

ARTICLE IX.

Eat slowly *and with appetite*: drink with moderation, that each may walk steadily as he goes out.

ARTICLE X.

Leave all quarrels at the door; what *enters at one ear must go out at the other* before passing the threshold of the Hermitage. If any member violate the above rules, for each fault witnessed by two persons, he must drink *a glass of fresh water (ladies not excepted)*: furthermore, he must read aloud a page of the *Telemachiad* (a poem by Trediakofsky). Whoever fails during one evening in three of these articles, must learn by heart six lines of the *Telemachiad*. He who fails in the tenth article must never more re-enter the Hermitage.

[14] The richness and splendour of the Court at the Winter Palace in the early 1780s, from *Travels into Poland, Russia, Sweden and Denmark* by William Coxe.

On every court day the great-duke [Paul, later Paul I] and duchess have also their separate levées at their own apartments in the palace. Upon particular occasions, such as her own and the empress's birth-day, foreigners have the honour of kissing her imperial highness's hand; but upon common days that ceremony is omitted.

In the evening of a court day, there is always a ball at the palace, which begins between six and seven. At that time the foreign ladies kiss the empress's [Catherine the Great's] hand, who salutes them in return on the cheek. Her majesty, unless she is indisposed, generally makes her appearance about seven; and, if the assembly is not very numerous, plays at Macao in the ballroom; the great-duke and duchess, after they have danced, sit down to whist. Their highnesses, after a short interval, rise; approach the empress's table; pay their respects; and then return to their game. When the ball happens to be crouded; the empress forms her party, as I have before mentioned, in an adjoining room, which is open to all persons who have once been presented.

The richness and splendour of the Russian court surpasses description. It retains many traces of its antient Asiatic pomp, blended with European refinement. An immense retinue of courtiers always preceded and followed the empress; the costliness and glare of their apparel, and a profusion of precious stones, created a splendour, of which the magnificence of other courts can give us only a faint idea. The court-dress of the men is in the French fashion: that of the ladies is a gown and petticoat, with a small hoop, the gown has long hanging-sleeves and a short train, and is of a different colour from the petticoat. The ladies wore, according to the fashion of the winter of 1777 at Paris and London, very lofty head-dresses, and were not sparing in the use of rouge. Amid the several articles of sumptuousness which distinguish the Russians nobility; there is none perhaps more calculated to strike a foreigner than the profusion of diamonds and other precious stones, which sparkle in every part of their dress. In most other European countries these costly ornaments are (excepting among a few of the richest and principal nobles) almost entirely appropriated to the ladies; but in this the men vie with the fair sex in the use of them. Many of the nobility were almost covered with diamonds; their buttons, buckles, hilts of swords, and epaulets, were composed of this valuable material; their hats were frequently embroidered, if I may use the expression, with several rows of them; and a diamond-star upon the coat was scarcely a distinction. This passion for jewels seems to pervade the lower ranks of people, for even private families abound with them; and the wife of a common Russian burgher will appear with a head-dress or girdle of pearls, and other precious stones, to the value of two or three hundred pounds. I will only mention a few more particulars; when the solemnity of the occasion added some variety to the general sameness which characterises a court.

The empress, on days of high ceremony, generally wears a crown of diamonds of immense value; and appears with the ribbands of the order of St Andrew and Merit, both of them flung over the same shoulder, with the collars of those orders, and the two stars emblazoned one above the other upon her vest.

On certain anniversaries the empress dines in public; two of these days occurred in the course of our stay at Petersburgh. The 2nd of December being the feast of the Ismailof regiment of guards, her majesty, who as sovereign is colonel of the corps, gave, according to annual custom, a grand entertainment to the officers. Being desirous to be present, we repaired to court at twelve. Her majesty was dressed in the uniform of the regiment, which is green trimmed with gold lace, made in the form of a lady's riding habit. As soon as all the officers of the regiment had kissed her hand; a salver of wine was brought in by one of the lords in waiting, and the empress presented a glass to each officer, who received it from her hands, and, after a low obeisance, drank it off. At the conclusion of this ceremony her majesty led the way, about one o'clock, into an adjoining apartment, in which a sumptuous dinner was spread: she took her place in the middle of the table; and the officers were ranged on each side according to their respective ranks. The empress helped the soup herself; and paid the greatest attention to her guests during the whole repast.

[15] A review witnessed from the Winter Palace by the American Minister John Quincy Adams in 1812, from *The Memoirs of John Quincy Adams.*

25th (January). At twelve o'clock I went with Mr Smith to the Winter Palace, expecting an ordinary circle on account of the Empress's [Elisaveta Alexeyievna's] birthday, instead of which we were regaled with the most unpleasant and dangerous part of the ceremony, which had been postponed from the sixth, and which I had flattered myself we should escape this year. We were introduced first to the Hermitage, by the door from the Grande Millione, and soon after were conducted to the Great Hall upon the quay to witness the filing off of the troops before the Emperor [Alexander I]. The two Empresses came sufficiently muffled up in furs, and went out upon the balcony. Reamur's thermometer was from ten to twelve degrees below zero – the precise degree of cold which was alleged last week for omitting the parade and the Court. It was indispensable to follow them out upon the balcony, bareheaded, without pelisse, with silk stockings and thin shoes. They both immediately and strongly recommended to us to go into the hall, and after a very few minutes I took them at their word; not, however, until I had been thoroughly chilled by the zephyr from the quay. The troops were more than an hour filing off; and Count Maistre and the Chevalier Bezerra stood it out almost the whole time. The other members of the Corps Diplomatique all withdrew into the hall, which was itself abundantly cold. The French Ambassador, who has been very ill, and several days confined even to his bed, was out on horseback in the suite of the Emperor. He came up, however, before the troops had all passed, and in time to make his compliments to the two Empresses. The true courtiers stuck to the balcony at the risk of their lives, but I thought my privilege as a republican would be an apology for me, and that I should be doubly ridiculous to stand there, cap in hand, shrugging my shoulders before the two Empresses, and my teeth chattering and my limbs shivering with cold. About three o'clock we were released, and I came home.

[16] Nicholas I kisses seven hundred subjects at Court on Easter Day, 1826, from *Original Letters from Russia, 1825–1828* edited by Charlotte Disbrowe.

FROM MRS DISBROWE.
4 May,
ST PETERSBURG, 22 April, 1826.

Now, to begin my Easter history, for like the rest of the Russian world, we have thought it necessary to make this quite an epoch, to be beguiling ourselves with the illusion that we are particularly happy and superlatively amused. I must date from last Saturday at midnight, when, accompanied by John and my Sposo, I went to the Imperial Chapel, in full puff, and had the exquisite satisfaction of seeing Nicholas the 1st slobber some hundreds of old and young, tall and short, thin and thick, ugly and handsome dutiful subjects of the male kind; such a ceremony. It began with the Archimandrite, and terminated with Count Salahoub, Maitre des Ceremonies, of whom Papa no doubt has a tender recollection. The Empresses were not present. The young one was ill, and the Dowager did not like to appear in public, so that the scene was not so splendid as it usually is. The maids of honour who did attend were, generally speaking, old and ugly. The Emperor kissed about seven hundred on both cheeks, and it really was a most extraordinary spectacle to see these people come up to him in regular files or rather strings, to receive the accolade; and how thoroughly His Imperial Majesty rubbed and wiped and rubbed again his mouth which had been in such constant exercise for about two hours and a half. Luckily the variety of heights and breadths combined occasioned some diversity of motion, or he certainly would have had a *torticolis* after it, It was over about three o'clock, but our expedition did not end there, for on quitting the palace we observed a tremendous fire, and supposing it to be at no great distance, we thought to take a look at it; but after proceeding about four versts we gave up the plan. The Emperor however went, as is the custom on such occasions, and did not get home till six o'clock. Twelve brick houses were burnt, about an equal number of wooden ones, and many horses perished. It began about ten o'clock, when almost every person was in the churches, and no assistance could be procured for some time.

Owing to Halker's discretion I saw no genuine celebration of Easter Sunday. He prevented the *esvoscheks* (coachmen) and *d'vornecks* from presenting me their offerings in person, so I received the eggs in a very humdrum way, and paid ten roubles for each de même. I forgot to say that the Emperor kisses the Archdeacons and Deacons three times, in token of the Trinity, one on each cheek, and the third on the *chin*. I hear he did not shave for the two preceding days, in order to ward off as much contact as possible.

[17] A Christmas Ball in the Winter Palace's *Salle Blanche*, as witnessed by Lady Londonderry in 1836, from *The Russian Journal of Lady Londonderry, 1836–7.*

Saturday 7th, New Style, December 26th, Old. On this day the long looked for ball which had been postponed from December 6th Old Style took place. Only a part of the Palace was thrown open and that was lighted by ten thousand candles.

The *Salle Blanche* is a gallery one hundred and thirty feet by forty nine with columns supporting a gallery which was filled with spectators. The room is of dazzling whiteness and without a line of gilding and with four immense stoves which had externally the appearance of banners and standards. The pillars were wreathed with candles, the whole a perfect blaze of light, and three thousand here produced literally the effect of daylight in which they themselves seemed to burn dim and blue.

When the company was assembled the doors opened and the Imperial family walked in and rarely does one find united so much grace and beauty. The Empress [Alexandra Feodorovna] was dressed in white with *colonnes* of large single diamonds round her gown from her waist to her feet. She had a *couronne du moyen age* at the back of her head and a small low one on her forehead, the shape of the whole perfectly classic, not a jewel or colour but these enormous diamonds which she called *mes cailloux*, and which, except on her, must have been taken for the pickings of a great glass lustre. Altogether I never saw such a combination of simplicity and splendour.

Prince Charles of Prussia, the Empress's brother, had arrived and in compliment to the Emperor wore the light blue ribbon, the great cordon of *St André*, the first order in Russia, the Emperor and the *Héritier* having on the orange ribbon, the Black Eagle of Prussia. Great attention is paid to these details and much importance attached to them. The Grand Duchesses Marie and Olga looked lovely, their beautiful skins, fair hair, graceful figures, simple *toilettes* and amiable high bred manner delighted everyone.

The polonaises began and continued some time. They are very agreeable for those who do not dance. When the Emperor [Nicholas I] took me I endeavoured to thank him for his *cadeaux* and his kindness in thinking of me at all. '*Mais, Madame, c'était une injure d'en doûter.*' He said my letter was *charmante*, and the Empress who said the same, added, '*C'était trop bon pour lui*'. The ball began at nine. After the polonaises were quadrilles and at twelve o'clock we passed through a *Salle des Maréchaux* and a long gallery with between three and four hundred pictures of Dawe's to the supper room, an enormous *salle* with scagliola columns and blue glass lustres and lighted by four thousand candles. This was really fairyland – the endless vista, the quantities of messy plate, the abundance of lovely flowers, and, to crown all, the whole having the appearance of an *orangerie*, the supper tables being so constituted as to let the stems of the immense orange trees through so that we literally sat under their shade and perfume. The scene was perfect enchantment and eight hundred and fifty sat down to supper without the slightest confusion or squeeze. The Empress, according to the strict old etiquette of Russian hospitality, went round all the tables and spoke to every person until she fainted away. She soon recovered and after we returned to *la Salle Blanche* she retired with the rest of the Imperial family and thus ended this magnificent fête . . .

New Year's Day
Friday 13th. This being the Russian New Year's Day, the great ball at Court was to have taken place but unfortunately the Empress was taken ill and it was put off. It was a great disappointment to me not to see this unique fête as it had been described to me so as to excite my utmost curiosity.

The whole of the Hermitage and Winter Palace are thrown open and lighted up and crowds of the commonest and dirtiest people admitted. Above forty thousand tickets are issued and coachmen, servants, moujiks, etc. are all allowed to enter, walk about and take refreshment.

The crowd, the heat, the smell, the squeeze are not to be imagined and nothing can penetrate the solid mass except when the Emperor appears, and holding up a finger requests his children to let him pass and the crowd falls back. It is spoken of as the most beautiful and touching sight to see the Sovereign in the midst of his subjects, the love and veneration shown, and the propriety of conduct of all these people high and low, rich and poor – not a case of drunkenness or dishonesty. Though all the treasures of the Palace are left open, not a bit of plate is ever missed.

Ice
From the Michael Palace we went to take leave of the Ficquelmonts, and lastly of Lord Durham from whence we returned home tired and worn. I found Count Orlov had called twice to bring me the Emperor's autograph and General Kisselov had also called and brought me a little bust of the Emperor Alexander. I was very sorry to have missed them; indeed all the kindness shown us, the entreaties to us to prolong our stay and the regrets at our departure made me quite grieved to go. A singular sight in St Petersburg is a train of little carts each loaded with one enormous, thick, square block of ice, all as if turned out of one mould of the clearest, transparent sea green, and when the sun plays on them as brilliant as aquamarines. Sometimes these huge blocks are set up like a sort of Stonehenge or miniature Giant's Causeway

on the Neva. I asked Madame Stroganov one day what they were for. '*Mais je les appelle les violettes de Petersburg*', was her reply because it is a sort of hope of spring when people begin to fill their icehouses. Another peculiar scene I have often wished to sketch is a Russian hall and stairs during the ball above, the steps regularly lined and the space below filled with servants – immense creatures in large cocked hats and enveloped in the skins of wolves, bears, foxes, hyenas, racoons, etc. and looking like wild beasts or savages each carefully nursing his mistress'[s] rare and costly fur and holding it with a sort of reverential respect almost during his sleep.

On Thursday 9th we left St Petersburg. Its climate is certainly as pernicious as the deadly upas tree; the severe cold, the damp exhalations attendant on its marshy position, and the sudden changes of temperature make it most trying to the strongest constitutions, but it is a wonderfully magnificent city and a most agreeable séjour. The colossal scale of everything – its palaces, institutions, buildings, fêtes, etc. strike the mind with wonder, while the kindness, cordiality and friendly hospitality of the people warm the heart. They are the most intelligent, agreeable, *distingués* clever persons imaginable.

[18] The great fire of 1837 which led to the rebuilding of the Winter Palace in one year, from *Pictures of St Petersburg* by Edward Jerrmann.

The next day the Emperor [Nicholas I] returned to the scene of destruction. Within the walls the fire still raged. It had been allowed to burn on, whilst all efforts were directed to saving the Hermitage, fortunately with complete success.

Long gazed Nicholas in deep sorrow at the grave of one of the prime ornaments of his beautiful city. At last he raised his head, passed his hand over his brow, and said, quite cheerfully, 'This day year will I again sleep in my room in the Winter Palace. Who undertakes the building?'

All present recoiled from the challenge. There stood around the Emperor many competent judges in such matters, but not

one had the courage to undertake that which seemed impossible. There was a brief pause, and then General Kleinmichael,
an aide-de-damp of the Emperor's, stepped forward and said,
like the Duke of Alba to Don Philip, 'I will!'

'And the building is to be complete in a year?', asked the
Emperor.

'Yes, Sire!'

''Tis good! Set to work!'

An hour later the still burning ruins were being cleared
away. The destruction of the building had occurred in December, 1837; by December, 1838, it was rebuilt. Three months
later it was occupied by the court.

Kleinmichael had kept his word: the building was completed, completed in the time specified! but – at what a price!
Only in Russia was such a wonderful work possible; only in
Russia, where the will of the 'Master' is a decree of Provi-
dence; only in Russia, where they spare nothing, recoil from
nothing, to fulfil his commands.

Under the Empress Elizabeth the palace had taken eight
years to build; Kleinmichael completed it in one. True it is
that almost the whole of the masonry resisted the fire, but the
whole of the interior had to be reconstructed, and what a task
that was! The work went on literally day and night; there was
no pause for meals; the gangs of workmen relieved each
other. Festivals were unheeded; the seasons themselves were
overcome. To accelerate the work, the building was kept, the
winter through, artificially heated to the excessive temperature of twenty-four to twenty-six degrees Réaumur. Many
workmen sank under the heat, and were carried out dead or
dying; a painter, who was decorating a ceiling, fell from his
ladder struck with apoplexy. Neither money, health, nor life,
was spared. The Emperor, who, at the time of the conflagra-
tion, had risked his own life by penetrating into the innermost
apartments to save the lives of others, knew nothing of the
means employed to carry out his will. In the December of the
following year, and in proud consciousness of his power, he
entered the resuscitated palace and rejoiced over his work.
The whole was constructed on the previous plan, but with
some improvements and many embellishments. With the
Empress on his arm, and followed by his whole family, he

traversed the apartments of this immense building, completed, in one year's time, by the labour of thousands of men. He reached the saloon of St George, the largest and most beautiful of all, and the royal family remained there longer than anywhere else, examining the costly gold mouldings of the ceiling, the five colossal bronze chandeliers, and the beautiful relievo over the throne, which represents St George slaying the dragon. The Empress was tired, and would have sat down; – the patron spirit of Russia prevented her: as yet there was no furniture in the hall, so she leaned upon the Emperor's arm and walked into the next room, followed by the entire retinue. The last of these had scarcely passed through the door when a thundering crash resounded through the palace, which trembled to its very foundations, and the air was darkened by clouds of dust. The timbers of the ceiling of the saloon of St George had yielded to the weight of the chandeliers; and the whole had fallen in, crushing everything beneath its enormous mass. The saloon, a moment before so brilliant, was a heap of ruins. The splendid palace was again partly destroyed, but the genius of Russia had watched over her destiny – the imperial family were saved.

[19] Nicholas I receives his war reports from the Caucasus in his study in the Winter Palace, from *Hadji Murad* by Leo Tolstoy.

It was half-past nine when in the haze of a twenty-degree frost Chernyshev's fat, bearded coachman in a blue velvet pointed cap drove up to the side entrance of the Winter Palace on the box of a small sledge identical to that in which the Emperor himself rode. He gave an amicable nod to his friend, Prince Dolgoruky's coachman, who, having dropped his master, had already been waiting a long time at the palace entrance with his reins tucked under his fat quilted rump while he rubbed his chilled hands.

Chernyshev was wearing a greatcoat with a soft grey beaver collar and a cocked hat with a plume of cock's feathers worn in the regulation manner. Throwing back the bearskin rug, he carefully lifted out his numbed feet (he wore no galoshes and took pride in never doing so) and, livening, walked with jingling spurs along the carpet and through the door respectfully opened before him by the porter. In the hall an old footman hastened forward to relieve him of his great coat, after which Chernyshev went to a mirror and carefully removed his hat from his curled wig. After regarding himself in the mirror he gave a twist to his curls at the front and sides with a familiar touch of his aged hands, straightened his cross, aiguillettes and the large epaulettes with the imperial cipher and, moving feebly on his aged, unresponsive legs, he began to climb the shallow, carpeted staircase.

Passing doors at which footmen in ceremonial dress obsequiously bowed to him, Chernyshev entered the Emperor's anteroom. He was respectfully greeted by the duty *aide-de-camp*, who had been recently appointed and was resplendent with his new uniform, epaulettes, aiguillettes and his ruddy, as yet unjaded, face with its trim black moustache and the hair at his temples combed forwards just like the Emperor's. Prince Vasilii Dolgoruky, the deputy Minister of War, with a bored look on his dull face (bedecked with moustache, side-whiskers and hair combed forwards at the temples just like the Emperor's), rose and greeted Chernyshev as he entered.

'*L'empereur?*', Chernyshev asked the *aide-de-camp*, with an inquiring glance at the door of the Emperor's study.

'His Majesty has just returned,' the *aide-de-camp* answered, evidently pleased with the sound of his own voice, then, gliding so softly that a glass of water on his head would not have spilled, he went to the door which swung silently open and, demonstrating with his whole being the veneration he felt for the place he was entering, he disappeared through the door.

Dolgoruky meanwhile had opened his dispatch-case and was checking through the papers inside.

Chernyshev, knitting his brow, walked up and down, easing his legs and remembering all the things he had to report to the Emperor. He was by the study door when it opened once more and the *aide-de-camp* appeared, even more resplendent and respectful than before, and signalled to the Minister and his Deputy that they should go into the Emperor.

The Winter Palace had long since been restored after the fire, but Nicholas continued to reside on the upper floor. The study in which he received ministers and the most senior officials who came to report to him was a very tall room with four big windows. A large portrait of Alexander I hung on the main wall. Two bureaux stood between the windows. Along the walls were several chairs and in the middle of the room an enormous desk, with an armed chair for Nicholas and ordinary chairs for his visitors.

Nicholas sat at his desk in a black frock-coat with shoulder straps and no epaulettes, his huge figure with its tightly-laced paunch thrown back in his chair. Without moving, he gazed lifelessly at his visitors. His long white face with the huge sloping forehead that bulged between the smoothly brushed hair at his temples (which was so artistically joined to the *toupée* covering the bald patch on his head) was particularly cold and fixed that day. His eyes, which were always dull, looked duller than usual; his lips compressed beneath the upturned points of his moustache, his plump cheeks freshly shaved around the regular sausage-shaped side-whiskers and supported by his tall collar, and his chin pressed down on the collar gave his face a look of displeasure, even of anger. The cause of this mood was tiredness. And the cause of his tiredness was that the night before he had attended a masked ball. Wearing his Horse Guards helmet topped with a bird, he had moved among the throng that pressed towards him but timidly withdrew before his huge, assured figure, and he had met again the masked lady – the one who at the previous ball had roused his senile passion by her white skin, beautiful figure, and tender voice, and who had then vanished after promising to meet him at the next masked ball. At yesterday's ball she had approached him and he did not let her go. He took her to the private chamber kept ready for this purpose, where they could be alone. Without speaking, Nicholas reached the door of the chamber and looked round for the attendant, but he was not there. Nicholas frowned and pushed the door open himself, allowing his partner to go in first.

'There is someone there,' said the masked lady, stopping. The chamber was indeed occupied. Sitting close to each other on a velvet couch were an Uhlan officer and a pretty young woman with blonde curls in a domino with her mask removed. Seeing the angry figure of Nicholas drawn up to its full height, she hastily replaced her mask, and the Uhlan officer, transfixed with horror, not rising from the couch, stared blankly at Nicholas.

However accustomed Nicholas was to the terror he inspired in others, he always found it agreeable and sometimes took pleasure in confounding his terror-struck victims by addressing them in a paradoxically gentle way. He did so on this occasion.

'You are a bit younger than me, my boy,' he said to the officer, who was numb with terror. 'You can make room for me.'

The officer sprang to his feet, going pale and red in turn, and bending low, silently followed his partner out of the chamber, leaving Nicholas alone with his lady. The latter turned out to be a pretty and innocent girl of twenty, the daughter of a Swedish governess. She told Nicholas that ever since she was a child she had been in love with him from his portraits, that she worshipped him and had decided at all costs to make him take notice of her. And now she had succeeded and, as she put it, she wanted nothing else. The girl was conveyed to the place where Nicholas customarily kept his assignations with women and he spent over an hour with her.

That night when he had returned to his room and got into the hard, narrow bed, on which he prided himself, and covered himself with his cloak, which he considered (and declared) to be as famous as Napoleon's hat, he was unable to get to sleep. He recalled the frightened and exalted look on the white face of the girl, then he thought of the powerful, rounded shoulders of his regular mistress Nelidova and compared the two of them. That it was wrong for a married man to engage in debauchery was something that never occurred to him and he would have been very surprised if anyone had condemned him for it. But though he was convinced that what he had done was right and proper, it still left a nasty taste in his mouth, and in order to suppress his feelings, he turned his mind to a subject which never failed to soothe him – his own greatness.

Although he had gone to sleep late, he rose, as always, before eight. He performed his usual toilet, rubbed his large, well-fed body with ice and said his prayers, repeating the familiar prayers he had said as a child – 'Mother of God', 'I believe', 'Our Father' – attaching no significance to the words. He then went out by the side entrance on to the embankment wearing a greatcoat and peaked cap.

[20] A military review of the Imperial Guard and other regiments before the Winter Palace, from *Valse des Fleurs* by Sir Sacheverell Sitwell.

We hear bands of military music marching to the parade along the granite quays, coming from the barracks of the Preobrajenski regiment. Soon, martial music can be heard from other directions, giving an indescribable excitement to this winter afternoon. Forty thousand men of the Russian Imperial Guard are to be reviewed. Salvos of guns are firing from the fortress of St Peter and St Paul, across the Neva. We reach the square in time to see the troops converging and high officers arrive, some in sledges drawn by splendid horses, others in closed carriages along the snow. On alighting, they throw off their cloaks, exhibiting rows of ribbons, stars and decorations, over uniforms of green, and white, and scarlet. The regiment of the Chevaliers Gardes rides forth at this moment from the portico of their Manège or riding school, which is a classical building by Quarenghi, mounted on bay horses, dressed in their white uniforms, with black horsetail helmets and cuirasses carrying the Persian standards[1], and

[1] From the Persian war of 1828. The Russian ambassador Griboyedov was murdered in Teheran. On the conclusion of peace, the Persian gifts consisted of a long train of rare animals, Persian webs, gold stuffs, and pearls. They reached St Petersburg in winter. The pearls and gold stuffs and rich shawls were carried in great silver and gold dishes by magnificently dressed Persians. The Persian Prince Khosreff Mirza drove in an Imperial State equipage with six horses; the elephants, bearing on their backs towers filled with Indian warriors, had leathern boots to protect them from the cold, and the cages of the lions and tigers were provided with double skins of the northern polar bears. The greater part of this tribute of pearls was given to the monastery of St Alexander Nevski, at the end of the Nevski Prospekt, where it was used to ornament mitres and rich vestments.

preceded by an entire band of trumpeters. They proceed at the peculiar slowness of a horse's walking pace, and take up their station. Opposite to them, the Gardes à cheval in scarlet uniforms are assembling.

The Tsar, who rides out from the central archway of the palace with a great suite of officers in attendance, is received with three tremendous roulades of the trumpets and the drums. The drums beat again while he gallops down the line, his horse being already covered with foam. He then mounts a fresh charger and rides through the ranks by the side of the Tsarina's carriage-and-four which, after this, is drawn up before the centre of the line. The band of each regiment stations itself opposite the Emperor, and the march past begins. The curiosity of this performance is that you hear the Tsar's voice as each battalion goes past. He makes some remark to them: 'Well marched', or 'Very good', and the entire battalion shouts a reply. The cavalry come first, preceded only by the Tsar's personal bodyguard, mounted Circassians or Mamelukes of the Guard, some armed with carbines and some with bows and arrows. Scarlet or white predominate in their uniform, but each is dressed according to the fashion of his country. . . .

The Gardes à cheval and the Chevaliers Gardes come next: huge men, picked for their height: the Gardes à cheval in immense jack-boots and helmets that sparkle like steel, surmounted by double-headed gilded eagles, their gilt breastplates fastened over their snow-white tunics. As each battalion, marching past, comes to the salute, its regimental band immediately opposite the Tsar, bursts afresh into a frenzied rendering of the Russian national anthem, Boje Tsar chrani. This tune was composed for Nicholas I by Prince Lwow. Apart from the Marseillaise, there is no patriotic air that is so stirring and none that, in a few bars, paints a whole country and a people. In this, it is equal to the immortal Glinka. The reiteration of this noble anthem, twenty or thirty times over, each time with different instruments, never twice alike, thrills and intoxicates like nothing else. It is the expression of this nation of eighty million persons. Unlike the Marseillaise, this tune does not flag towards the middle; and we could contrast the recovery of that, with its 'aux armes' of

fanfares and of trumpets, to its magnificent peroration, with
the clashing and maddened cymbals breaking in, half way
through, and carrying this other intoxication to its triumphant
end. That it is a sort of drug or stimulant given to the troops
as they come past, no one can doubt. It bursts forth, again
and again, with sublime effect, and that clension or stroke of
genius towards the end. No one who saw a military review in
the old Imperial days can ever forget this.

After the Horse Guards come four regiments of Cuiras-
siers, a portion of each regiment being equipped as Lanc-
ers.... After them, a superb train of Horse Artillery,
drawing field guns that shine like telescopes or steel instruments, the caissons painted a light green colour, and a pair
of soldiers seated, back to back, on each. But, in the impos-
sibility of giving each regiment enough attention as it goes
past, we discuss them statically, as though they stood quite
still....

There are Hussars of the Guard, in scarlet uniforms and
mounted upon greys, a Hungarian invention of the eighteenth
century, in descent from the Pandours and irregular levies of
the Turkish frontier, the hussar uniform, indeed, being an
adaptation, conscious or unconscious, of the Magyar peasant
costume. The Hungarian magnates had their heyducks, or
bodyguards, dressed like that. After the hussar regiments were
formed by Charles VI and Maria Theresa, the custom spread
all over Europe, and to Russia.

In the eighteenth century no other body of men wore
whiskers or moustaches. For this, alone, they were conspicu-
ous in an age of powdered hair. The cult of the hussar was at
its height in Germany, of which the Black Brunswickers or
Death's Head Hussars are an example; while, during the reign
of Frederick the Great, there were twenty five hussar regiments in the Prussian army, more than one contemporary
work upon military costume being given up to the minute
delineation of their differences in colour, their dolmans or
slung jackets, and their exceptionally high, cylindrical, hussar
caps, a detail which was characteristic of the time, but had
become much shortened by 1868. Here before us, in the
square of the Winter Palace, we have three hussar regiments;
the scarlet whom we mentioned, whose officers have silver

facings to their uniforms, and two others. One of them is the Heir Apparent's own regiment, led by the giant Tsarewitch in person; white hussars, in white dolmans with gold facings. This prince, six foot five inches tall and strong in proportion, the future Alexander III, who became Tsar upon the assassination of his father in 1881, was last of the huge Romanovs. It is probably true to say that it was the physical height and strength of these giant men, from Alexander I, that supported the Russian monarchy through the nineteenth century until the accession of the puny Nicholas II. . . .

So much for the cavalry. The infantry are, mostly, grey coated, as in the Crimean war, and wear the bachlik, one of the typical features of Russian costume, worn, even by the ancient Scythians, as can be seen on the silver vases in the Hermitage, a grey hood with tails crossed upon the breast like pelts, and put over the head at night in the snow and wind of a Russian winter. Several regiments of grenadiers come first, the leading company of each breaking into a hoarse cheer as it passed by the Tsar. It is not good marching; not to be compared to our Brigade of Guards, but has a servile, grey monotony and the sense of limitless numbers, if needed, for the slaughter. Another regiment runs past, at the double; but, in all the regiments of grenadiers, so difficult to know one from another, there is, to the foreigner, something typically Russian in the shaggy shape of their bearskins, and in the knowledge that this is, particularly, a Russian invention, coming we would suppose, from the first bear hunters, in the Urals. . . . Some of the finer infantry are kept till last. They are the Preobrajenski, or regiment of the Transfiguration; a Praetorian Guard of grenadiers for they have the right of entry, at all times, into the Winter Palace. These bearded men have the look of veterans of 1812. Last of all come the Pavlovski, one of the oddest of the freaks of militarism, for they are a snub-nosed regiment, founded by the mad Paul I, and confined to those who reproduced his Kalmuck features . . .

The review ends with a furious charge of Cossacks, the square being nearly empty, for the other troops had marched to their different barracks. It is led by the Cossacks of the Guard in their scarlet caftans brandishing their swords,

which, with the curved blades, flash like silver. The officers of
the Cossack Guard, could we note them in detail, have golden
belts and bandoliers. No other Cossacks take part, except the
Ataman Cossacks, in sapphire blue uniforms, who are one of
the crack regiments of Russia.[1] They are the special regiment
of the Tsarewitch, for both Alexander II, and the future
Alexander III, wore the dress of Cossack Ataman at every
opportunity, as Nicholas I favoured that of the Gardes à
cheval. Alexander III, in fact was *en cosaque* all his life. The
fantasia ends with a flourish and a fusillade; and when the
last squadron has gone by the Tsar turns his horse, and with
the Tsarewitch following him, rides slowly off the square,
under the great archway of the Winter Palace. Once more the
snow has begun to fall.

[21] The private apartments in the Winter Palace used
by Alexander II and Nicholas II, from *Art Treasures in
Soviet Russia* by Sir William Martin Conway.

Far more interesting than the State Apartments are the rooms
in which the Tsars actually lived. They present not merely a
pathetic human interest but a psychological problem. Bear in
mind that the people who dwelt in them belonged to the
wealthiest family in the world. Whatever they desired they
could have. They possessed endless treasures of matchless
beauty and rarity. Everything in the Hermitage was their
personal property. They could have hung their living-rooms
with pictures by Raphael or Rembrandt. They could have
decorated them with the loveliest *objets d'art*, which were
stacked in thousands only a few yards away. They could have
furnished them with the handiwork of the most perfect workmen of France in the great days of the eighteenth century.
What they actually did was to hunt out some obscure set of
small rooms in some remote corner of the huge building and

[1] There were, in fact, in the Russian army, Cossacks of the Don, the
Caucasus, of Astrakhan, the Sea of Azov, the Black Sea, Orenburg, the Ural,
of Mestcherak (Bashkirs), and, as well, of Siberia and the trans-Baikal, who
guarded the frontier towards China. The uniform of most of these was the
full Cossack green. The Tsar was Ataman of all the Cossacks.

The Bronze Horseman and Evgeny, from
Alexander Pushkin's poem *The Bronze Horseman*.
By A. Benois

'The Czar Peter the Great founds the city of
Petersburg', by P.A. Novelli, *c.*1797

The Winter Palace, by K.P. Beggrow, *c.*1822

The Great Fire of 1837 at the Winter Palace
('*Der Winter Pallast in St Petersburg während des grosses Brandes*', 29 December 1837). By F. Wolff

A cavalry charge executed by the Tsar's Household Circassian Escort, on the Champ de Mars. Illustration from *La Sainte Russie* by Comte Paul Vassili

The Tsar Paul I drilling his soldiers before the Mikhailovsky Castle (where he was later to be assassinated). By A. Benois

The Great Flood of 7 November 1824: an engraving by an unknown artist from *Pushkin's Petersburg* by A.M. Gordin

On the Senate Square, the Tsar Nicholas I takes command of his loyal troops facing the mutinous regiments, 'the Decembrists', on 14 December 1825. By C.Collmann

The poet Alexander Pushkin conversing with the hero of his poem, Eugine Onegin, by the gates of the Summer Garden: behind them is the Fortress of St Peter and St Paul. From the frontispiece of the first edition, 1833

Alexander I attends the *Te Deum* at the Kazan
Cathedral for the deliverance of his people from
Napoleon in 1812, by I. Ivanov

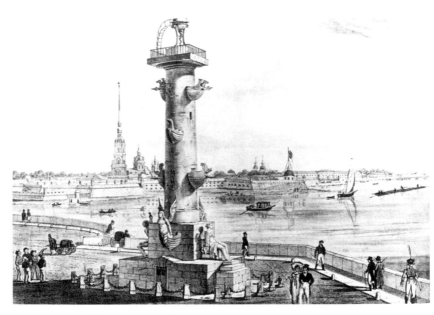

The Fortress of St Peter and St Paul, with the
Rostral Column in the foreground, by I. Ivanov

to furnish them in the simplest, least tasteful, and most bourgeois style of their day.

A narrow spiral staircase leads down to the single room, no larger than a Bloomsbury dining-room, in which Nicholas I lived, worked, slept and apparently also ate. A yet smaller adjacent ante-room served for his aides-de-camp. The little iron bedstead on which he died stands close to his desk. For ornaments he had a bronze statuette of a child, made by its mother who gave it to him, some poor pictures, and a French coloured print or two. His moth-eaten coat still hangs on a chair. His little wardrobe would hold few clothes. Inside at the back is a mirror which opens like a door and discloses another picture – ye gods! That I will by no means attempt to describe. The spiral staircase continuing down leads to a bath-room and to two or three tiny rooms in which he could receive a guest. A private door opens to the garden.

Alexander II's apartments are larger but little more luxurious. He also seems to have worked in his bedroom, or slept in his study, whichever way you like to put it. The bed was hidden behind a piece of wall round which you could walk to either end of it. Bed and floor are stained with his blood, for it was here that he was carried to die. There is a washing-stand close to his desk.

On the latter is a calendar still showing the date of his last day, his pens, ink-pot, blotting-pad, photographs, and all his little things just as he left them. It is an ugly room and contains nothing of beauty or value. The blue bedroom of his wife is adjacent. It has no view. Then comes a gold and red reception room from which you can look out, and then a dining-room with a top light rather well decorated in plaster work. The suite also contained one or two rooms for secretaries and books; that is all. The broken-backed carriage against which the assassin's first bomb exploded is preserved on the ground floor of the palace.

The rooms of the last Tsar Nicholas II possess a no less pathetic interest and are marked by a like simplicity. They contain a billiard table, a piano, a library and a study in which a heavy wooden staircase leads to a book-gallery. The ornaments placed about are very common-place, the kind of things you might buy at a bazaar. The single luxury is a small swimming bath. In the dressing-room are many Easter eggs and cheap cigar-cases, and there are many framed photographs, including those of King George V and Queen Mary, which stand on a little shelf in a prominent position. There are also in the study many personal photographs in cheap frames – of his wife as a German student, of the King of Denmark, and so forth. In the Tsaritsa's bedroom are again Easter eggs and icons, all of the latter being bad works of art except one small bas-relief in stone. Little seats for the children are grouped about the fireplace. The toilet appliances are quite simple. The drawing-room at the corner of the Palace commands a splendid view. Notwithstanding that the public seems to have obtained access to these rooms during the Revolution and ripped one or two painted portraits of unpopular persons, all the small objects were uninjured and remain as they were left. It is scarcely possible to imagine a more striking contrast than that offered by the private rooms of the Emperors and the stately halls into which they emerged, doubtless most unwillingly, on great occasions. There they could entertain a company which sometimes numbered 3,000 persons. Their own rooms would be overcrowded with a dozen visitors.

[22] The proclamation of the 1914 War in the Winter Palace's St George's Gallery: the crowd kneels before the Tsar on the balcony; from *An Ambassador's Memoirs 1914–1917* by Maurice Paléologue.

August 2, 1914.

At three o'clock this afternoon I went to the Winter Palace where the Tsar was to issue a proclamation to his people, as ancient rites decree. As the representative of the allied power, I was the only foreigner admitted to this ceremony.

It was a majestic spectacle. Five or six thousand people were assembled in the huge St George's gallery which runs along the Neva quay. The whole court was in full-dress and all the officers of the garrison were in field dress. In the centre of the room an altar was placed and on it was the miraculous ikon of the Virgin of Kazan, brought from the national sanctuary on the Nevsky Prospekt which had to do without it for a few hours. In 1812, Field-Marshal Prince Kutusov, before leaving to join the army at Smolensk, spent a long time in prayer before this sacred image.

In a tense, religious silence, the imperial cortège crossed the gallery and took up station on the left of the altar. The Tsar asked me to stand opposite him as he desired, so he said, 'to do public homage in this way to the loyalty of the French ally.'

Mass began at once to the accompaniment of the noble and pathetic chants of the orthodox liturgy. Nicholas II prayed with a holy fervour which gave his pale face a movingly mystical expression. The Tsaritsa Alexandra Feodorovna stood by him, gazing fixedly, her chest thrust forward, head high, lips crimson, eyes glassy. Every now and then she closed her eyes and then her livid face reminded one of a death mask.

After the final prayer the court chaplain read the Tsar's manifesto to his people – a simple recital of the events which have made war inevitable, an eloquent appeal to all the national energies, an invocation to the Most High, and so forth. Then the Tsar went up to the altar and raised his right hand toward the gospel held out to him. He was even more grave and composed, as if he were about to receive the sacrament. In a slow, low voice, which dwelt on every word he made the following declaration:

'Officers of my guard, here present, I greet in you my whole army and give it my blessing. I solemnly swear that I will never make peace so long as one of the enemy is on the soil of the fatherland.'

A wild outburst of cheering was the answer to this declaration which was copied from the oath taken by the Emperor Alexander I in 1812. For nearly ten minutes there was a frantic tumult in the gallery and it was soon intensified by the cheers of the crowd massed along the Neva.

Suddenly the Grand Duke Nicholas, generalissimo of the Russian armies, hurled himself upon me with his usual impetuosity and embraced me till I was half crushed. At this the cheers redoubled, and above all the din rose shouts of *Vive la France! . . . Vive la France! . . .*'

Through the cheering crowd I had great difficulty in clearing a way behind the sovereigns and reaching the door.

Ultimately I got to Winter Palace Square where an enormous crowd had congregated with flags, banners, ikons, and portraits of the Tsar.

The Emperor appeared on the balcony. The entire crowd at once knelt and sang the Russian national anthem. To those thousands of men on their knees at that moment the Tsar was really the autocrat appointed of God, the military, political and religious leader of his people, the absolute master of their bodies and souls.

As I was returning to the embassy, my eyes full of this grandiose spectacle, I could not help thinking of that sinister January 22, 1905, on which the working masses of St Petersburg, led by the priest Gapon and preceded as now by the sacred images, were assembled as they were assembled today before the Winter Palace to plead with 'their Father, the Tsar' – and pitilessly shot down.

[23] The working conditions in the General Staff (opposite the Winter Palace) at the outbreak of the 1914–1918 War, from *The Fourth Seal* by Sir Samuel Hoare.

So far as I remember there were no less than fifteen public holidays in the month of May and five on end in the last week of August owing to a perfect covey of saints' days and national anniversaries. During all these holidays the General Staff came to a standstill. Upon the Church festivals that were not important enough to be honoured with a whole holiday, services of considerable length would be held in the General Staff chapel, for no Government office was without its chapel and religious observances. Even when the Department was working, the hours were uncertain, and it was never easy to make an appointment with a Russian colleague. I remember, for instance, that at the time of my arrival, the Quartermaster General, the senior officer of the General Staff, made a common habit of arriving at his office at about eleven at night, and of working until seven or eight the next morning.

For those of us who worked by day such a mode of life made cooperation difficult.

Our rooms looked out upon the Winter Palace and the great Square in front of it. We found ourselves, therefore, at the very centre of the Russian bureaucracy. In the same huge block were the offices of the Governor of Petrograd, the Ministries of Foreign Affairs, and Trade and Industry, and the Headquarters of the Gendarmes. Beneath our windows were constantly drilling platoons of Russian recruits who, whatever the weather and however deep the mud, would charge across the square, and lie on their faces, as though they were advancing to take German trenches.

To one who like myself is an amateur of baroque, the scene was most satisfying, the great brick-red Rastrelli Palace, the endless block of brick-red offices, all of a piece with it, and a brick-red baroque arch to connect the centre of government with the city at large. True to Russian type, the façade was the best part of the building. At the back of the General Staff was a network of smelly yards and muddy passages that made entrance difficult and health precarious. Inside, the bureaucracy showed its unshaken power by maintaining a temperature that in those days of fuel shortage was far beyond the reach of any private house. As the windows were double and sealed up from the end of the summer until the spring, the power of the bureaucrats seemed to grow stronger as the year advanced.

Our caps and goloshes were left in the keeping of a Finnish gendarme in a stuffy waiting-room. The Finn's other duty was to bring us tea during the day. Hour by hour, there arrived, in every room of the General Staff glasses of tea and, unless the supply had run short, large quantities of sugar to take with it. The effect of prohibition had been to make some of the older officers require increasing quantities of sugar, and I well remember a general whose tower of sugar always overtopped the tea in his glass.

Soon after my arrival, two tiresome events happened in the Mission. One of my goloshes was missed from the waiting-room, and the samovar simultaneously struck work. Meanwhile, Petrograd had run short of goloshes, and the streets were a sea of mud, whilst the samovar either produced nothing, or tea of a curiously unpleasant taste.

At length, after several days of discomfort, the Finn entered my office with my lost golosh in his hand. He had been engaged upon the half-yearly cleaning of the samovar, and had found my golosh in it. His only sentiment seemed to be one of irritation with me for allowing my golosh to impede his duties as tea maker to the Mission.

There was a certain ritual in our work. As it was an offence of almost unparalleled enormity for a Russian officer to be seen without a sword, we had constantly to wear swords. When a Russian officer visited our office, or we a Russian office, it was necessary to shake hands with everyone in the room both on arrival and departure.

[24] The 1917 Revolution: the seizure of the Winter Palace by the Red Guards, from *Ten Days that Shook the World* by John Reed.

We went towards the Winter Palace by way of the Admiralteisky. All the entrances to the Palace Square were closed by sentries, and a cordon of troops stretched clear across the western end, beseiged by an uneasy throng of citizens. Except for far-away soldiers who seemed to be carrying wood out of the Palace courtyard and piling it in front of the main gateway, everything was quiet.

We couldn't make out whether the sentries were pro-Government or pro-Soviet. Our papers from Smolny had no effect, however, so we approached another part of the line with an important air and showed our American passports, saying, 'Official business!' and shouldered through. At the door of the Palace the same old *shveitzari*, in their brass-buttoned blue uniforms with the red-and-gold collars, politely took our coats and hats, and we went upstairs. In the dark, gloomy corridor, stripped of its tapestries, a few old attendants were lounging about, and in front of Kerensky's door a young officer paced up and down, gnawing his moustache. We asked if we could interview the Minister-President. He bowed and clicked his heels.

'No, I am sorry,' he replied in French. 'Alexander Feodorovich is extremely occupied just now. . . .' He looked at us for a moment. 'In fact, he is not here. . . .'

'Where is he?'

'He has gone to the front. And do you know, there wasn't enough gasoline for his automobile. We had to send to the English Hospital and borrow some.'

'Are the Ministers here?'

'They are meeting in some room – I don't know where.'

'Are the Bolsheviki coming?'

'Of course. Certainly they are coming. I expect a telephone call every minute to say they are coming. But we are ready. We have *yunkers* in the front of the Palace. Through that door there.'

'Can we go in there?'

'No. Certainly not. It is not permitted.' Abruptly he shook hands all round and walked away. We turned to the forbidden door, set in a temporary partition dividing the hall and locked on the outside. On the other side were voices, and somebody laughing. Except for that the vast spaces of the old Palace were as silent as the grave. An old *shveitzar* ran up. 'No, *barin*, you must not go in there.'

'Why is the door locked?'

'To keep the soldiers in,' he answered. After a few minutes he said something about having a glass of tea and went back up the hall. We unlocked the door.

Just inside a couple of soldiers stood on guard, but they said nothing. At the end of the corridor was a large, ornate room with gilded cornices and enormous crystal lustres, and beyond it several smaller ones, wainscoted with dark wood. On both sides of the parqueted floor lay rows of dirty mattresses and blankets, upon which occasional soldiers were stretched out; everywhere was a litter of cigarette butts, bits of bread, cloth, and empty bottles with expensive French labels. More and more soldiers with the red shoulder-straps of the *yunker* schools, moved about in a stale atmosphere of tobacco-smoke and unwashed humanity. One had a bottle of white Burgundy, evidently filched from the cellars of the Palace. They looked at us with astonishment as we marched past, through room after room, until at last we came out into a series of great state-salons, fronting their long and dirty windows on the Square. The walls were covered with huge canvases in massive gilt frames – historical battle scenes. . . .

'12 October 1812' and '6 November 1812' and '16/28 August 1813'. . . . One had a gash across the upper right-hand corner.

The place was all a huge barrack, and evidently had been for weeks, from the look of the floor and walls. Machine-guns were mounted on window-sills, rifles stacked between the mattresses. . . .

For a while we stood at the window, looking down on the Square before the Palace, where three companies of long-coated *yunkers* were drawn up under arms, being harangued by a tall, energetic-looking officer I recognized as Stankievich, chief Military Commissar of the Provisional Government. After a few minutes two of the companies shouldered arms with a clash, barked three sharp shouts, and went swinging off across the Square, disappearing through the Red Arch into the quiet city.

'They are going to capture the Telephone Exchange,' said someone. . . .

It was getting late when we left the Palace. The sentries in the Square had all disappeared. The great semi-circle of Government buildings seemed deserted. We went into the Hotel France for dinner, and right in the middle of soup the waiter, very pale in the face, came up and insisted that we move to the main dining-room at the back of the house, because they were going to put out the lights in the café. 'There will be much shooting,' he said.

When we came out on the Morskaya again it was quite dark, except for one flickering street-light on the corner of the Nevsky . . .

Here the streetcars had stopped running, few people passed, and there were no lights; but a few blocks away we could see the trams, the crowds, the lighted shop-windows and the electric signs of the moving-picture shows – life going on as usual. We had tickets to the Ballet at the Marinsky Theatre – all the theatres were open – but it was too exciting out of doors . . .

In the darkness we stumbled over lumber-piles barricading the Police Bridge, and before the Stroganov Palace made out some soldiers wheeling into position a three-inch field-gun. Men in various uniforms were coming and going in an aimless way, and doing a great deal of talking. . . .

Up the Nevsky the whole city seemed to be out promenading. On every corner immense crowds were massed around a core of hot discussion. Pickets of a dozen soldiers with fixed bayonets lounged at the street crossings, red-faced old men in rich fur coats shook their fists at them, smartly-dressed women screamed epithets; the soldiers argued feebly, with embarrassed grins. . . .

After a few minutes huddling there, some hundreds of men, the Army seemed reassured and without any orders suddenly began again to flow forward. By this time, in the light that streamed out of all the Winter Palace windows, I could see that the first two or three hundred men were Red Guards, with only a few scattered soldiers. Over the barricade of fire-wood we clambered, and leaping down inside gave a triumphant shout as we stumbled on a heap of rifles thrown down by the *yunkers* who had stood there. On both sides of the main gateway the doors stood wide open, light streamed out, and from the huge pile came not the slightest sound.

Carried along by the eager wave of men we were swept into the right-hand entrance, opening into a great bare vaulted room, the cellar of the east wing, from which issued a maze of corridors and staircases. A number of huge packing cases stood about, and upon these the Red Guards and soldiers fell furiously, battering them open with the butts of their rifles, and pulling out carpets, curtains, linen, porcelain, plates, glassware. . . . One man went strutting around with a bronze clock perched on his shoulder; another found a plume of ostrich feathers, which he stuck in his hat. The looting was just beginning when somebody cried, 'Comrades! Don't take anything. This is the property of the People!' Immediately twenty voices were crying, 'Stop! Put everything back! Don't take anything! Property of the People!' Many hands dragged the spoilers down. Damask and tapestry were snatched from the arms of those who had them; two men took away the bronze clock. Roughly and hastily the things were crammed back in their cases, and self-appointed setinels stood guard. It was all utterly spontaneous. Through corridors and up staircases the cry could be heard growing fainter and fainter in the distance, 'Revolutionary discipline! Property of the People. . . .'

We crossed back over to the left entrance, in the west wing. There order was also being established. 'Clear the Palace!' bawled a Red Guard, sticking his head through an inner door. 'Come comrades, let's show that we're not thieves and bandits. Everybody out of the Palace except the Commissars, until we get sentries posted.'

Two Red Guards, a soldier and an officer, stood with revolvers in their hands. Another soldier sat at a table behind them, with pen and paper. Shouts of 'All out! All out!' were heard far and near within, and the Army began to pour through the door, jostling, expostulating, arguing. As each man appeared he was seized by the self-appointed committee, who went through his pockets and looked under his coat. Everything that was plainly not his property was taken away, the man at the table noted it on his paper, and it was carried into a little room. The most amazing assortment of objects were thus confiscated; statuettes, bottles of ink, bed-spreads worked with the Imperial monogram, candles, a small oil-painting, desk blotters, gold-handled swords, cakes of soap. clothes of every description, blankets . . .

Yunkers came out in bunches of three or four. The committee seized upon them with an excess of zeal, accompanying the search with remarks like, 'Ah, Provocators! Kornilovists! Counter-revolutionists! Murderers of the People!' But there was no violence done, although the *yunkers* were terrified . . . The *yunkers* were disarmed. 'Now, will you take up arms against the People any more?' demanded clamouring voices.

'No,' answered the *yunkers*, one by one. Whereupon they were allowed to go free . . .

'*Pazhal'st'*, *tovarishchi!* Way, Comrades!' A soldier and a Red Guard appeared in the door, waving the crowd aside, and other guards with fixed bayonets. After them followed single file half a dozen men in civilian dress the member of the Provisional Government. First came Kishkin, his face drawn and pale, then Rutenberg, looking sullenly at the floor; Tereshchenko was next, glancing sharply around; he stared at us with cold fixity. . . . They passed in silence; the victorious insurrectionists crowded to see, but there were only a few angry mutterings. It was only later that we learned how the people in the street wanted to lynch them, and shots were fired but the sailors brought them safely to Peter-Paul. . . .

In the meanwhile unrebuked we walked into the Palace. There was still a great deal of coming and going, of exploring new-found apartments in the vast edifice, of searching for hidden garrisons of *yunkers* which did not exist. We went upstairs and wandered through room after room. . . . The old Palace servants in their blue and red and gold uniforms stood nervously about, from force of habit repeating, 'You can't go in there, *barin*! It is forbidden – ' We penetrated at length to the gold and malachite chamber with crimson brocade hangings where the Ministers had been in session all that day and night, and where the *shveitzari* had betrayed them to the Red Guards. The long table covered with green baize was just as they had left it, under arrest. Before each empty seat was pen, ink, and paper; the papers were scribbled over with beginnings of plans of action, rough drafts of proclamations and manifestoes. Most of these were scratched out, as their futility became evident, and the rest of the sheet covered with absent-minded geometrical designs, as the writers sat despondently listening while Minister after Minister proposed chimerical schemes. I took one of these scribbled pages, in the hand-writing of Konovalov, which read, 'The Provisional Government appeals to all classes to support the Provisional Government – '

All this time, it must be remembered, although the Winter Palace was surrounded, the Government was in constant communication with the front and with provincial Russia. The Bolsheviki had captured the Ministry of War early in the morning, but they did not know of the military telegraph office in the attic, nor of the private telephone line connecting it with the Winter Palace. In that attic a young officer sat all day, pouring out over the country a flood of appeals and proclamations; and when he heard the Palace had fallen, put on his hat and walked calmly out of the building.

The Tauride Palace

[25] Prince Potemkin's farewell ball for Catherine the Great in the Tauride Palace, 28 April 1791, to celebrate the victory of the capture of Ismailia, from *Mémoires Secrets sur la Russie, particulièrement sur la fin du règne de Catherine II et le commencement de celui de Paul I* by C. P. Masson.

The delighted eye surveyed shrubs or plants from every country, or rested with admiration on an antique head, or noted with amazement a diversity of many-hued fishes swimming about in crystal vases. These marvels of art and nature are recreated a thousand times through a transparent obelisk, and are continuously reflected from a grotto banked with mirrors. The delicious temperature, the scented plants and the voluptuous silence of this magic spot throw the soul into gentle dreams and carry away one's imagination to the woods of Italy. The enchanted illusion is only destroyed by the view out of the windows onto the icicles and frosts, heightened by all the sharpness and bleakness of winter menacing this magnificent garden.

A statue of Catherine II in Paros marble rises majestically, in the middle of this Elyseum.

Before his departure for the southern Provinces where death awaited him, Prince Potemkin used this monument to his grandeur as the backdrop for the feast he gave in honour of his Sovereign. Her lover may have had secret intimations of his death, and wished to exploit to the end the fullness of the favour which he enjoyed.

The preparations for this party were incredible, as were all the undertakings fathered by his imagination. Months before he had retained artists of all kinds; every day more than a hundred persons gathered to rehearse the roles he had entrusted to them. Each rehearsal was itself a party.

At long last the due day dawned, to still the impatience of all in Petersburg. As well as the Empress and the Imperial family, Prince Potemkin had invited the Court, the foreign envoys, the country's nobility, and a great number of individuals of the leading ranks of society. A masked ball started the party at six o'clock in the evening. As the Empress's carriage approached, food, clothes, and drinks of all kinds were offered without restraint to the assembled crowds. A triumphant fanfare from three hundred musicians greeted the Empress as she stepped into the Hall; from there she went into the principal hall where the crowd followed her; she seated herself on a throne erected for her in the middle of the hall; it was decorated by transparent inscriptions. The crowd settled itself into the boxes and under the colonnade; the second act of this extraordinary spectacle then began.

Leading the youthful flower of the court, the Grand Dukes Alexander and Constantine danced a ballet. There were forty-eight participants of both sexes, all dressed in white, with splendid sashes, decorated with precious stones worth more than ten million roubles. Special songs on the same themes as those played earlier, were alternated with the ballet music. The famous Lepicq ended the ballet dancing a measure he himself had composed. Afterwards, one went through to another hall, decorated with Gobelin tapestries; an artificial elephant enthroned in the middle was covered with emeralds and rubies; his keeper was a richly adorned Persian. As he rang the bell, the curtain rose and one saw a magnificent theatre. Two ballets in a new style were danced and the show ended with a gay comedy which greatly entertained the guests.

Choral singing succeeded, then varied dancers, and an Eastern masque of the subjects subjected to the rule of the Empress, all in their different national costumes.

Soon after all the apartments, blazingly illuminated, were opened to the excited public. The palace seemed afire. The garden was covered with sparkling stones. Innumerable mirrors, pyramids and crystal globes reflected everywhere this magic spectacle. Six hundred persons sat down to a meal. The other guests were served standing: gold and silverware were used and exquisite food was served in sumptuous dishes. From antique bowls flowed precious liquors, and the tables were lit by costly chandeliers. The desires of every guest were anticipated by the elaborately dressed majordomos and servants.

Against her usual custom, the Empress remained until midnight; leaving earlier would, she feared, destroy the happiness of her lover. When she retired, choirs and harmonious music echoed to the very ceilings of the Palace in a hymn in her honour. She was so touched by this that she turned towards the Prince to show her satisfaction. Potemkin, aware of all that he owed to his sovereign, threw himself at her feet, took her hand and burst into tears. It was the last occasion in which he could express – in this place – his gratitude to the august author of his own splendour.

[26] The presentation to the Empress Elizabeth of Catherine Wilmot, 31 August 1805, from *The Russian Journals of Martha and Catherine Wilmot 1803–1808.*

The Emperor [Alexander I] & Empress came however to Petersburg, & the opportunity of going to Moscow fail'd (from a Wisp of circumstance too troublesome to disentangle in a letter) so that I was left without any excuse, and therefore my name was given in to the Countess Protassoff, Dame d'Honneur for a presentation.[1] This delay cost me 8 days, & till yesterday the *Imperial Operation was not perform'd.*

---

[1] Countess Anne Protassoff (1745–1826), daughter of Senator Count Stephan Protassoff and his wife, Mlle Anysie Orloff. Had been a Lady in Waiting at Court since the beginning of Catherine II's reign. Was one of

Two days before I went in *full puff* with Mme de P. to make an acquaintance with the Countess Protassoff who was to present me, & yesterday at 12 o'clock you may fancy me *toss'd out* in a dress of white crape & roman pearls & white cameo ornaments, my Nob *catamomfricated* by a French hair dresser (as I chose myself) with Scarlet Larkspur to the front. (I suppose it would not be worth a pin if I did not give you this description.) Well Miss H – THERE I was driven full speed in a coach & six to the Palace of the Tauride (a lovely place as I ever beheld) & conducted by Mme de P's Servants into an immense Marble Hall (larger than a Church Miss H –) full of Statues & Columns. You will think it extraordinary that I went *by myself* but it was the etiquette! much as I expostulated with Mme de P. & Mme de Scherbenin (Pss D.'s daughter) & everyone I knew. From the Hall a dozen Servants conducted me into a sumptuous looking apartment (full of Officers in Stars) through which I pass'd, & so to another which was empty & which led to the room of presentation. Two Lords in Waiting rose up, & one of them (in the white uniform of the Horse guards with a crimson order & half a dozen Stars) very politely began to speak french to me. One other Lady had arriv'd before me. Presently in flourish'd Genl *Kutusow*, uncle to Mme de Poliansky (who is Chief in command of the troops just marching against the French) & whom I had known. He is a most respectable old Gentleman & I felt quite at ease at having him for a Sanctuary.[1] Then in came a Lady bowing like a Man (tis the old Russian mode of salutation) with a diamond Cypher on her left shoulder, & in 10 minutes afterwards a pretty little Girl looking very modest & like a Victim. We all then began to talk at one another, to

Catherine's closest friends and was used by her to spy upon her son Paul's Court at Gatchina. Was a cousin of Alexis and Gregory Orloff, and on the latter's death brought up his two natural daughters in her house in St Petersburg.

[1] Prince Michael Kutusow-Smolensky (1745–1812), Russian soldier and diplomat. Disregard of his advice resulted in the disastrous campaign ending at Austerlitz later in 1805. After this he resigned his command, but returned in 1812, when his strategy was largely responsible for the Russian successes against Napoleon. For his services during the French invasion he was created Field-Marshal and Prince by Alexander I and given the title of Smolensky.

walk about the room, & to look at the beautiful Garden in which the Palace is situated.

After having waited three quarters of an hour, at length an opposite door open'd, & thence came the Empress Elizabeth follow'd by the *fat* Countess Protassoff at her heels. The Empress is the loveliest creature I almost ever saw & in both face & figure excessively like the print of Cordelia, King Lear's daughter.[1] At her entry the Ladys rose & the Gentlemen retired. She was dress'd in white embroidery & immense pearls in her beautiful light brown hair. She has the humility, modesty, and sweetness of an Angel in her demeanour, & when we were presented & would fain have kiss'd her hand she struggled from the Ceremony & in her turn stoop'd down & kiss'd our cheeks. She spoke french to all, excepting one Russian lady to whom she spoke Russ. Her voice is very sweet & low, & she speaks as quick as lightening. Appropriate *trifles* were all of course she utter'd. She ask'd me 'how I lik'd Petersburg' & hoped it 'had given me a good impression'. I said '*it had*', (was not that witty?). She said 'she had heard of my Sister at Moscow, & that she understood I intended soon to take a long Journey for the gratification of seeing her.' I said 'yea'! & that I only delay'd at Petersb for the honor of being presented to her Imperial Majesty. She then bow'd, & after staying about qr of an hour (all parties standing in a Semi-circle by her) she withdrew with a mob of attendants at her heels, lovely interesting elegant Creature that she is!!

---

[1] Possibly from a picture by Angelica Kauffman.

The Michael Palace

[27] A ball given by the Grand Duchess Helen in 1839, from *Russia, abridged from the French, of the Marquis de Custine.*

July 19, 1839.
Scarcely had we rested from the fatigues of the court ball, when we had to attend, in the Michael Palace, another fête given yesterday by the Grand Duchess Helena, sister-in-law of the Emperor [Nicholas I], wife of the Grand Duke Michael, and daughter of Prince Paul of Wurtemberg, who lives at Paris. She is spoken of as one of the most distinguished personages in Europe, and her conversation is extremely interesting. I had the honour of being presented to her before the ball commenced, when she only addressed a word to me, but during the evening, she gave me several opportunities of conversing with her . . .

The whole length of the garden front of the Michael Palace is ornamented by an Italian colonnade. Yesterday, they availed themselves of a temperature of twenty-six degrees to illuminate the spaces betwixt each pillar of this exterior gallery with clusters of small lamps, arranged in a manner that had a very original effect. The lamps were formed of paper in the shape of tulips, lyres, vases, etc. Their appearance was both tasteful and novel.

At each fête given by the Grand Duchess Helena, it is said that she invents something altogether new. Such a reputation must be troublesome, for it is difficult to maintain. This princess, so beautiful and intellectual, and so celebrated throughout Europe for the grace of her manners and the charms of her conversation, struck me as being less natural and easy than the other females of the Imperial family. Celebrity as a woman of wit and high intellectual attainment, must be a heavy burden in a royal court. She is an elegant and distinguished-looking person, but has the air of suffering from weariness and lassitude. Perhaps she would have been happier had she possessed good sense, with less wit and mental acquirements, and had continued a German princess, confined to the monotonous life of a petty sovereignty.

Her obligation of doing the honours of French literature at the court of the Emperor Nicholas, makes me afraid of the Grand Duchess Helena.

The light that proceeded from the groups was reflected in a picturesque manner upon the pillars of the palace, and among the trees of the garden. The latter was full of people. In the fêtes at Petersburg, the people serve as an ornament, just as a collection of rare plants adorns a hot-house. Delightful sounds were heard in the distance, where several orchestras were executing military symphonies, and responding to each other with a harmony that was admirable. The light reflected on the trees had a charming effect. Nothing is more fantastically beautiful than the golden verdure of foliage illuminated during a fine night.

The interior of the grand gallery in which they danced was arranged with a marvellous luxury. Fifteen hundred boxes of the rarest plants, in flower, formed a grove of fragrant verdure. At one of the extremities of the hall, amid thickets of exotic shrubs, a fountain threw up a column of fresh and sparkling water: its spray, illumined by the innumerable wax lights, shone like the dust of diamonds, and refreshed the air, always kept in agitation by the movement of the dance. It might have been supposed that these strange plants, including large palms and bananas, all of whose boxes were concealed under a carpet of mossy verdure, grew in their native earth, and that the groups of northern dancers had been transported by enchantment to the forests of the tropics. It was like a dream; there was not merely luxury in the scene, there was poetry. The brilliancy of the magic gallery was multiplied a hundred-fold by a greater profusion of enormous and richly-gilded pier and other glasses than I had ever elsewhere seen. The windows ranged under the colonnade were left open on account of the excessive heat of the summer night. The hall was lofty, and extended the length of half the palace. The effect of all this magnificence may be better imagined than described. It seemed like the palace of the fairies: all ideas of limits disappeared, and nothing met the eye but space, light, gold, flowers, reflection, illusion, and the giddy movement of the crowd, which crowd itself seemed multiplied to infinity. Every actor in the scene was equal to ten, so greatly did the mirrors aid the affect. I have never seen any thing more beautiful than this crystal palace; but the ball was like other balls, and did not answer to the gorgeous decorations of the edifice. I was surprised that such a nation of dancers did not devise something new to perform on the boards of a theatre so different from all the others, where people meet to dance and to fatigue themselves, under the pretext of enjoyment. I should like to have seen the quadrilles and the ballets of other theatres. It strikes me that in the middle ages, the gratifications of the imagination had a greater influence in the diversions of courts than they have at present. In the Michael Palace the only dances that I saw were the polonaises, the waltz, and the degenerated country-dances called quadrilles in the Franco-Russian. Even the mazourkas at Petersburg are less lively and graceful than the real dances of Warsaw. Russian gravity cannot accommodate itself to the vivacity, the whim, and the *abandon* of the true Polish dances.

Under the perfumed groves of the ball-room, the Empress [Alexandra Feodorovna] reposed herself at the conclusion of every polonaise. She found there a shelter from the heat of the illuminated garden, the air of which, during this summer night, was as stifling as that of the interior of the palace.

When any one speaks in public with the Emperor, a large

circle of courtiers gathers at a respectful distance, from whence no one can overhear the sovereign's conversation, though all eyes continue fixed upon him.

It is not the prince who is likely to embarrass you when he does you the honour of conversing: it is his suite. . . .

The Emperor continued – 'We do not find it very easy to prosecute this work; submission may cause you to believe that there is uniformity among us, but I must undeceive you; there is no other country where is found such diversity of races, of manners, of religion, and of mind, as in Russia. The diversity lies at the bottom, the uniformity appears on the surface, and the unity is only apparent. You see near to us twenty officers, the two first only are Russians; the three next to them are conciliated Poles; several of the others are Germans; there are even the Khans of the Kirguises, who bring me their sons to educate among my cadets. There is one of them,' he said, pointing with his finger to a little Chinese monkey, in a whimsical costume of velvet all bedizened with gold.

'Two hundred thousand children are brought up and instructed at my cost with that child.'

'Sire, every thing is done on a large scale in this country – every thing is colossal.'

'Too colossal for one man.'

'What man has ever stood in nearer relation to his people?'

'You speak of Peter the Great?'

'No, Sire.'

'I hope that you will not be content with merely seeing Petersburg. What is your plan of route in visiting my country?' . . .

I left the ball of the Michael Palace at an early hour. I loitered on the staircase, and could have wished to remain there longer: it was a wood of orange-trees in flower. Never have I seen any thing more magnificent or better directed than this fête; but there is nothing so fatiguing as admiration too greatly prolonged, especially if it does not relate to the phenomena of nature, or the works of the higher arts.

The Mikhailovsky Castle

[28] The murder of Paul I in 1801, from the *Memoirs* of General Bennigsen, one of the conspirators.

It was already about a year that one of the powerful men thought it possible to maintain there was no longer any hope of the Emperor's ever accepting any reasonable advice. Count Pahlen, who shared with his master in the exercise of unlimited power, was certainly more than any one else in a position to know that while each day was marked by a plethora of violent acts, these were approaching a kind of cruelty which made some remedy indispensable in order to check the course of destructive despotism. Undoubtedly, convinced of its terrible consequences, Pahlen [who was] in charge of foreign affairs, of the police, and of the administration of St Petersburg, decided to speak to the Grand Duke Alexander about it. He presented to him all the perils which threatened both from within and without if no other order of things was established ... In reply to this first declaration the Grand Duke intimated that he could certainly not deny the aberrations of the Emperor, but that this prince was his father, and that whatever disaster might be expected in case the Emperor should retain his title any longer, he could not make up his mind to deprive him of it . . .

But after more than twenty-six people had disappeared within the first months of the year 1801, Pahlen repeated his arguments with greater insistence. Forced by circumstance, and having been promised that his father's life would be safe, the Grand Duke reluctantly consented that the Emperor should be imprisoned, and approved that he should be made to sign an abdication document, and that he should be taken to the Fortress of St Petersburg securely guarded . . . provided only that he was given a guarantee with regard to his father's life. Difficult as it was to agree to this condition definitely, Pahlen nevertheless promised the Grand Duke that Paul's life should on no account be endangered, and he wanted to perform the task on Sunday, 22nd March; but the Grand Duke insisted it should be done on the Monday, since on that day guard duties at the Mikhaylovsky Palace would be entrusted to that battalion of the Semyonovsky Guards of which the Grand Duke himself was in command and which was very devoted to him. Consequently Pahlen submitted to the wish of His Royal Highness. . . .

A few hours before the conspiracy broke out Pahlen increased the number of conspirators by drawing into their circle young men of the best families who that very morning had been degraded to the ranks and cruelly flogged as a punishment for errors which would scarcely have needed to be reprimanded. He himself hurried to release them from the cells of the Fortress and took them for supper to General Talyzin, the commander of the Preobrazhensky Guards Regiment, who, like the commander of the Semyonovsky Guards Regiment, Major-General Depreradovich, had drawn into the plot nearly all his officers. Counting on the discipline of their soldiers they did not risk to confide in them earlier. During the supper there prevailed the same terrible joy as at the feast of Atreus and Thyestes; excessive drunkenness made passions seethe.

Plato Zubov, the so-called last favourite of Catherine II, and General Bennigsen also attended this feast, and they assumed command of one part of the conspirators, whilst it was left to Pahlen to lead the rest. The number of people in both parties may have amounted to 60, most of whom were flushed with alcohol. About midnight the conspirators set out. Zubov and Bennigsen went straight to the Mikhaylovsky Palace, while Pahlen and his detachment made a *détour* in order to fetch the first battalion of the Semyonovsky Regiment. The latter had to intercept the Emperor in case he should escape through the apartments of the Empress and make an attempt to get away from this side, and it must be admitted that he would have had sufficient time to do it because the time wasted by Pahlen before the battalion of the Semyonovsky Regiment was assembled by him gave the Emperor a chance of escaping from the side which was still not guarded.

Zubov and Bennigsen let the Adjutant Argamakov walk in front. Since he had to submit daily reports to the Emperor Argamakov knew the stairs which led straight to the door of an antechamber in which two life-hussars and a valet were sleeping. As they walked along the passage which led to the room a sentry shouted: 'Halt, who goes there?' Bennigsen said to him: 'Be silent, you wretched man. You can surely see where we are going.' The sentry wrinkled his forehead and actually guessed what was going on. This sentry only shouted the words: 'Round – passed,' and in such a manner that if the Emperor heard the noise he could think a round was passing. The Adjutant Argamakov ran on faster and knocked softly at the valet's door, who without opening it enquired what he wanted. 'I have come to submit the usual report.' – 'Are you crazy? It is just midnight!' – 'Really? It is six o'clock in the morning. If you won't open you will get me into a nice lot of trouble with Emperor.' Finally the valet opened the door, but as soon as he saw seven or eight people rushing in with bare swords he took refuge in a remote corner. One of the hussars was more courageous and intended to defend himself. He was hurled to the ground by a blow on the head with a sword, and the other one vanished. Bennigsen ordered someone to watch over the stunned hussar so that he should not rise and start making a noise. Then Bennigsen and Zubov penetrated into the room of the Emperor. Not seeing him in bed, Zubov exclaimed, 'He has escaped!' Bennigsen, less excited, searched about with greater attention, discovered the unfortunate prince behind two wings of a folding screen, approached him, saluted with his sword, and explained to him that by order of the Emperor Alexander he was arrested, that his life would be spared, but that it was of the greatest importance for him not to put up the slightest resistance. Paul did not reply anything, and only by the light of a night-light one could see the confusion and terror which were depicted on his face. Bennigsen searched the room without loss of time, and found that only one door led to the apartments of the Empress; that, of the three other doors, one was the door of a wardrobe without exit, and two were doors of cupboards in which the banners and standards of the garrison and also a number of swords belonging to arrested officers were kept. While Bennigsen was putting the keys of these doors into his pocket, Zubov was repeating in Russian: 'Sire! In the name of the Emperor Alexander you are arrested'; whereupon Paul replied in a broken voice: 'What does that mean – arrested?' An instant later he added: 'What have I done to you?' One of the conspirators shouted: 'You have tortured us for four years!' The unfortunate prince was wearing a cotton night-cap; he had only a flannel bedjacket over his shirt, and was standing barefoot before the conspirators, who had their hats on their heads and their swords in their hands; those who had decorations wore them on their uniforms . . .

Zubov had scarcely stammered out his words when a great noise arose without anyone knowing what the cause of it was. Zubov fled to express his fears to the Grand Duke. His Royal Highness was living below the apartments of his father, and only his brother Constantine, and the two Grand Duchesses, i.e. their wives, were with him. Constantine had been initiated into the secret only that night, for although he did not love the Emperor, there had been fears as to his ability to keep it. These four persons were waiting for the outcome of this terrible moment with the greatest anxiety . . . Bennigsen, who on his part had remained in the Emperor's room with a few companions . . . did not utter a word and remained motionless.

In this state of stupor he was found by seven or eight of the conspirators who, intoxicated with wine, had lost their way and were now pushing in with great noise. Prince Yashvil', Major-General of the Artillery, who had been dismissed from the service some time before, entered at the head [of the group], rushed furiously at his sovereign, and in throwing him down simultaneously upset the folding screen and the night-light. Bennigsen, who during this tumult in the dark had thought that Paul was attempting to flee, or to resist, called out to him: 'For heaven's sake, Sire! Don't attempt to escape, otherwise you are in peril of your life, and you will be murdered if you put up the slightest resistance!' Meanwhile Prince Yashvil', Gordanov, Tatarinov, Prince Vyazemsky, and Skaryatin were grappling with the Emperor. At first he managed to rise from the floor, but then he crashed down again near a marble table. In falling he hurt his cheek and side. General Bennigsen alone avoided joining in this terrible *mêlée*; he called out to Paul once more not to defend himself and rushed into the antechamber to fetch a light. On re-entering after scarcely a moment's absence he saw Paul already strangled with a sash. His murderers later maintained that he had put up little resistance; he had only pushed his hand between the sash and his neck, and said in French: 'Messieurs au nom de ciel, épargnez mod! Laissez-moi le temps de prier Dieu!' These were his last words. So ended the man who could have turned the destiny of the world in a different direction and who a few hours earlier was making all the inhabitants of his vast empire tremble.

When Bennigsen saw that he no longer showed any sign of life he ordered him to be put on his bed, and covered his head with a blanket . . . After having issued the order not to admit anyone Bennigsen hurried away to report to the Emperor Alexander at what a price he had assumed power. His Majesty gave way to sentiments of the deepest pain and despair. While Bennigsen was issuing all the necessary instructions, Pahlen arrived at the big staircase in order to bar the way to Paul, and was informed that this prince had already departed from life . . . General Depreradovich, who had brought the other battalions of the Semyonovsky Regiment, divided them into several detachments, one of which occupied the hall between the apartments of the deceased Emperor and those of the Empress.

Pahlen reached the Emperor Alexander when this prince

was exclaiming, beside himself: 'People will say I am the murderer of my father; I had been promised that his life would not be harmed; I am the most unfortunate creature in the world!' More preoccupied with securing the fate of the living emperor than with dedicating tears to the dead one, Count Pahlen said to Alexander: 'Sire, you must bear in mind more than anything else that an emperor owes his title only to the sympathy of his people; one moment of weakness could provoke great consequences. There is not a moment to be wasted in order to get you acclaimed by the troops.' – 'And my mother,' said the Emperor, 'what has become of her?' – 'Sire,' replied Pahlen, 'I will go to her.' He actually hurried away to the Empress and instructed the Mistress of the Robes, Countess von Lieven, to report the recent happenings to the Empress. It may be considered as one of the strangest things that all the horrors enacted close by had not in the least interfered with her slumbers. When she was awakened by the Countess Lieven in the middle of the night she had as yet no premonition of what she was about to hear. She thought someone had come to prepare her for the news of the death of her daughter, the Palatine of Hungary. 'No, Madame,' said the Countess. 'Your Majesty must survive an even greater misfortune. The Emperor has had a stroke, he is dead.' – 'No, no,' exclaimed the Empress, 'he has been murdered!' – 'Yes, Madame,' replied the Countess. Hereupon the Empress dressed and intended to rush into Paul's apartment. In the hall between her room and that of the Emperor she found a lieutenant of the Semyonovsky Guards Regiment, Poltoratsky by name, who ... explained to the Empress that she could not pass. In the end she returned to her room, from where Pahlen escorted her to her son. The short span of time which the walk lasted was not sufficient to bring her to her senses; she declared that in consequence of her coronation she was the ruling empress and that allegiance should be sworn to her. While waiting for his mother, the Emperor Alexander could already have lost the most precious time, and seeing her in such a state he said to Pahlen: 'There we have a new embarrassment.' Pahlen did not permit anything to delay him; moreover he forced the Emperor to hurry away immediately. The same carriage which had been prepared to take Paul I to

the Fortress served to take Alexander I from the Mikhaylovsky Palace to the Winter Palace in order to receive the homage
of all the state dignitaries. Pahlen and Zubov climbed on to
the back of the coach, which was followed by battalions of
the Guards. Bennigsen was left with the Dowager Empress in
order to divert her from the ideas which preoccupied her. . . .

Bennigsen had spent more than an hour trying to restore
her to her placid dignified temper. Finally he succeeded in
persuading her that her good name must suffer from any vain
attempt she might make to snatch from her son a dignity
which the will of the nation had assigned to him. As soon as
the Dowager Empress consented to swear allegiance to her
son, the Emperor, everything proceeded as smoothly as if
Paul had died in accordance with the laws of nature.

The Bronze Horseman, and the Decembrist Revolt on Senate Square

(then called St Isaac's Square)

[29] Falconet's views about his statue of Peter the Great, from *Travels into Poland, Russia, Sweden and Denmark* by William Coxe.

'I have endeavoured,' said Monsieur Falconet to Mr Wraxall, 'to catch as far as possible, the genuine feelings of the Muscovite legislator, and to give him such an expression as himself would have owned. I have not decked his person with emblems of Roman consulage, or placed a marechal's baton in his hand: an ancient dress would have been unnatural, and the Russian he wished to abolish. The skin on which he is seated, is emblematical of the nation he refined. Possibly,' said M. Falconet, 'the czar would have asked me why I did not put a sabre into his hand; but, perhaps, he made too great use of it when alive, and a sculptor ought only to exhibit those parts of a character which reflect honour on it, and rather to draw a veil across the errors and vices which tarnish it. A laboured panegyrick would have been equally injudicious and unnecessary, since history has already performed that office with impartial justice, and held up his name to universal regard; and I must do her present majesty the justice to say, she had taste and discernment enough perfectly to see this, and to prefer the present short inscriptions to any other which could be composed.'

[30] A description of the Bronze Horseman by Eleanor Cavanagh, the Irish maid of the Wilmots, from *The Russian Journals of Martha and Catherine Wilmot 1803–1808.*

I'll never forget how beautiful Petersburg look'd the first day. Cork is a *Flay* to it; & the River as large as the Lee 5 times over; I don't believe they call it by that name tho'! We slept that Night at Mr Raikes's in a great Church of a House; very civil People, & all as one as Mr Read or Mr Anderson down at Fermoy! They gave me plenty of *Convaniencies* to wash out the things we *dirted* in the Ship, & indeed the Soap too was good enough. I'll engage I got Tai & fine Craim (& plenty of it) for my breakfast, & Miss Raikes's Maid give me a nice border of a lace Cap & Miss Wilmot's white wrapper dress'd me up smart eneough to go with the Servants of the House down to see the Palace. I thought the *Screech* wou'd have Choak'd me when turning round my head what wou'd I see leaping over a *rail* Rock but a Giant of a Man on the back of a *Dragin* of a Horse. 'Stop him' (sais I), for I declare to God, Miss Henrietta, but I thought the Life wou'd have left me to see a live Christian making such a Fool of himself, when what did I hear but that he was a Marble Emperor! Some old Snake of a Man that they call Pater, or *Pater the Great*, or something like that!

[31] 'The Decembrists', from *Lermontov: tragedy in the Caucasus* by Laurence Kelly.

The Tsar Alexander [1] had died on 1st December 1825, in the far south, at Taganrog. In his will he had made the unexpected nomination of his younger brother, the Grand Duke Nicholas, not the elder Constantine, as his successor. Nicholas, hitherto a mere General of the Artillery Corps, had been warned by Alexander in 1819 that he might have power thrust on him, but neither date nor means had been spelt out to him by his mystical, irresolute, cryptic brother.

Three thousand soldiers of the Grenadier and Marine Guards and the Moskovsky Regiment, however, refused to take the new oath to Nicholas: it meant treason to the 'true' Tsar, whom they thought was Constantine. Inveigled overnight by a number of their officers into marching onto the Senate Square in St Petersburg for the 'sake of the Constitution', most of the soldiers had no idea of the real aims of their officers, who had been conspiring actively for over five years to take power and reform the state, with or without a Tsar. Aristocratic almost to a man, 'liberal' veterans in some cases of the taking of Paris in 1814, the mood of these amateur plotters is echoed in the writings of Baron Andrei Rosen, possibly the best known of the Decembrists to have left his memoirs:

> ... the flower of the Guards, and especially the younger intellectuals, had attempted this master stroke of 1825. With youthful enthusiasm, they clung to a number of highly gifted but impractical leaders; many officers held it a point of honour to share danger and want with them whom they knew to be devoted, noble champions of modern thought, consciousness of working with the best of their time was more powerful than the fear of death or exile; for the first time they had come into contact with the Ideal, and they could not withstand the lustre of an enterprise which it appeared secured for every one who took part in it a place amongst the best and the very noblest of their fellows.

The night before the *coup*, the poet of the movement, Ryleyev, was speaking 'on his favourite theme, love of the Motherland', 'his jet black eyes lit up with an unearthly glow, his speech flowing as smoothly as molten lava'; it was not surprising that another of the conspirators (Prince Alexander Odoyevsky) should exclaim in exalted tones: 'We shall die, oh, how gloriously we shall die!'

In the event the drawing-room leaders failed to match Nicholas' will power with an effective plan. As the day wore on, the mutinous infantry saw loyal batteries train their cannon onto them. Civilians, amazed and bewildered, surrounding them on every side of the Square, took no part. At dusk, Nicholas ended the deadlock with the order to his artillerymen to fire. Rank and file died on the Square, or were drowned in the Neva, whose thick ice was pounded by shot and opened. The rest were easily arrested as they fled. The leaders, officers and a few civilians, were rounded up. These were the 'Decembrists'.

By July 1826 sentences were executed on five ring-leaders, quartering was commuted by Imperial benevolence to hanging from makeshift gibbets on the ramparts of the Fortress of St Peter and Paul. A hundred and thirty others – 'les malheureux' – began the long, fettered hobble to Siberia.

[32] The Senate Square: the Decembrist Revolt of 1825 as described by the wife of the British Minister, Charlotte Disbrowe, from her *Old Days in Diplomacy*.

He [Constantine] will have nothing to do with the crown, and so today his brother [Nicholas I] is declared. Lord Strangford says this ought to be called the Imperial year; two Emperors of Brazil, two of Russia. Constantine may say what he will; but he certainly is an ex. He got into a great passion when told he was Emperor; asked if they thought him a man to be frightened into making a declaration, or that he did not willingly resign the crown for himself and children, when he signed a document to that effect on his marrying Princess Lowitz! This resignation was formally drawn up and signed by the late Emperor Paul; one copy deposited here with the Empress-Mother and Council, and one at Moscow with the Senate and Metropolitan. In spite of this document he was proclaimed in both places as soon as the death of the Emperor Alexander was known, and all the troops and people took the oaths, and the Grand Duke Nicholas was the first to swear allegiance to him.

Messrs Heckeren and Kielmansegge have arrived, and at their instigation I took off my mourning to go to see the ceremonies at the Kazan Church and hear the *Te Deum*. I had got to the top of the stairs, when, lo and behold!

appeared Sir Daniel Bayley with a tremendously long face, to tell us not to stir, for one of the regiments had refused to take the oath to Nicholas, bayonetted two of their officers and a general; say that Constantine is shut up in Petersburg, and that they will have no other Emperor but him. They are now this very minute drawn up in square, on the Place d'Isaac, have loaded with ball, and Heaven knows what will follow! The Chevalier Guards took the oaths to Nicholas very quietly, and are assembling to quell this insubordination. The general is killed, but I believe the officers are only wounded . . .

Half-past three. I have been walking on the Quay. The revolt is in the same state; frequent cheers are heard, but they will not receive the Emperor's aides-de-camp. It is said that even all the people declare for Constantine, but indeed I think the Government has been much to blame for trifling so long with the people, trying to keep them in ignorance of everything, and thus allowing them to become suspicious. It is said that General Miloradovich (Military Governor of the town) is wounded in the side. Troops are marching up from all sides to surround the rebels. They hardly deserve that name, poor misguided people. They [the Imperials] have just found among them they will retreat down this way most likely, poor creatures!

Half-past nine. It was dreadful to hear the firing. Every round went to my heart. I do not know particulars for certain, except that at this moment all is quiet, and some say the mutineers have retreated across the river and dispersed. They were the Moskovskiy Regiment, joined by a battalion of the Fin Regiment. Do you remember our listening to their band at the camp? More spectators than soldiers have been killed, about a hundred they say. There are no hopes of General Miloradovich and a wounded officer who was carried to Count Laval's. Both the bridges close to our house were guarded, and the principal firing was down the back line, and all communication between this cut off. Every approach to the Place d' Isaac was prevented.

16/28 December. The poor soldiers seem to have been entirely misled by their officers, and soon returned to duty. They have received a general pardon; but of course a similar clemency could not be extended to those who conducted them and excited them to revolt, and a great many offficers are arrested; I am told upwards of thirty.

We are all in colours again during three days to cheer the accession of the Emperor Nicholas and his charming Empress Alexandrine, daughter of the King of Prussia. I grieve that he had such a melancholy inauguration on Monday; he was very much affected, and the Empress wept the whole afternoon. It put an end to all rejoicings; no illuminations nor public ceremonies. However, I trust that all is at an end, and everything will go on quietly. I went out in a *traineau* for the first time today. The town presented a curious spectacle. The traces of the sad event on Monday were horrid: pools of blood on the snow, and spattered up against the houses; the Senate House dreadfully battered. The whole took place on the Place d'Isaac. Poor General Miloradovich still lingers.

[33] Extracts from *The Bronze Horseman: A tale of St Petersburg* by Alexander Pushkin. (The incident described here is based on fact: particulars relating to the flood have been borrowed from contemporary publications. See also 'The Great Flood of 1824', by Robert Lee, on page 115.)

INTRODUCTION

Where lonely waters, struggling, sought
To reach the sea, *he* paused, in thought
Immersed, and gazed ahead. The river
Swept grandly past. In midstream caught,
A peeling bark did bounce and shiver
Upon the waves. And here and there,
On moss-grown, boggy shores a rare,
Ramshackle hut loomed dark, the dwelling
Of humble Finn. . . . The sun's bright glare
In milky fog was shrouded; falling
On forests dense, its sickly ray
Ne'er pierced their murk.

Thought he: the haughty
Swede here we'll curb and hold at bay
And here, to gall him, found a city.
As nature bids so must we do:
A window will we cut here through
On Europe, and a foothold gaining
Upon this coast, the ships we'll hail
Of every flag, and freely sail
These seas, no more ourselves restraining . . .

A cent'ry passed, and there it stood,
Of Northern lands the pride and beauty,
A young, resplendent, gracious city,
Sprung out the dark of mire and wood.
Where Finnish fisherman, forlorn
Stepchild of Fortune, came, intruding
Upon the calm, to cast his worn,
Much mended net into the brooding,
Mysterious waters, now there rise

Great palaces and towers; a maze
Of sails and mastheads crowds the harbour;
Ships of all ports moor here beside
These rich and peopled shores; the wide,
Majestic Neva slowly labours,
In granite clad, to push its way
'Neath graceful bridges; gardens cover
The once bare isles that dot the river,
Its glassy surface calm and grey.
Beside this youthful rival drooping,
Old Moscow fades and is outshone,
A dowager in purple stooping
'Fore her who now ascends the throne.

I love thee, Peter's proud creation,
Thy princely stateliness of line,
The regal Neva coursing, patient,
'Twixt sober walls of massive stone;
The iron lacework of thy fences,
Thy wistful, moonless, lustrous nights,
Dusk-clothed but limpid. . . .

I love thy chaste,
Inclement winter with its bracing
And moveless air, the lusty bite
And pinch of frost, the sledges racing
On Neva's banks, the bloom of bright
Young cheeks, the ballroom's noise and glitter,
And, at a bachelor's get-together,
The hiss and sparkle of iced champagne
And punch bowls topped with bluish flame.
I love the dash and animation
Of Fields of Mars where, trim and staid,
Both foot and horse pass on parade,
Their symmetry and neat formation
A pretty sight. In battles charred,
Here flags sail by, triumphant flowing,
There helmets meet the eye, their glowing,
Well furbished sides by bullets scarred.
I love to hear the thunder crashing,
O gallant city mine and fair,
When to the royal house of Russia
The tsar's young spouse presents an heir;
When mark we, full of pride and glee,
Our latest martial victory,
Or when the Neva boldly smashes
Its pale-blue chains, and off to sea
The crumbling ice, exultant, rushes.

Stand thou, O Peter's citadel,
Like Russia steadfast and enduring,
And let the elements rebel
No more but be subdued; your fury
Contain, O Finnish waves, and quell
And may the feud of old begotten
Now and for ever be forgotten,
And undisturbed leave Peter's sleep! . . .

PART ONE

Chilled by the breath of bleak November,
The city dismal lay and sombre . . .
'Gainst granite banks its waves of lead

With plashing sound a restless Neva
Flung wildly as it fidgeted
And tossed like one abed with fever.
The hour was late: 'twas dark; the rain
Beat angrily against the pane;
The wind howled plaintively, unceasing . . .
. . . And now the haze
Of night thinned out, fast disappearing,
And o'er the town pale day did rise . . .
A fearful day!
               Throughout the night
The frenzied Neva had insanely
The storm been charging, trying vainly
To gain the sea, the tempest's might
Its efforts foiling. . . .
              In the morning
Crowds came to watch the rising domes
Of waves that, all defences scorning,
Lashed at the banks with spray and foam.
Barred from the bay by wind, the Neva
Turned, chafing, back, and with a roar,
By savage wrath and passion driven,
The islands flooded. . . . Ever more
Fierce grew the storm. The river, raving,
Did seethe and boil and fume and swell,
And like a beast, for vengeance craving,
Enraged, upon the city fell.
All fled before it; streets were emptied;
Canals rose high and overflowed;
Swift torrents into basements flowed
And cellars and, audacious, raided
The homes and warerooms they invaded. . . .
The city, to the waist submerged,
Like Triton from the floods emerged.

A siege! An onslaught! Onward sweeping,
The waves advance, like robbers creeping
In through the windows, broken by
Boats flailed by wind. . . . Where'er the eye
Can reach, a host of things comes drifting:

Logs, roofing, stalls, the wares of thrifty
Tradesmen, a bridge and furniture,
The prized belongings of the poor,
Huts, coffins from a graveyard. . . .

                    The late
And reverenced tsar the scepter wielded
Of Russia then, and grief so great
Was his that, burdened by its weight,
He said: 'Not e'en a prince is shielded
From God's displeasure, for is he
Before the elements defenceless. . . .'
And standing on his balcony,
He watched with pensive eye the senseless
And dire destruction wrought. . . . The square
Was one vast lake and everywhere
The streets were streams; with seeming malice
They toward it rushed as if to snare
The lonely isle that was the palace. . . .
The sovereign spoke – his generals brave,
'Cross deluged streets before them lying,
At once set forth, the floods defying,
The drowning, fear-crazed folk to save.

On Peter's square where, built but lately,
A mansion stood, most rich and stately,
Beside whose entrance lions two
Rose lifelike, huge, their paws uplifted,
Yevgeny who had somehow drifted
To this fine neighbourhood and who
Was hatless, with his face the hue
Of death, immobile sat and quiet
Astride a marble beast. . . .

Like one bewitched and chained, a being
Lost to the world, he sits there, seeing
Naught but the water round him, and
Is powerless e'en to move or stand!
And high above him, all undaunted
By foaming stream and flooded shores,

Deaf to the storm's rebellious roars,
With hand outstretched, the Idol, mounted
On steed of bronze, majestic, soars.

PART TWO

At last, with wild destruction sated
And worn with so much violence,
Its thirst and fury now abated,
No more the Neva hesitated
But with a studied negligence
Decamped, its plunder shedding. So
A brigand and his band of low
Cutthroats and thieves into a village
Might break, and there maraud and pillage,
And shout, and curse, and smash, and shoot
Till, spent at last and nigh prostrated,
They fly, their confidence deflated
By fear of capture, of their loot
The greater part behind them leaving. . . .

[34] Herzen's hatred of Peter the Great when he first visits St Petersburg, from *My Past and Thoughts: the Memoirs of Alexander Herzen*.

When he sent me off to Petersburg to attend to his business, my father repeated once more, as he said goodbye to me, 'For God's sake, be careful; be on the alert with everyone, from the guard of the *diligence* to the acquaintances to whom I am giving you letters. Do not trust anyone. Petersburg nowadays is not what it was in our time. There is sure to be a spy or two in every company. *Tiens-toi pour averti.*'

 With this commentary on Petersburg life I got into a *diligence* of the original pattern, that is, one which had all the defects subsequently eliminated by different ones, and drove off.

 When I reached Petersburg at nine o'clock in the evening, I took an *izvocchik* and drove to St Isaac's Square. I wanted that to be the place with which I was to begin my acquaintance with Petersburg. Everything was covered with deep snow, only Peter I on his horse, gloomy and menacing, stood out sharply against the grey background in the darkness of the night.

> And looming black through mists of night
> With stately poise and haughty mien,
> Pointing afar with outstretched hand,
> A warrior on a horse is seen,
> A mighty figure, bold and free.
> The steed is reined. It rears aloft
> And paws the air imperiously,
> So that its lord might further see. . . .
>   Ogarëv: Humorous Verse.

Why was it that the conflict of the 14th December took place on that square? Why was it from that pedestal that the first cry of Russian freedom rang out? Why did the square of soldiers press close round Peter I? Was it his reward . . . or his punishment? The 14th of December, 1825, was the sequel of the work interrupted on the 21st of January, 1725. Nicholas's guns were turned upon the insurrection and upon the statue alike; it is a pity that the grapeshot did not shoot down the bronze Peter. . . .

[35] The Bronze Horseman's leap into the future: a prophecy that the yellow hordes of Asia will 'encrimson' the fields of Europe, from *Petersburg* by Andrei Bely.

Beyond the bridge, against the background of St Isaac's, a crag rose out of the murk. Extending a heavy patinated hand, the enigmatic Horseman loomed; the horse flung out two hooves above the shaggy fur hat of a Palace grenadier, and the grenadier's shaggy fur hat swayed beneath the hooves.

A shadow concealed the enormous face of the Horseman. A palm cut into the moonlit air.

From the fecund time when the metallic Horseman had galloped hither, when he had flung his steed upon the Finnish granite, Russia was divided in two. Divided in two as well were the destinies of the fatherland. Suffering and weeping, Russia was divided in two, until the final hour.

Russia, you are like a steed! Your two front hooves have leaped far off into the darkness, into the void, while your two rear hooves are firmly implanted in the granite soil.

Do you want to separate yourself from the rock that holds you, as some of your mad sons have separated themselves from the soil? Do you too want to separate yourself from the rock that holds you, and hang, bridleless, suspended in air, and then plunge down into the chaos of waters? Or, could it be that you want to hurtle through the air, cleaving the mists, to disappear in the clouds along with your sons? Or having reared up, have you, oh Russia, fallen deep into thought for long years in the face of the awesome fate that has cast you here, amidst this gloomy north, where even the sunset itself lasts many hours, where time itself in turn pitches now into frosty night, now into diurnal radiance? Or will you, taking fright at the leap, again set down your hooves and, snorting, now out of control, carry off the great Horseman, out of these illusory lands into the depths of plainflat spaces?

May this not come to pass!

Once it has soared up on its hind legs, measuring the air with its eyes, the bronze steed will not set down its hooves. There will be a leap across history. Great shall be the turmoil. The earth shall be cleft. The very mountains shall be thrown down by the cataclysmic earthquake, and because of that earthquake our native plains will everywhere come forth humped. Nizhny, Vladimir, and Uglich will find themselves on humps.

As for Petersburg, it will sink.

In those days all the peoples of the earth will rush forth from their dwelling places. Great will be the strife, strife the like of which has never been seen in this world. The yellow hordes of Asians will set forth from their age-old abodes and will encrimson the fields of Europe in oceans of blood. There will be, oh yes, there will – Tsushima! There will be – a new Kalka!

Kulikovo Field, I await you!

And on that day the final Sun will rise in radiance over my native land. Oh Sun, if you do not rise, then, oh Sun, the shores of Europe will sink beneath the heavy Mongol heel, and foam will curl over those shores. Earthborn creatures once more will sink to the depths of the oceans, into chaos, primordial and long-forgotten.

Arise, oh Sun!

The Admiralty

[36] 'The Admiralty' – a poem by Osip Mandelstam, from *Mandelstam* by Clarence Brown.

A dusty poplar languishes in the northern capital,
the translucent clockface has lost itself in the foliage,
and in the dark greenery a frigate or acropolis,
the brother of water and sky, gleams from far away.

An aerial ship and touch-me-not mast,
serving as a straightedge for the successors of Peter,
its lesson is that beauty is no demigod's caprice:
it is the simple carpenter's ferocious rule-of-eye.

The four elements in their sovereignty are well-disposed
   to us
but man, in his freedom, has created a fifth.
Does not the chaste construction of this ark
deny the dominance of space?

The whimsical medusas cling angrily,
anchors rust like discarded ploughs –
and, lo, the bonds of three dimensions are all sundered
and opened are the seas of all the world.

The poem is classical more by implication than by statement. The Admiralty – or strictly, the tower of the Admiralty building, which is the only visual subject of the poem, incarnates the original ideology of Petersburg and its dual, synthetic and paradoxical nature: the 'northern capital' that is touched by the 'medusas', 'demigods', and 'acropolis' of the Mediterranean world. Peter's will alone (he ordered that the tower and the arch beneath it convey the form of Cyrillic, and Greek, initial of his name: π) ordained the irony that Russia's access to the sea routes of the world lie through the Baltic rather than the classic Pontine in the south, which was denied him. The poem is compact of the sciences and crafts (arithmetic, geometry, navigation, carpentry) upon which Peter's scheme depended: frigate, mast, ship, ruler, timepiece, plough, and anchor. But many of the words are also chosen with very concrete reference to actual details of the tower. If it is figuratively a ship that conveys Peter's empire to hegemony not only over the traditional four elements and the three dimensions of space but even transcendently beyond them to a fifth element and a fourth dimension, the ship is also the actual three-masted ship atop the spire, the elements are the actual statues symbolizing them on the tower, the clockface is actually there (four times), and the 'acropolis' is an architecturally apt description of the colonnaded structure just beneath. The spire – or 'needle', as Pushkin called it – does indeed serve as a point of reference (a rule) for the successors of Peter: it is the visual end-point for all three of the immense avenues that radiate from it – a fact that enables one to see in this exceedingly geometrical poem the other meaning of the word *lad'ia* – not only 'ship' but also 'rook' (the 'tower' of the chessboard).

The Neva

[37] The ice palace on the Neva where Prince Galitzin was forced to consummate his marriage in 1740 by the Empress Anne, from *The Three Empresses* by P. Longworth.

The winter of 1739–40 was unusually cold, and the scientists of the Academy embarked on a programme of experiments to test the properties of ice that was available in such abundance. Knowing this, a court Chamberlain called Alexander Tatishchev thought of combining it with a new entertainment for the court – building a palace of ice on which artists and artisans as well as scientists could exercise their skills. In the end it turned out to be a setting for another of the Empress's macabre jokes for which poor Golitsyn was again the butt.

The Prince, still only a court page, was in his forties now and long since a widower. But the Empress insisted that he should take another wife. Indeed she chose one for him – Avdotaya Ivanovna, nicknamed 'Bujenina' after Anne's favourite dish – roast pork done in a sauce of onions, vinegar and spices. Avdotaya was of Kalmyk origin, extremely ugly and wanted desperately to find a husband. The Empress not only answered her prayers but agreed to pay for the wedding, deciding that it should be made the greatest comic spectacle ever seen in Russia.

A rocket whistled into the air and exploded with a loud report above the city. Within seconds a whole sheaf of rockets was set loose; fountains of coloured fire began to flame, catherine wheels to circle madly. All St Petersburg was lit up in brilliant flashes of light. The New Year 1740 had arrived.

The Empress attended the usual round of functions, but her own special comedy was due to be staged a few days later. Already the city was alive with excitement and despite the bitter cold, large crowds gathered on the frozen river, hoping to catch a glimpse of what the hundreds of craftsmen were up to concealed behind thick lines of guarding troops.

Then one morning a huge and astonishing procession formed up in the streets. Goats, pigs, cows, camels, dogs and reindeer were seen harnessed to various strange vehicles each of which contained a representative pair from each of the 'Barbarous Races' in the Empire. There were Lapps and Kirghiz, Tunguscs and Tatars, Bashkirs and Finns – each couple in 'national dress'. But the centrepiece was an elephant with an iron cage on its back. The cage contained Golitsyn and his unlovely bride.

To the accompaniment of cymbals, bells and the occasional roaring of an angry beast, the procession passed the Palace and eventually arrived at Ernest Biron's covered riding school, where a banquet had been prepared for the captive bridal pair and their guests. By the Empress's express command each couple was served with its own traditional dishes – including such culinary delights as reindeer meat, horse-flesh and fermented mare's milk. There was entertainment too. A poet named Tredyakovski declaimed an ode composed specially for the occasion entitled: 'Greetings to the Bridal Pair of Fools', and each pair of guests was made to dance its own 'national dance' for the amusement of the onlookers. Then the procession formed up again to accompany the bride and groom to their home for the night – the palace made of ice.

No other material had been used in its construction – walls and steps, baroque balustrades, cornices and columns, even the decorative figurines and window-panes were made of ice. So was the furniture – a huge four-poster bridal bed, chairs, tables, chandeliers, a clock, a commode, a set of playing cards, with the markings coloured in, and a statue of a Cupid. Outside there were other marvels of engineering and the sculptor's art – flowers and trees complete with perching birds, ice cannon which fired real charges, a pair of dolphins which breathed out flames of fire (thanks to a device inside which pumped out naptha), and a life-sized model of an elephant equipped with a machine to squirt out water to a height of two hundred and fifty feet. Everything had been done to excite the eye and astonish the imagination – and all at a cost of only thirty thousand roubles.

The Empress accompanied the bridal pair inside, saw them undressed and laid upon their bed of ice. Then she withdrew. From her bedroom she had an excellent view of the Ice Palace, and next morning she saw Golitsyn and his wife emerge apparently none the worse for their experience. The stove installed inside their chilly bedroom, as the scientists of the Academy took careful note, had proved effective.

[38] The Blessing of the Waters (c. 1792) from *A Tour of Russia, Siberia and the Crimea* by John Parkinson.

Thursday, 17th January

We were present this morning at the blessing of the waters, a ceremony held in great veneration all over Russia, and performed on this day in every part of the Empire professing the Greek religion. Mass being first said in the Chapel Royal, a numerous procession consisting of several Bishops and priests intermixed with a variety of other persons and brought up by little parties of soldiers conveying the colours of their respective regiments, set off from the Chapel, passed through the palace, and advanced along a scaffolding erected for the purpose to an octagon pavilion erected on the Canal which encompasses the Admiralty. The Archbishop, after the proper service had been performed descended by a ladder, dipped a cross into the water down to which a hole had been cut through the ice, baptised a child, and sprinkled with holy [water] the colours which had been carried in procession. A number of canons were fired to announce either the commencement or the completion of the ceremony, during [which] I observed that the people by crossing themselves expressed a great deal of devotion. They did the same particularly as the cross passed by and indeed kept their heads uncovered almost the whole time of [the] procession, both as [it] went and as it returned. For after the ceremony they returned in the same order. The crowd of people was immense; the area before the Canal was almost entirely filled; there were likewise a great many spectators on the top of the palace as well as on a low building adjoining to Count Bruce's. In general they make a point of conscience not to be absent on this occasion. The soldiers who had been on duty near the Pavilion made almost the circuit of the Area after this and passed in review under the Empress's windows.

To day the weather was not very severe; when it happens to be so it is exceeding hard service to those poor fellows, who remain on their posts from eight in the morning without any extraordinary cloathing. There have been instances of [a] great many lives being lost. For which reason, if the cold is very severe, the Empress [Catherine the Great] now defers the ceremony. I had the curiosity to go up to the Pavilion about half an hour after the water had been blessed and was much amused to see the anxiety with which the people were procuring it in Jugs and bottles; some were drinking, others washing their faces, and one man had dipped his whole head in and drenched his locks most completely. As the procession returned several persons were employed in sprinkling the holy water over the crowd on each side. Sir Watkin as a stranger by his own account was particularly favoured.

The Bishops, or at least those whom I took for them, wore a sort of Crown. The other priests, as well as the rest of the procession, were bareheaded. The priests wore gaudy vestments by which they were distinguishable as well as by their beards and their hair floating at a great length down their shoulders.

[39] Casanova sees a baby drowned at the Blessing, from *Memoirs of Jacques Casanova de Seingalt*.

Melissino and I were present at an extraordinary ceremony on the Day of the Epiphany, namely the blessing of the Neva, then covered with five feet of ice.

After the benediction of the waters children were baptised by being plunged into a large hole which had been made in the ice. On the day on which I was present, the priest happened to let one of the children slip through his hands.

'*Drugoi!*' he cried.

That is, '*Give me another.*' But my surprise may be imagined when I saw that the father and mother of the child were in an ecstasy of joy; they were certain that the babe had been carried straight to heaven. Happy ignorance!

[40] A 'regretful', 'pensive' and 'forgetful' Eugene Onegin strolls along the Neva Embankment, from Sir Charles Johnston's translation of *Eugene Onegin* by Alexander Pushkin.

Stanza XXXV

And Eugene? half-awake, half-drowsing,
from ball to bed behold him come;
while Petersburg's already rousing,
untirable, at sound of drum:
the merchant's up, the cabman's walking
towards his stall, the pedlar's hawking;
see with their jugs the milk-girls go
and crisply crunch the morning snow.
The city's early sounds awake her;
shutters are opened and the soft
blue smoke of chimneys goes aloft,
and more than once the German baker,
punctilious in his cotton cap,
has opened up his serving-trap.

Stanza XLVII

How often, when the sky was glowing,
by Neva, on a summer night,
and when its waters were not showing,
in their gay glass, the borrowed light
of Dian's visage, in our fancies
recalling earlier time's romances,
recalling earlier loves, did we,
now sensitive, and now carefree,
drink in the midnight benediction,
the silence when our talk had ceased!
Like convicts in a dream released
from gaol to greenwood, by such fiction
we were swept off, in reverie's haze,
to the beginning of our days.

Stanza XLVIII

Evgeny stood, with soul regretful,
and leant upon the granite shelf,
he stood there, pensive and forgetful,
just as the Poet paints himself.
Silence was everywhere enthralling;
just sentries to each other calling,
and then a drozhky's cropping sound
from Million Street came floating round;
and then a boat, with oars a-swinging,
swam on the river's dreaming face,
and then, with an enchanting grace,
came distant horns, and gallant singing.
Yet sweeter far, at such a time,
the strain of Tasso's octave-rhyme!

[41] The Great Flood of 1824, from *The Last Days of Alexander and the First Days of Nicholas* by Robert Lee.

At nine o'clock in the morning I attempted to cross the Voskresenkiy Bridge of boats, on my way to the General

Naval Hospital, on the Vyborg side, but was unable owing to the great elevation. I then paid some professional visits; and at eleven called on Prince Naryshkin, who had already given orders to remove the furniture from his lower apartments, the water then being above the level of the Fontanka Canal, opposite to his residence. From this time the rise was rapid; and at half-past eleven, when I returned to my house, in the Great Millionaya, the water was gushing upwards through the gratings of the sewers, filling the streets and courtyards with which every house is provided. A servant took me on his back from the drozhki, my horses at that time being above their knees, and conveyed me to the landing of the staircase. The wind now blew in awful gusts; and the noise of the tempest with the cries of the people in the streets was terrific. It was not long ere boats were seen in the streets, with vast quantities of firewood and other articles floating about. As there was an ascent to my coachhouse and stables, the water there attained but to four feet in depth; in most, however, it was necessary to get both horses and cows up to the landing-places of the stairs in order to save them, though the loss of animals was great. Now and then a horse was seen swimming across from one pavement to another, the deepest part of the streets of St Petersburg being in the centre. The number of rats drowned on this occasion was inconceivable; and of dogs and cats not a few. The crisis seemed to be from one to three in the afternoon, at which hour the wind having veered round a couple of points to the northward, the waters began to abate; and by four o'clock the tops of the iron-posts, three feet in height, by the sides of the pavement, made their appearance. The reflux of the water was tremendous, causing much damage, and carrying off firewood, boards, lumber, and all sorts of rubbish, with various articles of furniture. From the commencement of the inundation the report of the signal cannon, fired first at the Galleyhaven, at the entrance of the river, then at the Admiralty dockyard, and lastly at the fortress, was continued at intervals as a warning to the inhabitants, and added not a little to the horror of the scene. At five o'clock persons were seen on the pavements carrying lanterns, and the rattling of equipages was heard an hour afterwards. The depth of water in the different parts of the city varied from four to nine and ten feet; but along the border of the Gulf of Finland, and especially in the low suburb of the Galleyhaven before alluded to, the depth was from fourteen to eighteen feet, and many of the small wooden houses built on piles were carried away, inmates and all. A few were floated up the Neva, rocking about with poor creatures clinging on the roof. Some of these perished; others were taken off, at a great risk, by boats from the Admiralty yard, which had been ordered out by the express command of His Imperial Majesty, who stood during the greatest part of the day on the balcony of the Winter Palace, giving the necessary orders. The government ironworks, near the shore of the gulf, and two miles distant, were almost annihilated, and the loss of life was great. This establishment was afterwards removed to the left and elevated bank of the Neva, five versts above the city. Vessels of various kinds, boats, timber, &c floated over the parapets of the quays on the banks of the Neva and canals, into the streets and squares, and were for the most part afterwards broken up for fuel. As the lower part of most houses in St Petersburg is occupied by shopkeepers and artizans of various descriptions, so these unfortunate people sustained much loss, and until their dwellings were considered to be sufficiently dried by means of stoves, found refuge and maintenance with their neighbours in the upper apartments. A German shoemaker with his family lived below me, and in this way became my guests for the space of eight days. The wind continued providentially to get round to the north during the night of the Igth, and a smart frost taking place on the following morning, rendered the roads and streets extremely slippery, but doing much good by the dryness it produced. On the 20th, the Emperor Alexander, ever benevolent and humane, visited those parts of the city and suburbs most afflicted by this catastrophe; and in person bestowed alms and consolation to the sufferers, for the most part of the lower classes, and in every way afforded such relief, both then and afterwards, as won for him the still greater love and admiration of his people and of the foreign residents in St Petersburg. To assist the Emperor's benevolent views, a subscription was entered into, and the British residents came forward, as usual, with their wonted liberality. As nothing official was published as to the actual loss of lives on this melancholy occasion, it is impossible to state otherwise than by report. The authorities were shy on this subject; but from what information I could obtain, twelve or fifteen hundred persons must have perished. Owing to the damp and unwholesome state of the lower parts of the houses and cellars, the mortality during the subsequent winter was nearly doubled, from typhus chiefly, as also from affections of the lungs.

The Cathedral Church of
Our Lady of Kazan

[42] *Te Deum* for the deliverance of Moscow in 1812, and the state funeral of Marshal Kutusov in 1813, from the American Minister John Quincy Adams' *Memoirs*.

October 28, 1812.

About noon I went with Mr Smith to the Kazan Church, and attended the Te Deum for Marshal Koutouzof's, or rather for General Bennigsen's victory, and for the delivery of Moscow. The Duke of Serra Capriola and Baron Armfeldt were in the highest exultation of glory. Armfeldt had a letter from his son, who was with Bennigsen at the battle, written the day after, in all the insolence of victory. Armfeldt went about reading it to anybody who would hear him. Without moving from where I stood, I heard him read it seven times. Prince Plato Zuboff, the last favourite of Catherine, was also there. I had seen him at Berlin in 1797 and 1798. I did not know him again, and asked who he was. He has been in disgrace ever since the present Emperor's [Alexander I's] accession, but his estates in Poland, where he resided, being now over-run, he is again admitted in court. Count Romanzoff apologized to me for having permitted Mr Harris yesterday to take me a paper with bad news. I congratulated him on the occasion of the Te Deum, which he said it was to be hoped would be followed by important consequences, and especially that it would correct some opinions concerning the Russians, which had been industriously disseminated. I suppose he alluded to the reputation of the military skill of their generals. The music of the Te Deum was remarkably fine. After it was finished, the Emperor, the Empress and Empress-mother, the Grand Dukes Constantine, Nicholas and Michael, and the Grand Duchess Ann, made their prostrations and adorations to the miraculous image of the Virgin. When the Emperor left the church to return to the palace, he was greeted with three shouts by the crowd of people who surrounded the church. The city was illuminated again in the evening.

1813 (June)
Received an invitation from Princess Golenishtcheff Koutouzof Smolensky to attend the funeral service for her husband, the late Field-Marshal, at the Kazan Cathedral, Friday morning, and a notice from the Grand Master of the Ceremonies, Narishkin, that an apartment for the Corps Diplomatique would be reserved at Countess Strogonoff's house to see the funeral procession, at three o'clock p.m. tomorrow. . . .

23rd
The process was as magnificent as anything of the kind I had ever seen. The body had been embalmed at Bunzlau, and transported to the Monastery of St Serge, at Strelna, about ten miles from the city. At eleven this morning it was placed on a car and drawn by horses to the Tarakanoffka River, the bounds of the city, beyond the Peterhof gate. There the procession was formed. The car bearing the coffin, under a crimson velvet canopy, was drawn by the people. The nobility, the clergy, the high civil and military authorities, and the merchants of the city (bearded Russians) marched in the procession, which was closed by detachments of troops, about five thousand infantry and one thousand cavalry. The body was deposited on the catafalque in the Kazan Church.

24th

After dinner, Mrs Adams and Charles went with me to the Kazan Church, where we saw the preparations for the funeral ceremony at the interment of Prince Koutouzof Smolensky. The catafalque is in the centre of the church, immediately under the dome – a cubic basis, and about twelve feet high, with steps to ascend at the four corners. There is an arch in the middle of it, high enough for a man to pass through; the coffin is placed at the summit, on bars, over a cavity large enough to let it down by machinery. The coffin is said to weigh sixty poods – about a ton avoirdupois. It is surrounded by trophies – French eagles and standards, and bashaw's horsetails. All around the basis are rows of large tapers to be lighted. The whole fabric, which is of painted wood, appears to be rested on four fluted Corinthian pillars at the four corners. A figure of Fame or of an Angel, with a crown of laurel in one hand, hovers over the coffin, suspended by a rope from the summit of the dome. On the two sides of the catafalque are ranged stools, with velvet cushions, on each of which is placed some mark of dignity which he had acquired – the sword, the Marshal's truncheon, the orders of the Russian Black and Red Eagles, the Austrian order of Maria Theresa, and the Russian orders of St Andrew, St Alexander Newsky, St George of the first class, St Ann, and St Wladimir. The church was much crowded, but, by the civility of the Master of the Police, General Gorgoly, we saw everything. The Marshal's truncheon and sword-hilt are superbly studded with diamonds, and the eagle and the star of the order of St Andrew are entirely of diamonds. But the highest distinction of all is the order of St George of the first class, a plain cross, suspended by a black-and-yellow ribbon. He was the only person in the Empire who possessed it. The Emperor himself hung it on his neck, on arriving at Wilna, last December. It is reserved exclusively for commanders-in-chief of armies, and for achievements of the most signal importance.

[43] The state funeral of Tsar Alexander I (1826) from *Original Letters from Russia, 1825–1828*, edited by Charlotte Disbrowe.

FROM MR JOHN KENNEDY.

(ST. P.) $\frac{8}{20}$ March, 1826.

Last Saturday we attended the ceremony of the entrance of the body of the late Emperor [Alexander I] into the Cazan Church. We were previously assembled in the church, and remained there from half-past ten till three, excepting during the time we braved the cold and frost and a thick snow storm on the steps, watching the procession. *The Herault de Joie* in complete golden armour formed a striking contrast to the gloomy colour of the black cloth and large chapeaux rabattus, the same as worn by our coal heavers in London.

The different armorials of the different provinces and dependent states of Russia were on shields overhanging each side of a horse, one horse for each representation, and appliqués on black cloth, which, covering the animal entirely, extended two yards beyond him, and was supported by two train bearers.

The funeral car was gold, surmounted by a lofty catafalque. The coffin, when removed into the church and carried up the steps of the catafalque prepared for it, and which resembled a small temple, tastefully arranged, proved too heavy for the aide de camps, and was borne by about twenty old soldiers.

The Empress Mother came in just before, not having been able to follow on foot according to her intention. The Emperor [Nicholas I] and Empress followed immediately; then the Field Marshal, Duke of Wellington and the principal officers with the regalia. The church had, when lighted up, a much finer appearance than we had expected, but every body suffered excessively from cold, having generally supposed that, notwithstanding the total want of stoves, the crowd would make it even oppressive, whereas the crowd were not allowed to enter. The poor soldiers on duty suffered from seven in the morning all the evils of a freezing inaction, and one actually let drop his bayonet, which struck Prince Sapieha on the chin and cut it. The cold had a very different effect on one of the chief priests of the Catholic Church, for, wishing to blow his nostrils, when in the act of blessing, and not being able to get his handkerchief, he took the opportunity when leaning forward of pouring a blessing on the passing throng by a gentle, but not genteel pressure of the fore finger on the bony division of the nose.

Perfect quiet and decorum prevailed amongst those who witnessed the procession, as every body could not, and indeed few could, break through the strong guard placed at every avenue leading into those streets through which it should pass.

The body has been declared too disfigured to be opened to public view, but during certain hours of the day every body may walk round the coffin, going in at one door and passing . . .

The Imperial family went to the church twice every day whilst the body was in the Cazan. They knelt round the coffin during the prayers, and kissed it both on their arrival and departure. It was astonishing to see how firmly and actively the old Empress walked up and down the catafalque. The Empress Alexandrine seemed much more feeble. At Tscharkozelo, the hat and sword the Emperor last wore were laid on the coffin, and I was much more affected at seeing them than any thing else. Here the crowns of Cazan Tauride and the imperial crown and sceptre, and all the orders Alexander ever held, were placed on cushions and stands on the catafalque. The aide de camps who accompanied the body from Taganrog look quite worn out; and yet they say the burial is quite a second loss to them; they had become attached and so accustomed to watching the body. They kept watch alternately, night and day, and always stood on the bier when it travelled.

Ilia, the coachman, who had driven the Emperor for upwards of twenty years, obtained permission to conduct the funeral car from Taganrog to the grave. He was a very interesting person. I could distinguish his grey, bushy beard, which, according to etiquette, ought to have been cut off; but he cried three days about it, and was so miserable, that he was allowed to keep it. It is said that the circumstance of his conducting the bier tended more than anything to tranquillise the people about the real death of the Emperor, for it had been reported that he was not dead, but imprisoned, and that the funeral, etc., was an imposition; but when they saw Ilia, they were convinced that he would not have been deceived, and sure that he would not have been prevailed on to drive aught but the body of his late master. The Emperor was buried on the 14th, just the twenty-fifth anniversary of his accession, and of the death of his father, the Emperor Paul, and exactly a century since the death of Peter the Great.

I must tell you a fine sentence of the Emperor Nicholas, and then leave great folks. He has received many anonymous letters telling him his life is in danger, etc, etc, and some one advised him to attend to them. 'Non, on veut me faire tyran ou poltron; je ne saurais être ni l'un ni l'autre.'

Court Church,
Konyushennaya Street

[44] Pushkin's duel, death, and funeral at the Court
Church in January 1837, from *The Diary of a Russian
Censor* by Alexander Nikitenko.

January 29, 1837
An important and terribly sad event in our literature: Pushkin
died today of a wound he received in a duel.

Last night I was at Pletnyov's: it was from him that I first
heard of this tragedy. D'Anthès, a cavalry officer and Pushkin's opponent, was the first to fire, the bullet entered Pushkin's stomach. Nevertheless Pushkin managed a return shot
which shattered d'Anthès's hand. Today, Pushkin is no longer
in this world.

I still haven't heard a good account of all the details. This
much is beyond doubt: we have borne a grievous, irreplaceable
loss. Pushkin's most recent works are admittedly somewhat
weaker than his earlier ones, but he might have been going
through a period of transition, the result of some inner revolution, after which would have ensued a period of new grandeur.

Poor Pushkin! Here is how you have paid for the right of
citizenship in those aristocratic salons where you frittered

away your time and gifts! You should have gone the way of humanity, and not of caste; once a member of the latter, you could not help but obey its laws. You were meant for a higher calling.

30 January. What noise, what confusion in opinions about Pushkin! What we have is no longer a single black patch on the threadbare tatters of a singer, but thousands of patches, red, white, black, of all colors and shades. Still, here is some information about his death, culled from the most reliable source.

D'Anthès is a shallow man, but an adroit, friendly Frenchman who has sparkled in our salons as a star of the first magnitude. He would often visit the Pushkins. We all know that the poet's wife is beautiful. D'Anthès, as a Frenchman and a frequenter of salons, became too friendly with her, and she did not have enough tact to draw a line between herself and him, a line beyond which no man must pass in his relations with a woman who does not belong to him. In society there are always people who feed on the reputations of their friends: they welcomed this opportunity and spread rumours of a relationship between d'Anthès and Pushkin's wife. These reached Pushkin and, of course, troubled his already agitated soul. He forbade d'Anthès's visits. The latter was insulted and declared that he was visiting not Pushkin's wife but his sister-in-law, with whom he was in love. Thereupon Pushkin demanded that he marry the young girl, and the match was arranged.

In the meantime the poet received, on successive days, anonymous letters that congratulated him on being a cuckold. In one letter he was even sent a membership card in the society of cuckolds, with an imaginary signature of President Naryshkin. Moreover, Baron von Heckeren, who had adopted d'Anthès, was very dissatisfied with his marriage to Pushkin's sister-in-law, who, it was said, was older than her husband and without means. To von Heckeren are ascribed the following words: 'Pushkin thinks that with this marriage, he has split up d'Anthès and his wife. On the contrary he has merely brought them close together, thanks to a new family relationship.'

Pushkin flew into a rage and wrote von Heckeren a letter, full of insults. He demanded that the latter, as a father, curb his young man. The letter was of course read by d'Anthès – he demanded satisfaction and the affair ended beyond the city limits, at ten paces. D'Anthès was the first to fire. Pushkin fell. D'Anthès ran towards him, but the poet, gathering up his strength, ordered his adversary to return to his place, aimed at his heart but hit his hand which d'Anthès, either owing to an awkward movement or out of precaution, had placed over his chest.

Pushkin was wounded in the abdomen, the bullet entering his stomach. When he was brought home, he summoned his wife and children, blessed them and requested Dr Arendt to ask the emperor not to abandon them and to pardon Danzas, his second.

The emperor wrote him a letter in his own hand, promising to take care of his family and do all for Danzas that was possible. In addition he asked that before his death he do all that a Christian should. Pushkin demanded a priest. He died on the 29th, Friday, at 3 p.m. In his reception room, from morning till night, visitors gathered, seeking information about his condition. It became necessary to post bulletins.

31 January. I went to see the minister today. He is very busy trying to quell the loud cries over Pushkin's death. He is also very displeased with the elaborate tribute printed in 'The Literary Supplement' of the *Russian Veteran.*

And so, Uvarov cannot even forgive a dead Pushkin for *Lucullus's Recovery.*

I just received an order from the chairman of the Censorship Committee not to permit anything to be printed about Pushkin without first submitting the article to him or the minister.

The funeral is tomorrow. I received a ticket.

1 February. Pushkin's funeral. It was a real 'people's' funeral. Anyone and everyone in St Petersburg who thinks or reads thronged to the church where the mass was being sung for the poet. This took place in the church on Konyushennaya Street. The square was covered with carriage and people, but not a single homespun or sheepskin coat was to be seen among them.

The church was filled with notables. The entire diplomatic corps was present. Only those in uniform or holding tickets were admitted. Every face expressed sadness – at least on the surface. Alongside me stood Baron Rosen, Karlhof, Kukolnik and Pletnyov. I said my last farewell to Pushkin. His face had changed significantly, for decay had set in. I left the church with Kukolnik.

'At least we managed to move up ahead,' he said, pointing to the crowd coming to pay homage to the remains of one of its finest sons.

Platon Obodovsky fell on my breast, sobbing like a child.

But here, as usual, there were some very clumsy arrangements. The populace was fooled: they were told that the mass for Pushkin was to be sung in Saint Isaac's – so it was written on the admission tickets – while the body was in fact taken from the apartment at night, in secret, and put in the church on Konyushennaya Street. At the university a strict order was received stating that professors must not absent themselves from their courses and that students must be present at lectures. I could not restrain myself and expressed my distress about this to the superintendent. Russians cannot mourn their countryman who honored them with his existence! Foreigners came to bow at the poet's coffin, while university professors and Russian youth were forbidden to do so. In secret, like robbers, they had to steal their way to it.

The superintendent told me that it would be better if the students were not present at the funeral: they might band together and carry Pushkin's coffin – they could 'go too far,' as he put it.

Grech was severely reprimanded by Benkendorf for this statement which appeared in the *Northern Bee*: 'Russia owes a debt of gratitude to Pushkin for his twenty-two years of service in the field of literature.' (Issue no. 24.)

Kraevsky, editor of 'The Literary Supplement' to the *Russian Veteran*, also ran into difficulty for several lines printed in tribute to the poet. I received an order to delete in their entirety several such lines scheduled for publication in the *Reader's Library*.

Amidst universal sympathy and deep universal mourning for the deceased, all these measures were being taken. They were afraid – but of what?

The ceremony ended at 12:30. Then I went to my lecture. But instead of my regular lecture, I delivered a lecture to the students on Pushkin's contributions to our literature. What will be, will be!

12 *February*. Details about Pushkin's last moments have come to me from reliable sources. He died honorably, like a man. As soon as the bullet had entered his body, he knew that this was the kiss of death. He did not groan, and when Dr Dal advised him to do so he replied: 'So, this nonsense really can't be licked? Besides, my groans would upset my wife.'

He kept asking Dal: 'Will it be over soon?' And very calmly, without any mincing of words, he would refute Dal when the latter tried to reassure him with the usual words of comfort. A few minutes before his death, he asked to be raised and turned to the other side.

'My life is over,' he said.

'What's that?' asked Dal, not quite hearing his words.

'My life is over,' repeated Pushkin. 'Can't breathe.'

After uttering these words, his labours ceased, for he had stopped breathing. His life was over; the light on the altar had gone out. Pushkin died well.

About three days after the requiem mass for Pushkin, he was taken in *secret* to the country. My wife was returning from Mogilev, and at one depot not far from St Petersburg she saw a simple cart; on the cart was straw, under the straw a coffin wrapped in best matting. Three gendarmes were scurrying about in the depot yard, pleading that the horses be reharnessed more quickly for they had to ride on further with the coffin.

'What's that?' my wife asked of one of the peasants there.

'God only knows what! You see, some fellow by the name of Pushkin was killed, and they are speeding him away on this post chaise in matting and straw – may God forgive them! – like a dog.'

The measure prohibiting publication of anything about Pushkin is still in effect and the public is very disturbed by it.

[45] Description of Pushkin's duel on the Islands, from the Commentary to *Eugene Onegin* by Vladimir Nabokov.

Pushkin's second was his old schoolmate, Lieutenant Colonel Konstantin Danzas, and that of d'Anthès was Viscount Laurent d'Archiac, a secretary of the French embassy. The duel took place on Wednesday, January 27. Both sleighs arrived in the vicinity of the so-called Commandant's Villa about 4 P.M., with dusk already dulling the frosty air. While the two seconds and d'Anthès were engaged in trampling out a twenty-yard-long path in the snow, Pushkin, enveloped in a bearskin pelisse, sat waiting on a snowdrift. The seconds marked the ten-yard boundary with their shed carricks, and the duel began. Pushkin at once walked up his five paces to the boundary. D'Anthès made four paces and fired. Pushkin fell on Danzas' military carrick, but after a pause of a few seconds raised himself on one arm and declared he had enough strength to fire. His pistol had stuck barrel down in the snow; another was given him, and Pushkin took slow careful aim at his adversary, whom he had ordered to come up to the boundary. The shock of the ball, which hit d'Anthès in the forearm, bowled him over, and Pushkin, thinking he had killed him, exclaimed, 'Bravo!' and threw his pistol up into the air. He was carried to the livery coupe that had conveyed the passionately anxious Dutch minister to the vicinity of the ground (Heeckeren then quietly transferred himself to one of the hack sleighs).

D'Anthès later had a distinguished career in France. In *Les Châtiments*, bk iv, no vi, a fine diatribe of thirty resounding Alexandrines 'Ecrit le 17 Juillet 1851, en descendant de la tribune,' Victor Hugo qualified the members of Napoleon III's senate, including d'Anthès, as follows (ll 1–2, 7):

> Ces hommes qui mourront, foule abjecte et grossière,
> Sont de la boue avant d'être de la poussière.
> . . . .
> Ils mordent les talons de qui marche en avant.

The Fortress of St Peter and St Paul

[46] Peter the Great pardons a courtier incarcerated there, from the knout, at the request of his favourite Italian greyhound Lisette, from *Original Anecdotes of Peter the Great . . .* by J. V. Stählin-Storckburg.

In the cabinet of natural history of the academy at Petersburgh, is preserved, among a number of uncommon animals, Lisette, the favourite dog of the Russian Monarch. She was a small, dun-coloured Italian greyhound, and very fond of her master, whom she never quitted but when he went out, and then she laid herself down on his couch. At his return she showed her fondness by a thousand caresses, followed him wherever he went, and during his afternoon nap lay always at his feet.

A person belonging to the court, having excited the anger of the Czar, I do not know by what means, was confined in the fort, and there was reason to suppose that he would receive the punishment of the knout, on the first market day.

The whole court, and the Empress herself, thought him innocent, and considered the anger of the Czar as excessive and unjust. Every means was tried to save him, and the first opportunity taken to intercede in his favour. But so far from succeeding, it served only to irritate the Emperor the more, who forbade all persons, even the Empress, to speak for the prisoner, and above all to present any petition on the subject, under pain of incurring his highest displeasure.

It was supposed that no resource remained to save the culprit. However, those who in concert with the Czarina interested themselves in his favour, desired the means of presenting a petition, without incurring the penalty of the prohibition.

They composed a short but pathetic petition in the name of Lisette. After having set forth her uncommon fidelity to her master, she adduced the strongest proofs of innocence of the prisoner, intreated the Czar to take the matter into consideration, and to be propitious to her prayer, by granting him his liberty.

This petition was tied to her collar, in such a manner as to be easily visible.

On the Czar's return from the admiralty and senate, Lisette as usual came leaping about him; and he perceived the paper, folded in the form of a petition. He took, and read it – 'What!' said he, 'Lisette, do you also present me petitions? Well, as it is the first time, I grant your prayer.' He immediately sent a *denchtchick* (servant) to the fort with orders to set the prisoner at liberty.

Source: Miss Anne Cromer; then chambermaid to the Empress, and since governess of the Princess Natalia, sister of Peter II.

[47] The interrogation, sentences and executions of the Decembrists in the Fortress of St Peter and St Paul, from *The First Russian Revolution, 1825* by Anatole Mazour.

Nicholas [I] as prosecutor. – Nearly every person arrested was presented to the new Emperor, who, after a few questions, attached an order indicating to the Commandant of the Fortress, Alexander Sukin, the treatment each prisoner was to receive: whether he was to be kept in chains, placed under special surveillance, or allowed more liberty. These orders, one hundred and fifty of them, often written on small pieces of paper, are preserved and they constitute a remarkable record. They show the keen interest that Nicholas took in the whole affair and his determined effort to obtain at any price maximum evidence from every person detailed; they display the bestial vengeance of this gifted gendarme in the purple robe. 'Ryleev,' reads the note accompanying him, 'to be placed in the Peter and Paul fortress, but his hands not tied; no communication with others, give him writing paper and whatever he writes daily deliver to me personally.' 'Upon receiving Bestuzhev, as well as Obolensky and Shchepin,' reads another, 'order them to be manacled.' A third reads: 'Yakushkin to be treated severely and not otherwise than a villain.'

Treatment of the prisoners changed as they became more willing to confess. Those who showed any stubbornness were not only rigorously handled but often deprived of food, left on bread and water, as was the Decembrist, Semënov. The harsh prison régime, the scanty diet, the heavy chains, and the damp cell often achieved the purpose sought and even more: few of the members could endure the dreadful trials and many began to break down, to confess, and to involve others. Even today some of the confessions represent heartbreaking documents, manifestly written by men on the verge of total mental or physical collapse. Only characters like Yakushkin's were able to stand firm and resist the strain, but men like him were few.

Physical discomfort as a means of extracting evidence did not suffice for Nicholas; he was an artist who assumed a pose befitting the character of each defendant. His talent enabled him to deceive even La Ferronnays, the French Ambassador, before whom he shed tears, pretending to be an innocent and inexperienced Sovereign forced by conditions to occupy a throne to which he had never aspired, and one whom evil plotters wished to betray. However, he assured the Ambassador that, notwithstanding his lack of experience in political affairs, he had the most honest intention to rule justly and was determined upon the extermination of all sedition in the country. So well did he dramatize the scene that La Ferronnays hastened to inform his government that Russia had an enlightened Peter the Great on its throne.

If Nicholas could deceive such a skilled diplomat as La Ferronnays, there is little wonder at his still greater success with the Decembrists, who took his pretended sympathy at its face value. Before all the defendants Nicholas put on a show rarely equaled by any prosecuting attorney ... Violently hating every member, no matter how remotely he had been associated with the events, even years afterward Nicholas could not speak of the Decembrists without evident irritation.

Execution of sentences. – On July 3, 1826, at three o'clock in the morning, the sentence was administered. All the prisoners were called for the ceremony of military degradation: insignias were stripped, uniforms were taken off, and the men were given special robes; each man's sword was broken over his head and thrown into a bonfire built for that purpose. Afterward, the execution of the five men began. The hanging was accompanied by a horrifying episode. During the night it had rained and the ropes were wet; the executioner did not tighten the noose enough, and three of the five men, namely, Muraviev-Apostol, Ryleev, and Kakhovsky fell down when the stools were pulled from under their feet. Muraviev-Apostol, whose legs were broken, remarked bitterly: 'Poor Russia, she cannot even hang decently!' Kakhovsky swore. General Chernyshev, in charge of the execution, immediately ordered that the men be taken back to the scaffolds. Shortly afterward the five bodies were taken down and buried in a secret place, which still remains unknown.

It should be noted that not even the dead Decembrists were spared: Ippolit Muraviev-Apostol, Shchepillo, and Kuzmin, who perished in the uprising in the South, could not escape the all-reaching hand of the official Nemesis. The verdict demanded that on their graves be placed, not crosses, but scaffolds with inscriptions indicating 'the eternal disgrace' of their names ...

The exile of all the privates of the Moskovsky and Chernigovsky regiments began in February, 1826. About fifteen hundred soldiers were sent to the Caucasus, where war with Persia was imminent; a few, after undergoing severe corporal punishment, were sent to the East. On July 13, 1826, there began the exodus to Siberia of the first party of convicts.

Among them were Prince Trubetskoi, Prince Obolensky, Yak-
ubovich, Peter and Andrei Borisov, Prince Volkonsky, and
Artamon Muraviev, all of whom were chained and sent to
the Nerchinsk mines. The party was soon followed by others.
Some of the wives of the prisoners, determined to drink the
bitter cup with their husbands, trod the long road to Siberia,
setting an example of heroic devotion and leaving a monument to Russian womanhood.

Thus ended the first act in the drama of the struggle for
liberty in Russia.

[48] The imprisonment, ceremony of military degradation, and departure for Siberia of the Decembrists
(1826), from *The Rebel on the Bridge*, a biography of
Andrei Rozen, by Glyn Barratt.

Rozen, to continue with his tale, came to the Crownwork
(*Kronverk*) Curtain of Peter-and-Paul Fortress on January 5,
1826, exhausted by emotional stress and sheer physical hunger. He found himself placed in a cell compared with which
his anteroom had been a veritable scene of luxury. In itself, it
has been rightly stressed, incarceration in the Fortress's damp
casemates (most covered to a depth of several feet by the
tremendous floodtides of November 7–9, 1824), was frequently enough to break a spirit – or a life. What with the
wretched diet, chains, and endless silence, few men could
endure the trial and, breaking down, many involved ex-
comrades. Even today, their statements are oppressive documents, written by men obviously on the verge of physical and
mental collapse. Always there was suspense, always some fear
for wives and families, and always ignorance of what others
had already said to implicate their friends. Many men collapsed under the strain, or from the noisome air and scanty
food. . . .

Altogether, 579 persons had been brought to trial in connection with the risings of December 14, 1825 and January
1826, of whom 290 were acquitted. Of the remaining 298 (at
least 30 of whom were from the Baltic provinces), 121 were
selected as the most responsible conspirators, 61 being ex-

members of the Northern Society. The sentence in respect to these 'chief criminals', passed on July 9 and made public three days later, was that the five who later hanged should be quartered, thirty-one men losing their heads. Predictably, the sentences recommended by the Court were modified by Nicholas. He had, after all, to demonstrate his clemency. But the fates of the Decembrists had been settled long before the Special Court had held its final session, in the mind of Nicholas.

To return to Rozen's narrative:

Thus dawned July 13. Before sunrise, I was taken to the Fortress courtyard, where stood a large detachment of the Pavlovsky Bodyguards, and another of the garrison artillery. From there, I was taken to the Square, where some of my companions in misfortune stood already; the remainder were gradually brought out. I was delighted to see old acquaintances again. We all embraced, and every man sought out his closest friends. I looked in vain for Ryleyev . . . Prince S. G. Volkonsky walked about, talking cheerfully; Baten'kov went up and down, lost in thought; Prince Obolensky had been thriving in the Fortress, and his cheeks were glowing . . . I saw no one in despair; even the sufferings mirrored on the faces of the sick now held their peace. Beyond the square, Generals-Adjutant Benkendorf and Levashev and a few more officers restlessly walked up and down . . .

At last, in four groups separated by rows of soldiers, we were led through the Fortress gate on to the glacis of the Crownwork Curtain . . . A gallows was now visible above the rampart; I recognised the carpenters' work which I had seen from my own casemate without fathoming its purpose. Our sections were arranged at equal distances. Near each division burned a funeral pyre, an executioner standing by. General-Adjutant Chernyshev was on horseback; on this morning he was not rouged, and his face was pale.

A general was with each division; our former Brigadier, G. A. Golovin, was attached to ours. We were each called out singly, according to the order of the categories. One by one we had to fall upon our knees while an executioner broke our sword over our head, tore off our uniform, and cast the broken sword and the clothes on to the burning funeral pyre. I hastily stripped off my uniform as I knelt down, before the executioner could touch me, the general meanwhile shouting at him, 'Tear it off!', but it was already done. The swords had been filed through beforehand . . .

This ceremony lasted over an hour. Then they made us put on striped dressing-gowns, such as are worn in hospitals, and took us back to the Fortress in the order in which we had left it. On the glacis there had been no one to look at us, but at the gate a crowd pressed round. As we were taken back, the gibbet on the Crownwork rampart was awaiting its victims; but no one was to be observed nearby. We turned our eyes towards it, and prayed that God would grant an easy death to our companions. I was taken to the cell in the Crownwork Curtain, no 14, in which Konrad Ryleyev had passed his last night on this earth.

So ended the initial phase of Rozen's expiation. For the moment, Rozen had no choice but to watch autumn to winter, and wonder when, if ever, he would leave Peter-and-Paul Fortress. Meanwhile, other men were going . . .

On July 25, my wife obtained permission to let me see her newborn son in the Commandant's house; although in tears, she was composed and firm. My son, aged six weeks, lay on the Commandant's sofa; his blue eyes and the smiles round his mouth seemed to bring us messages of comfort. My wife asked me about the time and place of our reunion. I begged her not to follow me out to Siberia at once, but to wait until our boy could walk unaided and until I could tell her something of our new place of abode.

Every third day, four men and no more were dispatched. We were allowed, when September came, to see our relatives for one hour a week till we should leave. My wife visited me every Wednesday, and my brothers also came at times, one of them from Estonia. My youngest brother, a cadet in the First Cadet Corps, also came; he wept bitterly and regretted deeply, among other things, that by my condemnation I had lost the privilege of ever winning the Cross of St George. I passed seven months in this manner, every day expecting to be taken off to Siberia. A whole year of imprisonment already gone, and still I must needs wait! . . .

So began 1827. Rozen read the contents of the Fortress library; Cook's voyages, old newspapers, many of Scott's Waverley novels. Some twenty of his comrades, he was told, had been removed to Finnish fortresses. He wondered why. His gums were white and swollen. His brother-in-law came from Estonia with reindeer skins, which Anna turned into an overcoat. His spirits sank still lower, as another month began. But at last, on February 5, his turn arrived. He had a final meeting with his wife, who gave him 'a small wooden cross from Jerusalem', and at night was taken to the Commandant's house, where Repin, Glebov and Mikhail Kyuhkel'beker greeted him. All four were overjoyed, and talked until the entry of General Sukin with a sentry:

> The artilleryman, who was following him, was holding up the ends of his cloak, which were gathered mysteriously in his hands. The Commandant announced to us that, in accordance with the Sovereign's command, he was to dispatch us to Siberia, and, he was grieved to say, in chains. At these last words the artilleryman let fall the ends of his cloak, and the chains meant for us rattled to the floor . . . After this, we went out; it was not easy to go down the steps with chains on. I held firmly on to a rail, but one of my comrades stumbled and very nearly fell. The town-major then brought some red cords, which had served to tie up quills; one end of the cord was attached to a ring which joined the bars and links of the iron chains; the other was fastened to our girth, to enable us to move with speed. Gendarmes were waiting at the steps to put us each into a sled; and so began our journey of 6,600 versts. The moon and sparkling stars lighted us on our way. We passed over the River Neva at a slow trot . . .

[49] Fyodor Dostoyevsky is taken from the Fortress of St Peter and St Paul to a mock-execution, from *Dostoyevsky: His Life and Work* by Ronald Hingley.

Early in the morning of 22 December 1849 Fyodor Mikhay-
lovich Dostoyevsky, officially described as 'Lieutenant of
Engineers, retired', was ordered out of his cell in the Petropav-
lovsky Fortress in the Imperial Russian capital, St Petersburg.
He was then taken across the River Neva, by carriage in a
convoy flanked by mounted Cossacks, to the Semyonovsky
Square in the south of the city. Blinking in the wintry sun-
shine, the twenty-eight-year-old former army officer – and, it
seemed, unsuccessful novelist – was paraded on the snow
with twenty friends and former associates. They were surrounded on all four sides of the huge square by troops.

Dostoyevsky and his friends had been arrested several
months earlier for treason. Their conspiracy against the Russian state had consisted of little more than debating judicial
reform, serf emancipation, socialism and revolution in informal discussion circles. But to discuss these subjects at all,
however privately, in the Tsar-Emperor Nicholas I's later
reign had been to take a grave risk. Perhaps the spice of
danger had been the chief attraction to the young author,
gambler and hypochondriac who now waited, shivering on
the snow after embracing the other accused. Dostoyevsky was
fair-haired, freckled, with small, deep-sunk eyes under a high-
domed forehead; shortish of stature, but broad-shouldered
and of fairly strong build. He wore the rumpled civilian
clothes in which the police had arrested him the previous
April. Paler even than usual after eight months in the dun-
geons, he formed with his friends a sharp contrast to the
glittering battalions and squadrons massed on all sides.
Orders cracked, drums rumbled ominously.

The presiding General stepped forward and began reading
from a document. Only now did the twenty-one young men
learn that they had been tried and condemned in their absence
– to immediate death by firing squad! 'Criminal conversations
... reading a felonious missive ... full of impudent
expressions directed against Supreme Authority and the
Orthodox Church ... plotting to write anti-government articles and to disseminate them by means of a home lithographic
press': these were the main charges for which Dostoyevsky
personally had to pay the penalty!

That the young men were to be executed three at a time,

with Dostoyevsky himself in the second batch, soon became evident after they had been arrayed in the prescribed white 'shrouds' with long, trailing sleeves and hoods. The first victims were each secured to a post, their arms were bound behind their backs by the sleeves, and the hoods were pulled over their faces. At the word of command, three guards detachments took aim at almost point blank range and the order to fire was instantly expected. But then an aide-de-camp galloped across the square bearing a sealed packet. A drum roll halted the proceedings, and the condemned men heard the presiding General laboriously intone the last-minute commutation of their sentences: most to periods of *katorga* (Siberian hard labour and exile). Two days later the political criminal and future great novelist, his ankles secured by the customary fetters, had begun his two-thousand-mile journey to a new life as a convict at Omsk in Siberia.

The mock execution had been a cruel farce, deliberately staged to teach the culprits a lesson on the detailed instructions of the Emperor; he had, perhaps, even maliciously chosen the General, a notorious stutterer, who haltingly read out the sentences. Thus, at the whim of this crowned martinet, specialist in gallows humour and hounder of imaginative writers, did the young Dostoyevsky spend several minutes in full expectation of imminent death. During that time, as he later indicated, all his previous life passed in review through his mind.

[50] Prince P. Kropotkin, then a young page at Court, attends the lying-in-state of the Empress Alexandra Feodorovna, Nicholas I's widow, in the Church of the Fortress in 1860, from his *Memoirs of a Revolutionist*.

No sooner all these troubles were over, than the death of the Dowager-Empress the widow of Nicholas I. – brought a new interruption in our work.

The burial of crowned heads is always so arranged as to produce a deep impression on the crowds, and it must be owned that this object is attained. The body of the empress was brought from Tsárkoye Seló, where she died, to St

Petersburg, and here, followed by the imperial family, all the high dignitaries of the state, and scores of thousands of functionaries and corporations, and preceded by hundreds of clergy and choirs, it was taken from the railway station through the main thoroughfares to the fortress, where it had to lie in state for several weeks. A hundred thousand men of the Guard were placed along the streets, and thousands of people, dressed in the most gorgeous uniforms, preceded, accompanied, and followed the hearse in a solemn procession. Litanies were sung at every important crossing of the streets, and here the ringing of the bells on the church towers, the voices of vast choirs, and the sounds of the military bands united in the most impressive way, so as to make people believe that the immense crowds really mourned the loss of the empress.

As long as the body lay in state in the cathedral of the fortress, the pages, among others, had to keep the watch round it, night and day. Three pages de chambre and three maids of honour always stood close by the coffin, placed on a high pedestal, while some twenty pages were stationed on the platform upon which litanies were sung twice every day, in the presence of the emperor and all his family. Consequently, every week nearly one-half of the corps was taken in turns to the fortress, to lodge there. We were relieved every two hours, and in the daytime our service was not difficult; but when we had to rise in the night, to dress in our court uniforms, and then to walk through the dark and gloomy inner courts of the fortress to the cathedral, to the sound of the gloomy chime of the fortress bells, a cold shiver seized me at the thought of the prisoners who were immured somewhere in this Russian Bastille. 'Who knows,' thought I, 'whether in my turn I shall not also have to join them in some day or other?'

The burial did not pass without an accident which might have had serious consequences. An immense canopy had been erected under the dome of the cathedral over the coffin. A huge gilded crown rose above it, and from this crown an immense purple mantle lined with ermine hung towards the four thick pilasters which support the dome of the cathedral. It was impressive, but we boys soon made out that the crown was made of gilded cardboard and wood, the mantle was of velvet only in its lower part, while higher up it was red cotton, and that the ermine lining was simply cotton flannelette or swandown to which black tails of squirrels had been sewn, while the escutcheons which represented the arms of Russia, veiled with black crepe, were simple cardboard. But the crowds which were allowed at certain hours of the night to pass by the coffin, and to kiss in a hurry the gold brocade which covered it, surely had no time to closely examine the flannelette ermine or the cardboard escutcheons, and the desired theatrical effect was obtained even by such cheap means.

When a litany is sung in Russia all the people present lighted wax candles, which have to be put out after certain prayers have been read. The imperial family also held such candles, and one day the young son of the grand duke Constantine, seeing that the others put out their candles by turning them upside down, did the same. The black gauze which hung behind him from an escutcheon took fire, and in a second the escutcheon and the cotton stuff were ablaze. An immense tongue of fire ran up the heavy folds of the supposed ermine mantle.

The service was stopped. All looks were directed with terror towards the tongue of fire, which went higher and higher towards the cardboard crown and the woodwork which supported the whole structure. Bits of burning stuff began to fall down, threatening to set fire to the black gauze veils of the ladies present.

Alexander II lost his presence of mind for a couple of seconds only, but he recovered immediately and said in a composed voice: 'The coffin must be taken!' The pages de chambre at once covered it with the thick gold brocade, and we all advanced to lift the heavy coffin; but in the meantime the big tongue of flame had broken into a number of smaller ones, which now slowly devoured only the fluffy outside of the cotton stuff and, meeting more and more dust and soot in the upper part of the structure, gradually died out in the folds.

I cannot say what I looked most at: the creeping fire or the stately slender figures of the three ladies who stood by the coffin, the long trains of their black dresses spreading over the steps which led to the upper platform, and their black lace veils hanging down their shoulders. None of them had made the slightest movement: they stood like three beautiful carved images. Only in the dark eyes of one of them, Mdlle. Gamaléya, tears glittered like pearls. She was a daughter of South Russia, and was the only really handsome lady amongst the maids of honour at the Court.

[51] 1881: The funeral of the assassinated Tsar Alexander II in the Church of the Fortress of St Peter and St Paul, from *Voyageurs en Russie* by Eugène Melchior de Vogüe.

Transfer of the body to the Fortress
19th March. We went to see the procession at the Paskiewitchs', and then the ceremony at the Fortress. In the whole of this lengthy parade, from 11 a.m. to 3 p.m., not a single detail was truly impressive or truly moving; a wretched operatic staging, stuffed with so many archaisms that any grief or devotion became impossible.

These heralds, these gentlemen at arms in their gilt cuirasses, these coats of arms, orders and coronets, borne by civil servants of the Eighth rank, all these trappings are too removed from contemporary ways to be associated with present, real mourning. One is reluctantly prepared to see a dummy corpse paraded forth in this ill-rehearsed Wagnerian show. Jomini points out with reason that such a drama is impressive and eloquent enough in its own right, without any need for it to be decked out in all this medieval flummery. This may still be acceptable in England where they obstinately believe in it, whereas here it is but an official chore, where all the actors are consumed by cold and boredom. Only Valuef bore the Crown of Monomakh with conviction. The people were not allowed to follow, thanks to the measures taken by the police: the people, the only element that would have restored credibility: powerful, silent, black waves banked in the distance, the tide biding its hour.

At St Peter and St Paul's bored functionaries and diplomats had been waiting interminably. The corpse was carried in by all those numerous, robust princelings, a promising harvest for future assassinations. The Emperor, calm, dignified, admirable composure. As for the rest, harassed with their funeral duties. The marvellous anthem of the Russian Orthodox Church greeted the body. The unforgettable face of an old Archimandrite, an anchorite come to life from an icon of Mount Athos, with a macabre and flickering flame of life in his thin body: how I understood the holy fools of the Middle Ages. The wretched, hacked about corpse, disguised and covered by braid and gauze, was then placed under a dais of gold cloth. Its jawbone had come loose during the march. The officers of State took up their stations about the quartered trunk, each holding its Crown, orders or insignia. Shuvaloff, the unfortunate negotiator at Berlin, held the gauntlet of Russia. The ceremony over, we all kissed the coffin. Some wives, including mine, cried, but not heart-rendingly, there were too many alarums and excursions in the Church.

'What a chapter that would have been for Tolstoi, the conversations in the Church,' Boisdeffre pointed out to me. Only one moving moment, the last: after the Imperial family had left, the heartbroken wife dragged herself along the steps held up by Robinder; she kissed the body, and crushed by it all, collapsed. At last, we were overwhelmed by the incredible sorrow of this lost woman, who had risen to the steps of the throne and now falls back into the abyss. This was the only true sounding note that I can recall of this artificial day, a day intriguing to the idle bystander, a day that showed itself to be purely formal, those involved infected by the terror that overcomes one if caught up in catastrophe, a day unworthy of the major historical drama that caused it.

Obsequies of the Emperor.
27th March. Damnable weather, blizzard and icy winds. Four hours at the Fortress, from ten-thirty in the morning to half-past two.

All the princes of this earth, the heirs apparent of Germany and England, Denmark, the Arch-Duke Charles Louis, a horde of German princelings, magnificent Church rituals. Tragic train of thought in this Church: three layers: the courtiers on top, still devoured by their intrigues and ambitions, the corpses on the ground, the condemned below ground, in their cells, damning the rest. There lies the real disaster, this hatred brewing under our feet. What a grim, ill-matched world! and yet the priests chant 'Glory to God'. I chatted to Polovtsof, and Lieven: disorder, disquiet, the ill-defined worries of lesser souls. At two o'clock the poor relict of yesterday's power was lowered and sealed into his grave. The key was given to his Heir, so that he should not re-emerge. One more gloomy drama in Russia's history.

The Summer Garden

[52] Jacques Casanova de Seingalt waylays the Empress Catherine the Great for an informal discussion, from *Memoirs of Jacques Casanova de Seingalt*.

I thought of leaving Russia at the beginning of the autumn, but I was told by MM Panin and Alsuwieff that I ought not to go without having spoken to the Empress.

'I should be sorry to do so,' I replied, 'but as I can't find anyone to present me to her, I must be resigned.'

At last Panin told me to walk in a garden frequented by her majesty at an early hour, and he said that meeting me, as it were by chance, she would probably speak to me. I told him I should like him to be with her, and he accordingly named a day.

I repaired to the garden, and as I walked about I marvelled at the statuary it contained, all the statues being made of the worst stone, and executed in the worst possible taste. The names cut beneath them gave the whole the air of a practical joke. A weeping statue was Democritus; another, with grinning mouth, was labelled Heraclitus; an old woman, Avicenna; and so on.

As I was smiling at this extraordinary collection, I saw the czarina, preceded by Count Gregorius Orloff, and followed by two ladies, approaching. Count Panin was on her left hand. I stood by the hedge to let her pass, but as soon as she came up to me she asked, smilingly, if I had been interested in the statues. I replied, following her steps, that I presumed they had been placed there to impose on fools, or to excite the laughter of those acquainted with history.

'From what I can make out,' she replied, 'the secret of the matter is that my worthy aunt was imposed on, and indeed she did not trouble herself much about such trifles. But I hope you have seen other things in Russia less ridiculous than these statues?'

I entertained the sovereign for more than an hour with my remarks on the things of note I had seen in St Petersburg. The conversation happened to turn on the King of Prussia, and I sang his praises; but I censured his terrible habit of always interrupting the person whom he was addressing. Catherine smiled and asked me to tell her about the conversation I had had with this monarch, and I did so to the best of my ability. She was then kind enough to say that she had never seen me at the 'Courtag', which was a vocal and instrumental concert given at the place, and open to all. I told her that I had only attended once, as I was so unfortunate as not to have a taste for music. At this she turned to Panin, and said smilingly, that she knew someone else who had the same misfortune. If the reader remembers what I heard her say about music as she was leaving the opera, he will pronounce my speech to have been a very courtier-like one, and I confess it was; but who can resist making such speeches to a monarch, and above all, a monarch in petticoats?

The czarina turned from me to speak to M. Bezkoi, who had just come up, and as M. Panin left the garden I did so too, delighted with the honour I had had.

[53] The Summer Garden: Statute-Fair for Wives and Lottery of Marriage from *Russia: 1842* by J. G. Kohl.

Among the various modes of matchmaking in Russia I ought not to omit to mention that of Whit Monday. On that day a general meeting of lads and lasses takes place, at least of all those who are desirous of taking upon them the duties of a married life.

I went several times on such occasions to the summer gardens of St Petersburg to see 'the brides.' Along the principal walk were two rows of candidates: on one side were the young men, on the opposite side the young women: they appeared to consist for the most part of shopkeepers and servants, and were of course all of the inferior ranks in society. They were dressed in a great deal of finery badly put on, and a great many colours ill-assorted. The young men were, upon the whole, rather good-looking, but an uglier assemblage of young women it would be difficult to meet with anywhere, notwithstanding their painted faces and silk gowns.

Speaking of paint reminds me of a curious custom in Russia which may serve to show how very common its use is among the people: when a young man is paying his court to a girl he generally presents her with a box of both red and white paint, as a necessary addition to her beauty. Among the upper classes this habit is also very general, and I have often been present when ladies have most unceremoniously rouged their face before going into the drawing-room. The lower class use a great deal of white paint, which gives them an extremely ghastly appearance, and must be very injurious to the health, as it turns the teeth quite black; I was told that it consists of a preparation of mercury.

But to return to the 'brides' in the summer garden. There seemed to be very little laughing or merriment among them; there they stood, silent and almost motionless, with their arms hanging straight by their sides; they had evidently come upon a serious business, and were heroically intent on carrying it through. I noticed that behind the young people were the elders of the family, to whom now and then they addressed a few words.

Being anxious to know in what manner matches were made at this 'statute-fair,' I applied to an old lady of our party.

'Do you not see,' replied she, 'that the parents and friends of the candidates are behind them? Well, when a young man has fixed his choice on one of the girls, he informs his mother or father of it, who immediately proceeds to make all sorts of inquiries concerning her, as to the amount of her marriage-portion, quantity of wedding-clothes, what her household accomplishments are, &c: having received the necessary replies, and given information in return, if it meet with the approbation of the parties the affair does not take long to be arranged to the satisfaction of all.'

'But do you think they can be happy?'

'And why not?' replied my friend: 'having once determined upon taking a ticket in the matrimonial lottery, the chances are they enjoy as much felicity as generally falls to the share of other couples. Marriages, you know, the proverb says, are made in heaven.'

[54] Oblomov's hopeless courtship of Olga in the Summer Garden, from *Oblomov* by Ivan Goncharov.

But he set his mind at rest with the thought that Olga would most probably come with her aunt or with Maria Semyonovna, who was so fond of her and could not admire her enough. He hoped that in their presence he would be able to disguise his embarrassment, and he prepared himself to be talkative and gallant. 'And at dinner time, too,' he thought as he set out, none too eagerly, for the Summer Gardens. 'What an hour to choose!' As soon as he entered the long avenue, he saw a veiled woman get up from a seat and walk towards him. He did not think it was Olga: alone! Impossible! She would never do a thing like that and, besides, would have no excuse for leaving home unchaperoned. However – it seemed to be her way of walking: her feet moved so lightly and rapidly that they did not seem to walk but to glide; her head and neck, too, were bent forward as though she were looking for something on the ground at her feet. Another man would have recognized her by her hat or dress, but he could never tell what dress or hat Olga was wearing even after spending a whole morning with her. There was hardly anybody in the garden; an elderly gentleman was walking very briskly, apparently taking his constitutional, and two – not ladies, but women, and a nurse with two children who looked blue with the cold. The leaves had fallen and one could see right through the bare branches; the crows on the trees cawed so unpleasantly. It was a bright and clear day, though, and warm, if one were wrapped up properly. The veiled woman was coming nearer and nearer. . . .

'It is she!' said Oblomov, stopping in alarm and unable to believe his eyes.

'Is it you?' he asked, taking her hand. 'What's the matter?'

'I'm so glad you've come,' she said without answering his question. 'I thought you wouldn't come, and I was beginning to be afraid.'

'How did you get here? How did you manage it?' he asked, thrown into confusion.

'Please, don't! What does it matter? Why all these questions? It's so silly! I wanted to see you and I came – that's all!'

She pressed his hand warmly and looked at him gaily and light-heartedly, so openly and obviously enjoying the moment stolen from fate that he envied her for not sharing her playful mood . . .

The Nevsky Prospekt

[55] The Nevsky Avenue, from *Tales of Good and Evil* by N. Gogol.

There is nothing finer than Nevsky Avenue, not in St Petersburg at any rate; for in St Petersburg it is everything. And, indeed, is there anything more gay, more brilliant, more resplendent than this beautiful street of our capital? I am sure that not one of her anaemic inhabitants, not one of her innumerable Civil Servants, would exchange Nevsky Avenue for all the treasures in the world. Not only the young man of twenty-five, the young gallant with the beautiful moustache and the immaculate morning coat, but the man with white hair sprouting on his chin and a head as smooth as a billiard ball, yes, even he is enthralled with Nevsky Avenue. And the ladies . . . Oh, for the ladies Nevsky Avenue is a thing of even greater delight! But is there anyone who does not feel thrilled and delighted with it? The gay carriages, the handsome men, the beautiful women – all lend it a carnival air, an air that you can almost inhale the moment you set foot on Nevsky Avenue! Even if you have some very important business, you are quite certain to forget all about it as soon as you are there. This is the only place in town where you meet people who are not there on business, people who have not been driven there either by necessity or by their passion for making money, which seems to have the whole of St Petersburg in its grip. It really does seem that the man you meet on Nevsky Avenue is less of an egoist than the man you meet on any other street where want and greed and avarice can be read on the faces of all who walk or drive in carriages or cabs. Nevsky Avenue is the main communication centre of the whole of St Petersburg. Anyone living in the Petersburg or Vyborg district who has not seen a friend on the Sands or the Moscow Tollgate for years can be sure to meet him here. No directory or information bureau will supply such correct information as Nevsky Avenue. All-powerful Nevsky Avenue! The only place in St Petersburg where a poor man can combine a stroll with entertainment. How spotlessly clean are its pavements swept and, good gracious, how many feet leave their marks on them! Here is the footprint left by the clumsy, dirty boot of an ex-army private, under whose weight the very granite seems to crack; and here is one left by the miniature, light as a feather, little shoe of the delightful young creature who turns her pretty head towards the glittering shop-window as the sunflower turns to the sun; and here is the sharp scratch left by the rattling sabre of some ambitious lieutenant – everything leaves its imprint of great power or great weakness upon it. What a rapid phantasmagoria passes over it in a single day! What changes does it not undergo in only twenty-four hours!

Let us begin with the early morning when all St Petersburg is filled with the smell of hot, freshly baked bread and is crowded with old women in tattered clothes who besiege the churches and appeal for alms to the compassionate passersby. At this time Nevsky Avenue is deserted: the stout shopkeepers and their assistants are still asleep in their fine linen shirts, or are lathering their noble cheeks, or drinking coffee; beggars gather at the doors of the pastrycooks' shops where the sleepy Ganymede, who the day before flew about like a fly with the cups of chocolate, crawls out with a besom in his hand, without a cravat, and flings some stale pasties and other leavings at them. Workmen are trudging through the streets:

occasionally the avenue is crossed by Russian peasants, hurrying to their work in boots soiled with lime which not all the water of the Yekaterinsky Canal, famous for its cleanness, could wash off. At this time it is not proper for ladies to take a walk, for the Russian workman and peasant love to express themselves in vigorous language that is not even heard on the stage. Sometimes a sleepy Civil Servant will walk along with a briefcase under his arm, if the way to his office lies across Nevsky Avenue. It can indeed be stated without fear of contradiction that at this time, that is to say, until twelve o'clock, Nevsky Avenue does not serve as a goal for anyone, but is merely a means to an end: it is gradually filled with people who have their own occupations, their own worries, their own disappointments, and who are not thinking about it at all. The Russian peasant is talking about the few coppers he earns; old men and women wave their hands about or talk to themselves, sometimes with picturesque gestures, but no one listens to them or even laughs at them except perhaps the boys in brightly coloured smocks who streak along Nevsky Avenue with empty bottles or mended boots. At this time you can please yourself about your dress. You can wear a workman's cap instead of a hat, and even if your collar were to stick out of your cravat no one would notice it.

At twelve o'clock Nevsky Avenue is invaded by tutors and governesses of all nationalities and their charges in cambric collars. English Johnsons and French Coques walk arm in arm with the young gentlemen entrusted to their parental care and explain to them with an air of grave decorum that the signboards over the shops are put there to tell people what they can find inside the shops. Governesses, pale misses and rosy-cheeked mademoiselles, walk statelily behind slender and fidgety young girls, telling them to raise a shoulder a little higher and to walk straighter. In short, at this time Nevsky Avenue is a pedagogic Nevsky Avenue. But the nearer it gets to two o'clock in the afternoon, the fewer do the numbers of tutors, governesses, and children grow, until finally they are crowded out by their loving fathers who walk arm in arm with their highly-strung wives in gorgeous, bright dresses of every imaginable hue. These are by and by joined by people who have by that time finished all their important domestic engagements, such as talking to their doctors about the weather and the small pimple that has suddenly appeared on their nose; or enquiring after the health of their horses and the children, who, incidentally, seem always to be showing great promise; or reading in the papers the notices and important announcements of the arrivals and departures; or, lastly, drinking a cup of tea or coffee. They are soon joined by those upon whom enviable fate has bestowed the blessed calling of officials on special duties as well as by those who serve in the Foreign Office and who are particularly distinguished by their fine manners and their noble habits. Dear me, what wonderful appointments and posts there are! How they improve and delight the soul of man! But, alas, I am not in the Civil Service myself and so am deprived of the pleasure of appreciating the exquisite manners of my superiors. Every one you now meet on Nevsky Avenue is a paragon of respectability: the gentlemen in long frock-coats with their hands in their pockets; the ladies in pink, white and pale blue redingotes and hats. You will meet here a most wonderful assortment of sidewhiskers, a unique pair of whiskers, tucked with astonishing and extraordinary art under the cravat, velvety whiskers, satiny whiskers, and whiskers black as sable or coal, the latter, alas, the exclusive property of the gentlemen from the Foreign Office.

[56] Prostitutes sweep the Nevsky at 4 a.m., (*c.* 1850) from *Pictures of St Petersburg* by Edward Jerrmann.

Startling contrasts abound in St Petersburg. One morning, before four o'clock, I was driving to the Neva baths, when, on the Camino-Most, the stone bridge, my progress was impeded by a long process of these little emigrants, proceeding into the country in their carriages. Still under the influence of the impression this scene had made upon me, and meditating on the temptations and perils to which the children, and especially the daughters, of the poor are exposed in this age of luxury and corruption, I drove past the magnificent Kasansky, and reached the Newsky Prospect, stretching away, in its vast length, beyond the range of vision, and at that hour of the morning, hushed in a stillness which was not without a certain solemnity. Suddenly, to my astonished eyes, the strangest scene presented itself. I beheld before me an *alfresco* ball. A number of elegantly attired ladies, some in handsome shawls, and with feathers in their hats, were performing the strangest sort of dance, which they accompanied with a sort of bowing motion, incessantly repeated. I could recognise no French or German dance in their singular revolutions. Could it be some Russian national dance? What kind of dance could it be that was thus danced in broad daylight on the public highway, and without male dancers? A few men were certainly there, but merely as lookers-on. I touched the arm of my *Isworstschik*, called his attention to the group, and made an interrogative gesture. The explanation he gave me was doubtless very lucid and circumstantial, and would have been highly satisfactory, had it only been intelligible to me. Unable to understand a word he said, I ordered him, by the vigorous articulation of '*Pachol*' to drive up to the strange ball before the weary dancers should seek repose upon the stones at the street corners. Drawing nearer and nearer, I yet heard no sound of music; at last we reached the Anitschkow Palace, and found ourselves close to the scene of this untimely activity. A repulsive and horrible sight met my eyes. A number of young women, apparently still fresh and blooming, with ruddy cheeks – but whether of artificial or natural colours their incessant monotonous bowing movement prevented my distinguishing – elegantly dressed in silks, jewels, and feathers, were sweeping the Newsky Street under the superintendence of policemen. Some of them appeared overwhelmed with shame, others stared at me, at the *Isworstschik* and horse, with perfect indifference, and seemed rejoiced at our passage, which suspended for a moment their painful and disgraceful occupation. They were a detachment of nocturnal wanderers, who, when returning too tardily to their homes from pursuing their wretched calling, had fallen into the hands of the patrol, had passed the remainder of the night in the watch house, and were now atoning, broom in hand, their untimely rambles. I hurried off to the bath, glad to escape from this degrading and deplorable spectacle.

The Hay Market

[57] Raskolnikov wanders about the Hay Market (1860s), from *Crime and Punishment* by Fyodor Dostoyevsky.

The heat in the street was terrible: and the airlessness, the bustle and the plaster, scaffolding, bricks, and dust all about him, and that special Petersburg stench, so familiar to all who are unable to get out of town in summer all worked painfully upon the young man's already overwrought nerves. The insufferable stench from the pot-houses, which are particularly numerous in that part of the town, and the drunken men whom he met continually, although it was a working day, completed the revolting misery of the picture. An expression of the profoundest disgust gleamed for a moment in the young man's refined face. He was, by the way, exceptionally handsome, above the average in height, slim, well built, with beautiful dark eyes and dark brown hair. Soon he sank into deep thought, or more accurately speaking into a complete blankness of mind; he walked along not observing what was about him and not caring to observe it. From time to time he would mutter something, from the habit of talking to himself, to which he had just confessed. At these moments he would become conscious that his ideas were sometimes in a tangle and that he was very weak; for two days he had scarcely tasted food.

He was so badly dressed that even a man accustomed to shabbiness would have been ashamed to be seen in the street in such rags. In that quarter of the town, however, scarcely any shortcoming in dress would have created surprise. Owing to the proximity of the Hay Market, the number of establishments of bad character, the preponderance of the trading and working-class population crowded in these streets and alleys in the heart of Petersburg, types so various were to be seen in the streets that no figure, however queer, would have caused surprise. But there was such accumulated bitterness and contempt in the young man's heart that, in spite of all the fastidiousness of youth, he minded his rags least of all in the street. It was a different matter when he met with acquaintances or with former fellow students, whom, indeed, he disliked meeting at any time. And yet when a drunken man who, for some unknown reason, was being taken somewhere in a huge wagon dragged by a heavy dray horse, suddenly shouted at him as he drove past: 'Hey there, German hatter!' bawling at the top of his voice and pointing at him – the young man stopped suddenly and clutched tremulously at his hat. It was a tall round hat from Zimmermann's but completely worn out, rusty with age, all torn and bespattered, brimless and bent on one side in a most unseemly fashion. Not shame, however, but quite another feeling akin to terror had overtaken him.

St Alexander Nevsky's Monastery

[58] The American Minister John Quincy Adams attends the Anniversary of the Saint's Feast in 1810, from *The Memoirs of John Quincy Adams.*

September 11th, 1810.
It is the anniversary festival of St Alexander Newsky, a Prince of Novgorod, who reigned about the year 1250; and is also what they call the name-day of the Emperor [Alexander I]. At eleven o'clock I went with Mr W. Smith to the monastery, where the crowd was great, and the concourse of the people, from the Perspective to the church, on both sides of the street, was excessive. When we got to the church, we found it difficult to ascertain a proper place to stand in. None of the other foreign Ministers were there excepting Count Schenk, who came in some time after me, and who was as much embarrassed as myself. He took a place among the officers in attendance on the imperial family, which he found was not the proper one, and returned to where I had taken mine. Count Romanzoff, at length seeing me, came to me and stood next to me during the whole ceremony, and explained to me many parts of the performances. The silver shrine of the saint

is at the right hand of the chancel, as you go up the broad aisle to the altar. Before this shrine was spread a large carpet, on which the Emperor took his stand, with the Empress at his left hand; next to her the Empress-mother; then the Grand Dukes Nicholas and Michael, and the Grand Duchess Ann behind her mother. The Crown officers and attendants were ranged in a line beyond the Emperor, up to the steps to the shrine of the saint. Prince George of Oldenburg, husband of the Grand Duchess Catherine, the Prince of Würtemberg, brother of the Empress-mother, and a number of officers and strangers, stood before the chancel, on the right side of the aisle, and a number of ladies, and crowd of women at the left.

The ceremony was performed by the Archbishop and the other priests who usually perform at the Imperial Chapel, with the same choir of singers. But it was not a Te Deum, and differed in many respects from an ordinary mass. Count Romanzoff told me that the two candlesticks which the Archbishop occasionally takes in his hands, one with three lighted candles and the other with two, and which he waves downward crosswise, were symbolical of the Trinity, and of the double nature of Christ. Coxe, I think, mentions this. At a particular part of the ceremony a sort of embroidered cloth was waved, or rather shaken, over the altar. The Count said it was during the 'Credo', and to express the uncertainty of the time when the mystery of the descent of the Holy Ghost commences – the Greek Church not having thought the precise moment ascertainable.

After the mass was finished, the Emperor went up to the shrine of the saint, knelt, and kissed the silver coffin three times – twice at the side, and once on the top. The Empress, Grand Dukes, and Grand Duchess all followed in turn, and repeated the same adoration of the saint. The Grand Duchess Ann, a beautiful princess of about seventeen years of age, performed her part at once with the most complete prostration, the most grace, and the most dignity. As the Empress-mother descended the steps, the Emperor lent her his arm to assist her. There were then three small pictures, in frames, given to the Emperor and two Empresses, and small round loaves of bread to each of the members of the imperial family.

On going out of the church, the crowd was so great that the passage out to my carriage by the way at which we had entered was totally barred. I followed the crowd of the Imperial officers through the only passage-way that was open, supposing it led to another issue, until I found myself unexpectedly in the Archbishop's apartments where the Emperor and his suite had been invited to breakfast. One of the messengers of the Grand Master of the Ceremonies gave me notice that the attendance of strangers there was not usual . . .

[59] The Monastery of St Alexander Nevsky, from *Russia: 1842* by J. G. Kohl.

Petersburg has but two convents – this Smolnoi convent, which is a convent only in name – for the *demoiselles nobles*, on the first foundation of the establishment by the Empress Catherine, dispossessed the twenty nuns settled here – and the convent of St Alexander Newskoi, for monks. This convent is now one of the most celebrated in Russia, a *lawra*[1] and the third in rank, the other two superior to it being the *lawra* of the Trinity at Moscow, and the *lawra* of the Caves at Kiew. It is the seat of the metropolitan of Petersburg, and is situated near the Newa, at the farthest extremity of the Newsky Perspective, where it occupies a considerable area, with all its churches, towers, gardens, and cells, inclosed by a high wall. Peter the Great founded it himself in honour of the Grand-duke Alexander, who gained a great victory here over the Swedes and the Knights of the Sword, who was canonized after his death, and whose remains were removed hither in a silver coffin. Peter's successors enlarged the possessions and the buildings of the convent, and to Catherine it was indebted for its present beautiful cathedral, which is one of the finest churches in Petersburg. For the decoration of its interior, blocks of marble were brought from Italy, precious stones from Siberia, and genuine pearls from Persia; it was embellished moreover with good copies from Guido Reni and Perugino; and the altar-piece, an Annunciation of the Virgin

[1] This designation is given to the most sacred convents of the empire, the seats of Metropolitans; the other convents are called merely *monastir*.

Mary, is by Raphael Mengs, or, as the monk who conducted us said, by Arphaele.[1] In a chapel hang several pictures by 'Robinsa', that is, in English, not Robinson, but Rubens. '*On Italiansky* – he was an Italian,' added the good father, by way of explanation. Such paintings by foreign masters are scarcely ever heard of in Russian churches. From Robinson to cannibals is not too violent a leap and, therefore, we were the less alarmed when our guide, pointing to a corner of the church, told us that a cannibal was buried there. We read the inscription: it was the celebrated Russian general, Hannibal. The Russians, having no H, always change that letter into G, and almost into K or C.

Against two pillars of the church, opposite to the altar, are hung two admirable portraits of Catherine and Peter the Great, rather larger than life. These two, the founder and the finisher, are every where in Petersburg seen together, like husband and wife. And how, if they had really been husband and wife? Would Peter have put her down as he did his sister Sophia, or would Catherine have dethroned him as she did her husband, Peter III; or would Russia have gained doubly by them?

In a side chapel stands the monument of Alexander Newsky. It is composed entirely of silver, and, and, next to the Ikonastases of the Kasan church, it is the largest mass of that metal in Petersburg; for it is said to consist of no less a weight than 5000 pounds of pure silver. It is a hill of silver, fifteen feet high, upon which stands a silver catafalque; above it are silver angels, of the size of men, with silver trumpets and silver flowers; while a number of silver basso-relievos exhibit representations of the battle of the Newa. We placed two wax-tapers on the tomb of the saint, and rejoiced to see how steadily they burned in honour of him. This burning of lamps and tapers in the Russian churches is a pleasing custom: the little flame is a living emblem of the immortality of the soul; and, of all material things, flame is certainly the best representative of what is spiritual. The Russians have so thoroughly penetrated themselves with this idea, that they can never think of performing any religious act, either funeral,

[1] The Russians change the name Raphael to Arphaele.

baptism, or wedding, without the aid of torches, lamps, and tapers: with them fire is a pledge of the presence of the Holy Ghost; hence, in all their church ceremonies, illumination acts the principal part. On the tomb of St Alexander are also hung the keys of Adrianople: they are remarkably small, not much larger than the key of a cash-box, which, in fact, Adrianople has in some respect become for the Russians.

But the Newsky convent received a larger share of the presents sent by Persepolis to the Petropolis of the North, when Gribojedow, the Russian ambassador, was murdered at Teheran, than had been assigned to it out of the Byzantine tribute. It was a long train of rare animals, with Persian stuffs, cloth of gold, and pearls, that entered in the winter season. The pearls and the gold-dust were carried in large silver and gold bowls by magnificently-dressed Persians, and exposed to public view; so likewise were the costly shawls. The Persian prince, Khosrew Mirza, rode in one of the imperial carriages with six horses, which had been sent to meet him; the elephants bore upon their backs towers manned by Indian warriors, and huge leathern boots had been put on tinier legs to protect them from the snow; the tigers and lions were provided with double skins of northern ice-bears – at least, their cages. 'It was a fairy scene of the Arabian Nights,' was the cry among us, 'and the population of whole provinces had collected to witness the show.' – 'It was a bagátelle,' said the people of Petersburg, 'and the pearls were many of them false;' and the affair excited but little sensation. The elephants soon died of cold; and the pearls were partly presented to the *Risnitzi* (treasuries) of the convents. In the Newskoi convent we saw whole pailfuls of these pearls, and, besides them, what is usual in the Russian convents, a rich collection of mitres set with many precious stones, of pontifical habits of the Petersburg metropolitans, made of gold brocade, and souvenirs of individual metropolitans and princes, for instance, a handsome crosier, which Peter the Great himself turned for a present to the first metropolitan of Petersburg, another of amber, the gift of Catherine II, and many other costly rarities, all which were one to find them any where else, one would admire and describe, but which, among the mass of valuable objects, are passed over unnoticed. The library of the convent, of about 10,000 volumes, contains a great number of most important manuscripts, about which many a book unknown to us has been written, and many curious relics of Russian antiquity.

St Isaac's Cathedral

[60] Easter Saturday, from *Vanished Pomps of Yesterday* by Lord Frederic Hamilton.

Many of the Diplomatic Body were in the habit of attending the midnight Mass at St Isaac's on Easter Day, on account of the wonderfully impressive character of the service. We were always requested to come in full uniform, with decorations; and we stood inside the rails of the ikonostas, behind the choir. The time to arrive was about 11.30 p.m., when the great church, packed to its doors by a vast throng, was wrapped in almost total darkness. Though conscious of the presence of this dense mass of humanity, one *felt* it rather than saw it. Under the dome stood a catafalque bearing a gilt coffin. This open coffin contained a strip of silk, on which was painted an effigy of the dead Christ, for it will be remembered that no carved or graven image is allowed in a church of the Eastern rite. There was an arrangement by which a species of blind could be drawn over the painted figure, thus concealing it. As the eye grew accustomed to the shadows, tens of thousands of unlighted candles, outlining the arches, cornices, and other architectural features of the cathedral, were just visible. These candles each had their wick touched with kerosene and then surrounded with a thread of gun-cotton, which ran continuously from candle to candle right round the building. When the hanging end of the thread of gun-cotton was lighted, the flame ran swiftly round the church, kindling each candle in turn; a very fascinating sight. At half-past eleven, the only light was from the candles surrounding the bier, where black-robed priests were chanting the mournful Russian Office for the Dead. At about twenty minutes to twelve the blind was drawn over the dead Christ, and the priests, feigning surprise, advanced to the rails of the ikonostas, and announced to an Archimandrite that the coffin was empty. The Archimandrite ordered them to search round the church, and the priests perambulated the church with gilt lanterns, during which time the catafalque, bier, and its accessories were all removed. The priests announced to the Archimandrite that their search had been unsuccessful, where-upon he ordered them to make a further search outside the church. They went out, and so timed their return as to arrive before the ikonostas at three minutes before midnight. They again reported that they had been unsuccessful; when, as the first stroke of midnight pealed from the great clock, the Metropolitan of Petrograd announced in a loud voice, 'Christ is risen!' At an electric signal given from the cathedral, the great guns of the fortress boomed out in a salute of one hundred and one guns; the gun-cotton was touched off, and the swift flash kindled the tens of thousands of candles running round the building; the enormous congregation lit the tapers they carried; the 'Royal doors' of the ikonostas were thrown open, and the clergy appeared in their festival vestments of cloth of gold, as the choir burst into the beautiful Russian Easter anthem, and so the Easter Mass began. Nothing more poignantly dramatic, more magnificently impressive, could possibly be imagined than this almost instantaneous change from intense gloom to blazing light; from the plaintive dirges of the Funeral Service to the jubilant strains of the Easter Mass; from the darkness of the tomb to the glories of the Resurrection. I never tired of witnessing this splendid piece of symbolism.

It sounds almost irreverent to talk of comical incidents in

connection with so solemn an occasion, but there are two little episodes I must mention. About 1880 the first tentative efforts were made by France to establish a Franco Russian alliance. Ideas on the subject were very nebulous at first, but slowly they began to crystallise into concrete shape. A new French Ambassador was appointed to Petrograd in the hope of fanning the faint spark into further life. He, wishing to show his sympathy for the *nation amie*, attended the Easter Mass at St Isaac's, but unfortunately he was quite unversed in the ritual of the Orthodox Church. In every ikonostas there are two ikons on either side of the 'Royal doors'; the Saviour on one side, the Madonna and Child on the other. The new Ambassador was standing in front of the ikon of the Saviour, and in the course of the Mass the Metropolitan came out, and made the three prescribed low bows before the ikon, previous to censing it. The Ambassador, taking this as a personal compliment to France, as represented in his own person, acknowledged the attention with three equally low bows, laying his hand on his heart and ejaculating with all the innate politeness of his nation, 'Monsieur! Monsieur! Monsieur!' This little incident caused much amusement, as did a newly-arrived German diplomat, who when greeted by a Russian friend with the customary Easter salutation of 'Christ is risen!' ('Kristos voskress!') wished to respond, but, being ignorant of the traditional answer, 'He is verily risen,' merely made a low bow and said 'Ich auch,' which may be vulgarly Englished into 'The same here.'

The Smolny Convent
for Girls

[61] A leading literary figure, Alexander Nikitenko, attends the hundredth anniversary of the foundation of the Smolny Convent (1864) and the formal breakfast there after the Mass, from *The Diary of a Russian Censor* by Alexander Nikitenko.

31 October, 1843.
Discussions with the director of Smolny Convent. No, I've definitely decided to leave this institution. Even my dreams of doing some good here, too, are only dreams! My lectures made an impression and often aroused enthusiasm in my students. I liked them, and they liked me, but what good is all this if the whole system is a sham. In general, our institutes for women pay so little attention to the academic and moral aspects of the education, that an honest man becomes discouraged and feels that he is wasting his time. Their only concern is dancing, singing and curtsying. They turn the girls' heads with gold lace and red livery and so forth. Neither moral strength nor an awareness of their domestic and social responsibilities is developed in them. And they will be the mothers of our next generation. So, the result is that our

Russian nobility raises its sons to wield the whip and its daughters for Court debauchery. Of course, not all of them will be Court maids-of-honor, not all of them will bring the immorality and hurly-burly of pompous high society into their homes. But, much time will be needed to make good wives and mothers out of these chiseled dolls.

15 November, 1843.
The director of Smolny Convent invited me to mass today at her church, where the Metropolitan was due to perform the service. I went. I hadn't witnessed a bishop's service for a long time. The first impression was striking; it had a kind of dramatic grandeur. Then it became monotonous. The endless liturgical prayers were particularly wearisome. Oh, servile Byzantine! You have given us a religion of slaves! Damn you! Indeed, the best of Christianity drowns in this gilded rubbish of ritual which despots have invented to keep the prayer itself from reaching God. They are everywhere – and nothing but them! There are no people, ideas or universal equality! There is only an oppressive hierarchy, a dazzling splendor to divert the eyes, to confuse people. Yes, there is everything here except simple Christian simplicity and humanity.

5 May, 1864.
Celebration of the one hundredth anniversary of Smolny Convent. I had received an invitation several days ago. I called for Polinka Sukman at 9 a.m. She had been educated at Smolny Convent and had also been invited to the celebration; and since she is such a nice young lady, I thought it would be pleasant to take her with me. We were at Smolny Convent church by 9.40. A lot of old women, probably from the almshouse, stood by the fence. The convent's pupils and several busy officials were behind the balustrade. Prince von Oldenburg had already arrived. He came up to me in his usual unpretentious, kindly way and asked how long I had taught at the convent and whether my students were attending university lectures conscientiously. The church began to fill with dignitaries and alumni. I met many friends among both. The Metropolitan conducted the mass. The court choir boys sang. How lovely the church is! I haven't seen anything

comparable to the grandeur, simplicity and gracefulness of its architecture anywhere, except, perhaps, in the Pantheon in Paris. The emperor [Alexander II], empress, and entire imperial family came for the service. The church and the convent building were temporarily joined by a covered canvas gallery. All the invited guests passed through it into the convent's endless corridors, which led them to the main hall. Along both sides of the upper corridor pupils stood in two rows, producing a very interesting effect. In the main hall, opposite the entrance, shaded by beautiful greenery, stood a statue of Catherine II, and the entire hall was filled with tables set for breakfast. All the tables were occupied by women except one which had been set aside for dignitaries, among whom I, too, a little and obscure man, took my place, between a very high ranking figure, Yazykov, director of the Law Institute, and Minister of Justice Zamyatin.

Since this was mainly a woman's holiday and since I generally have a greater appreciation for educated women than for our so-called educated men, I devoted all my attention to the waves of women's heads which filled almost the entire hall. What a variety of faces and ages! Side by side with blooming youth of recent graduations sat the ruins of the beginning of the century, which had once known the bloom of youth, too. They say a 104-year-old woman was the last survivor of the convent's first graduating class. But she didn't come. Many familiar little faces, that some 15 or 20 years ago had radiated the charm and excitement of youth in bloom, flashed by me; but now, alas! – they were fading, partly faded or totally faded, which eloquently spoke of how I, too, had faded. And how many of them had faded and are fading in want and under the stress of daily misfortunes and eternal Many, when they noticed me, sent me their warm greetings and smiles, somberly marked by the sad imprint of time. The men sat down immediately at the table and were about to attack the pies, cutlets and so forth, when a gentle-man-in-waiting appeared and announced that we had to wait for the emperor. After some 20 minutes the emperor appeared, leading the empress and followed by the grand dukes and members of the court. The band began to play. The emperor bowed with his usual warmth and sat down at the table, which everyone else then proceeded to do. And the gluttony commenced. The feast didn't interest me at all; I was too absorbed in contemplating the meaning of this celebration. My thoughts turned to Catherine, to whom Russia owes its understanding of the great importance of women, to whom it is indebted for their transformation from a piece of sweet meat or pie filled with physical delights, into thinking, noble beings, into great instruments for the regeneration and humanization of our people. But suddenly, foolish Yazykov interrupts my thoughts by taking my plate and piling it with cutlets. So, I had to eat. Glasses of champagne appeared; a first toast to the emperor; and charming female voices began to sing, 'God save the Tzar.'

My fellow guests were glad that the singing had ended and they could return to the business of feeding their stomachs. The breakfast was sumptuous, with plenty of wine, and good wine, too. All from the palace. Court servants attended us.

When the breakfast ended the emperor left quietly with his family. We all scattered about the hall. I kept running into my former pupils.

I started for home at 2.30 and, on the way, stopped at the Sukmans' to deliver my companion to her parents. The Smolny Convent celebration left me with most pleasant memories.

The Imperial Manège

[62] Tsar Alexander II reviews his cavalry in the Imperial Manège, from *Russia in the Eighties* by J. F. Baddeley.

While the Emperor Alexander II lived it was his custom, when in St Petersburg during the brief social season from New Year's day to the beginning of Lent, to hold a *razvód*, or review of the troops of the day, in the great Michael *manège*, or riding-school, each Sunday. The ceremony took place before luncheon and was a very brilliant affair, being largely attended by the Court and by the ambassadors and staffs of the various embassies and legations with their wives and their daughters. Non-official foreigners had little chance of gaining admittance on these occasions; but on the Sunday after our arrival in St Petersburg Schouvaloff took me in and I enjoyed a sight soon to be numbered with things of the past. There were squadrons and companies splendidly mounted and equipped, Chevaliers-gardes, Gardes-à-cheval, snub-nosed men of the Paul Regiment, Horse-grenadiers, Preobrajénsky Guards and others,[1] but the main interest lay in the presence

[1] The Chevaliers-gardes and the Gardes-à-cheval answered to our Life

of the Emperor's Caucasian bodyguard, which in those days
was drawn from all the chief mountain tribes, including the
Pshavs, Tusheens and Khevsours. These wild riders performed
various manoeuvres and feats of horsemanship, culminating
in a frantic charge up the centre of the *manège* to the very
feet of the Emperor and his brilliant staff. A little less than
two years later, on the 1st March, 1881, the *razvód* was held
as usual in spite of warning: the Emperor then lunched with
the Grand Duchess Catherine at the Michael Palace, and on
leaving it to return to the Winter Palace was cruelly assassinated. His successor, for reasons of economy, did away with
the bodyguard as it then existed – formed of units from many
tribes each dressed in its own costume – and instituted instead
a force composed of Ossietines and Cossacks from the Térek
and Koubán rivers, all dressed alike in the blue *cherkess* for
ordinary wear, the scarlet for special occasions.[1] It was many
years later that I paid a visit to the Khevsours in their
mountain fastnesses, and had for guide, up a ten thousand-
foot snow-covered pass, one of the tribe clad in hauberk of
chain-mail, with iron shield, sword, dagger and rifle, and a
bridle decorated alternately with cowrie-shells and beads of
turquoise blue.

[63] The assassination of Alexander II by four terrorists
in 1881, from *Russia in the Eighties* by J. F. Baddeley.

Guards and Horse Guards. The Emperor Paul having himself a snub-nose
raised a new guard-regiment in which snub-noses were *de rigueur*. The
Preobrajénsky foot-guards, the premier Russian regiment, had been formed
by Peter the Great when a boy, at the village of Preobrajénskoe near
Moscow, at first as living toys. Their barracks were in the Milliónnaya,
opposite Schouváloff's house, separated from the Imperial Hermitage and
the Winter Palace by the narrow Winter Canal, but with access to both, by
gallery-bridges, as a reward for their fidelity in 1825, at the time of the
Decabrist rising.

[1] *Cherkess* is the Russian form of the name from which Europe has derived
the word Circassian. It belongs properly to the noble people who call
themselves *Adighe*; but is loosely applied by travellers to almost any
Caucasians. *Cherkess* is also used for the long loose-sleeved garment which,
with the silver-mounted belt and cartridge cases across the breast, forms a
well-known and picturesque article of attire. In the form *Cherkas* it was
applied to the Little Russian Cossacks; hence Novocherkask, on the Don.

(The Church of Christ Resurrected, an *église expiatoire*, was later built on the spot where Alexander II was mortally wounded.)

The preparations made by the assassins bear witness to their grim and ruthless determination, and at the same time prove the criminal negligence of the police. The Catherine street had been mined from a basement butter-shop, and the mine remained undiscovered until after the assassination, although the authorities had received warning and had actually sent a general of engineers to make investigations. It was proved subsequently that when this officer made his enquiries of the butter-man, really Kóbezeff, a leading Nihilist, there was nothing but a board between him and the mine, at which a naval lieutenant was even then working. But he was satisfied with the answers given, and reported 'all well.' In case the Emperor went the other way, three men armed with dynamite bombs were waiting about under the direction of the woman Peróvskaya. On the fatal day at a signal from her that the victim was coming that way two of the three moved on to the canal embankment. Then, as the carriage passed, one of them, Risakóff, threw a bomb which exploded just behind it, partly shattering the woodwork and wounding several of the mounted Circassian escort. The Emperor got out, unhurt. The coachman implored him to get back into the carriage, declaring that he could perfectly well drive it home. But the Emperor, solicitous for the wounded, took a step or two towards the pavement on the canal side, where the assassin was being held by some of the Circassians; then, looking round and seeing that no one was killed, crossed himself, saying, *sláva Bógu* ('Thanks to God'). The assassin thereupon exclaimed, *yeehehó li sláva Bógu* ('Is it thanks to God yet?'); and the Emperor having moved a few paces along the canal a beardless youth threw a bomb at his feet, mortally wounding himself and his victim. The Emperor, driven to the Winter Palace in a sledge, in the arms of his brother Michael, who had been following him at some distance, only partly recovered consciousness and died at 3.30. The murderer, Grinevétsky, not identified as such for some days afterwards, died the same evening in hospital, whither he had been taken in the belief that he was a chance victim only, of the bomb. The third man, Emiliánoff, I met at Khabaróvsk on the Amoor in 1909 – a mild intelligent grey-beard, who after years at the mines, had been set free. He had by a natural instinct run to the Emperor's help after the explosion of the second bomb.

The Yusupov Palace on the Moika Canal

[64] The assassination of Grigory Rasputin by Prince Yusupov in 1916 in the Yusupov Palace, from *First Russia, then Tibet* by Robert Byron.

On returning to the ground floor, a series of passages led us to the winter garden, where the Scientific Workers and the Trade Union of Educationalists were eating soup. Beyond this was a billiard-room copied from the Alhambra, and beyond that the apartments of old Prince Yusupov...

The way now led through a series of locked doors and empty rooms, till suddenly we found ourselves in a small octagon about ten feet across and eight feet high. Each of the eight sides consisted of a wooden door painted white and inset with a broad panel of plate glass, behind which was a curtain of frilled blue silk. One door led into a still smaller bathroom, beyond which was a no less diminutive bedroom. The walls of both these sinister little apartments were thickly padded. A second door revealed a plain square room with two windows looking out on the Moika. This was now used as a military classroom; there were posters on the walls of tactical exercises, first-aid, and how to affix your gas-mask; a rifle on a stand was pointing into the street. A third door opened on to a cavern of darkness. But the other doors gave access to blank walls only, so that, once in the octagon, it was a matter of some minutes to find which door provided a way out of it. In addition, I had noticed that one of the previous doors leading to the octagon had had to be carefully propped open, as it was self-locking.

These were Prince Yusupov's private apartments, and here came, on the night of December 16, 1916, the Grand Duke Dmitri Pavlovitch, Purishkevitch, and Dr Lazovert. The headquarters of the conspiracy, so to speak, were in the room looking out on to the Moika. Here Dr Lazovert placed crystals of cyanide of potassium in the chocolate cakes and the wine-glasses. But the scene of action was across the octagon in that black void. Peering in, I saw a tiny spiral staircase, barely two feet wide. The guide asked me not to descend, as it was slippery and dangerous. But I persisted, and found a cellar divided by an arch and covered in six inches of water; for a thaw had set in. From high up in the wall came a glimmer of daylight. According to Prince Yusupov, this dank apartment 'had originally formed part of the wine cellar. In day time it was a rather dark and gloomy chamber, with a granite floor, walls faced with grey stone, and a low vaulted ceiling . . . I ordered some antique furniture to be brought down from the storeroom.' A large fire was lit. From the roof hung lanterns with coloured glass panes . . .

Prince Yusupov, borrowing the Grand Duke's car, went to fetch Rasputin and arrived back with his guest about one o'clock. 'The prospect of inviting a man to my house with the intention of killing him horrified me', observes the Prince in his book. 'I could not contemplate without a shudder the part which I should be called upon to play – that of a host encompassing the death of his guest.' A nasty complacency lurks beneath these protestations. But the conspirators had worked on one another's emotions till they had reached the state of Messianic exaltation which accounts for most things in Russian history. All Russians are saviours by vocation. These three, thinking to deliver the imperial throne of an unholy counsellor, merely precipitated the extinction of all they hoped to rescue.

On entering the house, host and guest crossed the octagon and descended by the spiral staircase to the cellar. There Rasputin ate the cakes and drank out of the poisoned glasses, while his host played the guitar and sang. Upstairs, in 'the study', Grand Duke and deputy waited. At length the Prince rushed in with the news that the poison would not work. After some discussion, he took a revolver and returned to the cellar. The others followed and stood listening at the top of the stair. A report was heard and a thud. The Prince emerged; the deed was done.

After an interval he returned to look at the body. As he did so the face began to twitch and the eyes opened. Suddenly Rasputin jumped to his feet and seized the youth by the throat. Yusupov struggled, got away, and fled up the stairs, while the monk could be heard crawling up them too on all-fours. But instead of making for the octagon, Rasputin escaped by a door off the staircase into the courtyard of the palace. Purishkevitch ran out after him, to see the enormous figure lurching across the snow. 'Felix, Felix,' Rasputin was shouting, 'I shall tell the Tzarina.'[1] Purishkevitch shot twice and the figure collapsed. Meanwhile the Prince was being sick in the bathroom. On learning that Purishkevitch had succeeded after all, he seized a loaded stick and fell to battering the corpse in a savage frenzy. Purishkevitch was much moved by this spectacle. Then the police arrived, and they shot one of the best dogs to give colour to the bloodstains and the other shots. The dog's grave, said the guide, was still in the garden. We looked out. But the garden had been flooded, to make a skating-rink for the leisure of Scientific Workers and the Trade Union of Educationalists.

---

[1] The authenticity of this exclamation as recorded by Purishkevitch, is doubted by those familiar with Russian parlance. Rasputin, or anyone else for that matter, would normally have referred to the Empress as 'Elizaveta Feodorovna' (sic).

The Mariinsky Theatre
and Theatre Street

[65] The Imperial Ballet: Tamara Karsavina's education, from her *Theatre Street*.

1896.
On December 6th, the Emperor's [Nicholas II's] name day, all three imperial theatres gave a special matinee for all the schools. Huge samovars steamed outside the stage door. The theatre was an unusually pretty sight on these days, full of children and young people, tiers of boxes tightly packed with girls in uniform dresses, blue, red, pink with white fichus. The partners were reserved for boys, schools, Lyceum, military and naval cadets and pages, and the gallery for popular schools. Every child received a box of sweets with a portrait of either the Tzar, Tzaritza or Tsarevitch on the lid. In the interval, tea and refreshments were served in several foyers, and the waiting staff wore their gala red livery with the Imperial eagles. Cool almond milk, deliciously fragrant, was a special feature of this treat.

Back at school we compared notes on the respective performances. We were usually given a choice of the theatre, but only few of us wanted to go to the Michailovsky, though the

French company performing there was excellent. If the day of the treat fell on Wednesday or Sunday, there was a ballet given instead of opera, and we often took part in it. On one of such occasions we were taken in costume to the Imperial box to receive sweets. Alexandra Feodorovna and the Empress Dowager stood in the drawing-room at the back of the Imperial box and handed us the sweets. We came one by one, curtsied and kissed the hand of both Tzaritzas. The Tzar stood by. He asked, 'Who is the little girl that danced the golden fish?' and I stepped forward and made a deep curtsy. 'How is it,' he went on, 'that the Tzar Maiden's ring was found on you?' Ivanoushka, the hero of the Russian tale, the plot of which had been worked into the ballet, dives to the bottom of the seas to retrieve the ring which had been swallowed by a golden fish. I wore a fish head modelled in papier mâché, and there was a small opening in it with a lid where the ring was put. I explained how it worked, and bent down my head for him to see. He smiled, 'Thank you for explaining, I would have never guessed it.' His smile had a charm irresistible. I have heard many times that all who came into his presence felt alike fascinated by his personality. To me it was like being lifted to Paradise.

1902.
The theatres closed for the summer, the examination over, there was still more than a fortnight to wait for the 'Act', a ceremony marking our coming out on the 25th of May. The days got out of shape, long from inactivity and yet too short for dreams. We spent most of the time in our little garden, talking or reading. My mind constantly wandered away from the book. The little calendar scrawl thinned down rapidly; it ceased to exist on the 24th of May. On the eve of the great day we were late in breaking up the last evening in Pensionnerskaya; we put our hair in curl papers; gave favourite imitations of masters; boldly sang prohibited couplets of farewell, poor rhymed efforts of our collective brains.

Up betimes long before the morning bell, my first thought was for my pale coral dress waiting for me in my wardrobe. It had to wait for a while yet. For the last time we dressed in blue serge and plaited our hair. There was a church service in the morning and thanksgiving. After a hurried lunch we assembled in the big dancing room in the presence of parents and masters. Father Vassily said a farewell word. We came forward to receive prizes and certificates from the Inspector of classes.

Farewell to the 'toads' and masters; farewell to Varvara Ivanovna, all skirmishes forgotten – tender farewells on both sides. Farewells to the friendly maids; furtive adieux to all the rooms, nooks and corners; a short bit of prayer before the dormitory ikon. Secular garb, affectionate vows of eternal friendship – the last page of school life was turned.

Yet unwritten pages were to be bound in the same book. Theatre Street remained a consecrated ground of daily work, a link in the chain of continuity. A nursery of creative search, a haven of repair. The mirror-image of yesterday had vanished; the same mirror, unsparing, unflattering, guardian of zeal, will reflect the shape of tomorrow. Before this same mirror, under the same roof, in the aloofness of Theatre Street, began, continued and faded a dancer's career.

[66] A performance of Glinka's *Life for the Tsar* in 1914; the atmosphere in 1916; and a concert at the Mariinsky Theatre after the March Revolution in 1917; all from *An Ambassador's Memoirs 1914–1917* by Maurice Paléologue.

September 13, 1914.
In the evening I went to the Marie Theatre for a performance of Glinka's *Life for the Tsar*. The Director of the imperial theatres had invited my English and Japanese colleagues, the Belgian and Serbian Ministers and myself to be present this evening as a demonstration in honour of the Allies had been prepared. Before the curtain rose the orchestra played the Russian national anthem, the *Boje Tsaria Kranie*, which Prince Lvov composed about 1825, a hymn with a broad sweep which produces a noble, religious effect. How many times had I heard it before? But I had never realized so forcibly how foreign the melody of the national anthem is to

Russian music and how German it is – in the direct tradition of Bach and Handel. But that did not prevent the public from listening to it in a patriotic silence which ended in an outburst of prolonged cheering. Next came the *Marseillaise*, received with transports of delight. Then *Rule Britannia* which was likewise hailed with loud cheers. Buchanan was in the box next to mine and I asked him why the orchestra played *Rule Britannia* and not *God save the King*. He replied that as the latter was the same as the Prussian national anthem the authorities feared a mistake which would have shocked the public. Next came the Japanese national anthem, suitably greeted. I calculated that it was only nine years since Mukden and Tsushima! At the opening notes of the *Brabançonne* a storm of grateful and admiring cheers burst. Everyone seemed to be saying: 'Where should we be now if Belgium had not resisted?' The ovation to the Serbian national anthem was more restrained, in fact very restrained. Many people seemed to be reflecting: 'If it had not been for the Serbs we should still be at peace!'

Then we had to sit through the *Life for the Tsar*, a stale and frigid work with its too official loyalty and its too old-fashioned Italianism. The public enjoyed it all the same for Glinka's drama touches the very fibres of the Russian conscience.

Sunday, September 17, 1916.
Sylvia and *The Water-Lily* were given at the Marie Theatre this evening. In both works the lead is in the hands of Karsavina.

The sumptuous hall, with its blue and gold hangings, was quite full; the evening marked the opening of the winter season and the resumption of those ballets in which the Russian imagination loves to follow the interplay of flying forms with rhythmic movements through the music. From the stalls to the back row of the highest circle I could see nothing but a sea of cheery, smiling faces. In the intervals the boxes came to life with the irresponsible chatter which made the bright eyes of the women sparkle with merriment. Irksome thoughts of the present, sinister visions of war and the melancholy prospects of the future vanished as if by magic the moment the orchestra struck up. An air of pleasant unreality was in every face.

Thomas de Quincey, the author of the *Confessions of an Opium Eater*, tells us that the drug often gave him the illusions of music. Conversely, the Russians go to music for the effects of opium.

April 7, 1917

This afternoon, the Volhynian regiment, formerly a regiment of the Guard, which was the first to revolt on the 12th March and carried the rest of the garrison with it by its example, organized a concert at the Marie Theatre for the benefit of the victims of the revolution. An extremely polite invitation was sent to the ambassadors of France, England and Italy. We decided to turn up, to avoid the appearance of slighting the new regime; the Provisional Government was also present at the ceremony.

What an extraordinary change at the Marie Theatre! Would its clever stagehands have succeeded in producing such an amazing transformation? All the imperial coats of arms and all the golden eagles have been removed. The box attendants had exchanged their sumptuous court liveries for miserable, dirty grey jackets.

The theatre was filled with an audience of bourgeois, students and soldiers. A military orchestra occupied the stage; the men of the Volhynian regiment stood in groups behind.

We were ushered into the box on the left which was formerly the box of the imperial family, and in which I have so often seen the Grand Duke Boris, the Grand Duke Dimitri and the Grand Duke Andrew applauding Kchechinskaia, Karsavina, Spesivtsiava or Smirnova. Opposite us, in the Minister of the Court's box, all the ministers were gathered, wearing nothing more impressive than frock-coats. I could not help thinking of old Count Fredericks, with his blaze of orders and his exquisite courtesy, who is now kept a prisoner in a hospital, sorely stricken with a disease of the bladder and obliged to submit to the most humiliating attentions in the presence of two gaolers. My thoughts went also to his wife, the worthy Countess Hedwig-Aloisovna, who sought refuge in my embassy and is on her deathbed in an isolation hospital; to General Voyeikov, Commandant of the Imperial Palaces, who is a prisoner in the Fortress, and to all the brilliant aides-de-camp, *gardes-à-cheval* and knight-guards, who are now dead or in captivity or flight.

But the real interest of the audience was concentrated on the great imperial box in the centre, the gala box. It was occupied by some thirty persons, old gentlemen and several old ladies, with grave, worn, curiously expressive and unforgettable faces, who turned wondering eyes on the assembly. These were the heroes and heroines of terrorism who, scarcely three weeks ago, were living in exile in Siberia, or in the cells of Schlusselburg and the Fortress of SS Peter and Paul. Morozov, Lopatin, Vera Figner, Catherine Ismailovitch, etc. were there. I shivered to think of all that the little party stood for in the way of physical suffering and moral torment, borne in silence and buried in oblivion. What an epilogue for Kropotkin's *Memoirs*, or Dostoievsky's *Memories of the House of the Dead*.

The concert began with the *Marseillaise*, which is now the Russian national anthem. The theatre almost collapsed under the cheers and shouts of 'Long live the Revolution!', and 'Long live France!' was occasionally sent my direction.

Then we had a long speech from the Minister of Justice, Kerensky; it was a clever speech in which the subject of the war was wrapped up in socialist phraseology. The orator's style was incisive and jerky; his gestures were few, impatient and imperious. He had a *succès fou* which made his pale, drawn features seem to light up with satisfaction.

In the interval which followed, Buchanan said to me: 'Let's pay our respects to the Government box! It will look well.'

At the end of the interval we returned to our box. A murmur of sympathy and something like concentration passed through the theatre; it was a sort of silent ovation.

Vera Figner had appeared on the stage, in the conductor's place.

She was utterly unaffected, her grey hair coiled round her head, dressed in a black woollen gown with a white fichu, and looking like a very distinguished old lady. Nothing about her betrayed the fearsome nihilist she used to be in the days of her youth. She was of course of good family, connected with the nobility.

In calm, level tones, unaccompanied by any kind of gesture, and without a single outburst or the slightest trace of violence or emphasis, the acid note of vengeance or the pealing cry of victory, she reminded us of the countless army of obscure victims who have bought the present triumph of the revolution with their lives, all those nameless ones who have succumbed in state prisons or the penal settlements of Siberia. The list of martyrs came forth like a litany or a piece of recitative. The concluding phrases, uttered more slowly, struck an indescribable note of sadness, resignation and pity. Perhaps the Slav soul alone is capable of that intensity. A funeral march which the orchestra at once began seemed a continuation of the speech, the pathetic effect of which thus culminated in religious emotion. Most of those present were reduced to tears.

We took advantage of this general emotion to withdraw, as we were told that Cheidze, the orator of the 'Labour' group, was about to speak against the war and that heated disputes, etc might be anticipated. It was time to go. Besides, the ceremony had made a peculiarly poignant impression upon us: we did not want to spoil it.

In the empty passages through which I hastened I seemed to see the ghosts of my smart women friends who had so often been here to lull their restless minds with the novelties of the ballet, and who were the last charm of a social system which has vanished forever.

THE APPROACHES
TO ST PETERSBURG:
FOUR PALACES IN
THE COUNTRY

Peterhof

[67] Peterhof: Peter the Great's plans, and Le Blond's execution of them (1715), from *Palmyra of the North* by Christopher Marsden.

Peter entrusted to Le Blond the task of building for him a country palace to rival that which Schädel was erecting for Menshikov. He went further; he ordered two. So, while the German proceeded with Oranienbaum, the Frenchman set to work on two sites close by; both, like Oranienbaum, on the shore of the Gulf of Finland, one eleven and the other five miles on the Petersburg side of Oranienbaum. There, both with windows overlooking the sea from which the tsar could watch the evolutions of his fleet in the gulf, Strelna (then called Strellemouse, Strelna Muisa or Strena Moise) and Peterhof arose . . .

The *Versailles au bord de la mer* that Peter ordered of Leblond – has fared little better, the main palace having been almost entirely reconstructed under Elizabeth. There is hardly any of the original work recognizable on the exterior; but within, the walls, doors and mirror frames of Peter's study are still decorated with the exquisite, if rather severe, wood-

carving of Nicholas Pineau who, it will be remembered, came
from Paris with Le Blond. In one room were some remarkably
obscene paintings, discreetly enclosed behind shutters; they
were reputed to have been of Chinese origin. They have gone.
In spite of alterations, the site which Le Blond chose for his
structure gives the place such individuality that it is not
difficult to imagine its earlier appearance; and even the
enlarged Elizabethan building (which will find its own place
in its account) retains something of its original character of
an imitation of Versailles. The terrace, about forty feet in
height, upon which the palace stands, is formed by a natural
slope of the ground towards Neva Bay, and commands a
distant view of the Finnish coast. The high ground behind the
palace Le Blond laid out regularly in the Le Nôtre manner
with flower beds (which in 1926 were restored in accordance
with the original plans) and he put a large ornamental fountain in the centre, enlivened, as at Versailles, with vomiting
horses and dolphins. In front of the palace a huge cascade
rushes down in two arms between a grotto (later remodelled)
over six wide steps of coloured marble into a large basin. The
water was drawn from about six miles away in wooden pipes,
which were replaced by metal ones in the reign of Elizabeth.
From the basin a long canal, flanked by rows of trees,
fountains and statues, leads right through the lower garden to
the sea. Fountains and statues were arranged about the lower
garden in strict symmetry, as required by the French and
Dutch styles. A special feature was the fountain in the form
of a pyramid, composed of hundreds of little jets of water of
regularly varying height which together merged into a perfectly geometrical mass of water. It was the work of an expert
French *fontainier*, a certain M. Paul, who must have come in
Le Blond's party . . .

   In the gardens of Peterhof, the best-preserved relics of Le
Blond's activity are the three pavilions in the lower garden –
the Hermitage, Marly and Monplaisir. The first of these, the
Hermitage, which stands within a little moat and is 'guarded'
by a drawbridge, is a pleasantly light and airy pavilion on
two stories; its large round-headed windows and Corinthian
pilasters give it much delicacy and elegance. It is the earliest
of the Russian pavilions to be fitted with the French device

for lowering part of one floor to the floor below at the sound of a bell, so that a table, laid for twelve, could vanish and reappear without the tiresome presence of servants. The First Carpenter, a Frenchman named Michel, was responsible for this contraption. The second pavilion, Marly, bears no conceivable resemblance to its famous French namesake: it will be remembered that Peter visited the Mansart palace when he was in France in 1717 and was much impressed by its waterworks. It is plainer and more 'Dutch' than the Hermitage, but has an enchanting, quiet grace as it stands, white and cool, surrounded by its mirror-like pond. Inside it has more carved oak wainscoting by Pineau and a kitchen with Delft tiles. Finally, on the water's edge, is Monplaisir, a one-storied red-brick pavilion with windows overlooking the sea, from which Peter could gaze across the bay to the fortress of Kronstadt.

[68] Peter the Great's wood-cutting party at Peterhof in 1715 for the envoys at his Court, from *Mémoires pour Servir à l'Histoire de l'Empire Russien sous le Règne de Pierre le Grand* by F. C. Weber.

1715.
When we arrived at Cronslot, the Czar invited us to proceed to Peterhof, a country-house which he had recently built on the Ingrian coast. We were feasted as usual. His Majesty, who was restrained in his own drinking, gave us a well matured Hungarian wine at dinner. We could hardly stand, having drunk such a quantity already, but it was impossible to refuse another pint glass offered by the Czarina herself. This reduced us to such pitiful circumstances that our servants chose to throw one of us into the garden, another in the wood where we stayed till four p.m. in the afternoon, and where we were sick. We were woken up at four p.m. and we went back into the Palace where the Czar gave us each an axe and ordered us to follow him. He took us into a wood, planted with young trees.

Wanting to reach the sea, he had marked out a cutting and immediately started cutting wood down alongside us. Hardly able to cope with this type of work, especially after a debauch which had made us very tired, the seven of us, not counting His Majesty, finished off the alley in three hours. This violent exercise sweated us out of our alchoholic haze. No accident happened except that Mr. . . ., one of His Majesty's Ministers, lurching hither and thither, was knocked over by a tree which fell on him.

Having thanked us for our work, His Majesty paid for our supper that night. A second debauch followed; this time we fainted away and we were put to bed. After one hour's sleep, one of the Czar's favourites woke us up to visit the Prince of Circassia, in bed with his wife. We had to drink brandy and wine by his bed till four o'clock when we found ourselves at home, ignorant of how we got there.

At eight a.m., we went to Court to drink coffee but the cups were full of brandy. Afterwards we were taken to a mountain facing the Palace. A peasant helped us to mount eight miserable horses, without saddles or stirrups. Leading this grotesque cavalcade, using sticks to beat the horses, not worth four kopecks, a Russian nobleman got us somehow to the top of the mountain.

Their Majesties, looking through the windows, reviewed us; after wandering long in the woods and having drunk a full bucket of water to quench our thirst, we went to dine, i.e. to get drunk for the fourth time. As the wind was blowing quite hard, the Czar, fearing we should not be able to put out to sea if we delayed, decided it was time that we should leave.

[69] Count Stanislaus Poniatovsky spends the night at Monplaisir in July 1756 with the Grand Duchess Catherine, on her husband's orders; from *The Russian Journals of Martha and Catherine Wilmot 1803-1808*.

Sunday, 30th November.
Tonight I again heard the Empress Katherine's letter to the Princess D. who read them for Kitty & again I admired her spirited charming style of writing. *The Imperial conversation* which follow'd unfolded the following curious circumstances.

At the period of Katherine's intimacy with Poniatofsky[1] while she was Grand Duchess & he Polish Ambassador, 'tis a well known fact that he used to visit her at Oranienbaum & likewise that He was one night seiz'd by the Grand Duke's Guards & brought prisoner before him, that Peter[2] call'd a Council of War, & after various opinions (such as one recommending his being thrown into the Sea, another offering to fight him) & no decision it was refer'd to the Empress Eliz[th] and by her decreed that the Prisoner (who she affected to suppose could not be Poniatofsky) should be released without further notice.

This affair however had been spread abroad, & a great feast for the name day of Peter & of his son Paul (w[ch] come together) happening immediately after, at which all the partys were to appear, caused a general embarrassment. Count Poniatofsky wish'd to appease the G[d] Duke but had not even imagined any plan to effect it when a follower & friend of his M. de Branitsky, a Man who did a successful thing more frequently than a cleaver one (& does so still for he is alive), happening to dance with the Countess Eliz[th] Worontzow[3],

---

[1] Stanislaus Poniatowsky (1732–1798) last King of Poland, known as Stanislaus II. While Saxon Ambassador at St Petersburg he formed a notorious attachment for the Grand Duchess Catherine, whose influence, when she became Empress, was largely instrumental in raising him to the Polish throne. Noted for his handsome appearance and extravagance. Abdicated on the outbreak of Kosciuszko's rising in 1794 and died in St Petersburg.

[2] Later Czar Peter III, who was assassinated in the Revolution of 1762.

[3] Countess Elizabeth Woronzow (1739–1792), eldest daughter of Count Roman Woronzow and sister of Princess Daschkaw. While Maid of Honour to Catherine II, when Grand Duchess, she became the mistress of her husband, Peter, later Czar Peter III. This liaison provoked general astonishment at Court, as Elizabeth was both ugly and stupid in contrast with the other handsome and gifted members of the Woronzow family. Peter doubtless had his reasons for choosing her as a companion in preference to his clever and unscrupulous wife, and in spite of his supposed mental shortcomings he formed a far truer estimate of Catherine II's character than did his mistress's brilliant sister. 'My child,' he said one day to Princess Daschkaw, 'you would do well to recollect that it is much safer to deal with honest blockheads like your sister and myself than with great wits who squeeze the juice out of the orange and then throw away the rind.' For Elizabeth, it may justly be said that she did love Peter for himself, and not like the majority of persons in her position, for what could be got out of their paramours. It was thought by many that Peter intended to marry her and shut up his wife in a monastery on the very day of the *coup d'état* (June 29, 1762) which

Peter's mistress, say'd to her, 'What a pity it is to have this foolish story in circulation while your influence and goodness of heart could settle everything in a moment.' She enquired how. He told her by representing it as a matter of slight consequence to the G. Duke, & added, 'You would obtain a pension of 3000 roubles (about £300) if you succeeded'. The simple round-faced Dame made no reply, but when ask'd by Peter after the dance 'what the fellow had been saying' she told it all. Peter no sooner heard of a 'Pension' for her than he exclaim'd, 'Faith that's an honest Lad, but let *me* speak to him'. When Branitsky came across the room he told him nearly the same thing & desired him to come to a certain part of the Grounds Monte Plaisir at 2 o'clock with Poniatofsky & then he would confirm his promise of forgiveness. Branitsky repeated the affair to Count P. who refused to go imagining it must be some plan of the G^d Duke's to have him assassinated. However his friend at length prevail'd, he accompanied him to Monte Plaisir, & there met the G. duke who held out his hand to be kiss'd while he kiss'd his cheek (according to the Russian fashion). They were about to separate when Peter seizing Poniatofsky by the arm began to stride forward with all his might & main dragging along the astonish'd Count. At last they stop'd at Katherine's Apartments, & the despicable mean-spirited Peter ordering the Door to be open'd left the Count there & retired! Such is the Virtue, the Morality & the Magnanimity of the Great!

[70] Catherine II's letter to Count Stanislaus Poniatovsky in 1762, describing her *coup d'état*, from *Memoirs of Catherine the Great*.

---

raised Catherine to the throne. Though arrested along with the Czar she was later liberated, and after Peter's assassination, she was allowed to retire to Moscow, where the Empress showed how little jealousy she bore her by purchasing a house for her.

In 1765 she married colonel Alexander Poliansky, later Counsellor of State and Court Chamberlain, by whom she had two children. Of these, Alexander married Elizabeth, daughter of M. Ivan Ribeaupierre, and Anne married Baron D'Hoggier, Dutch Ambassador in St Petersburg.

August 2 (os) 1762.

I was in Peterhof. Peter III lived and got drunk at Oranienbaum. We had agreed in case of a betrayal not to await his return, but to assemble the Guard and proclaim myself as ruler. Zealousness on my behalf accomplished for me what a betrayal would have done.

On the 27th a rumour that I had been arrested spread among the troops. The soldiers became excited; one of our officers quieted them. Then a soldier came to a captain by the name of Passek, the leader of the groups, and told him that I was certainly lost. He assured him that he had news of me. The soldier, still disturbed on my account, went to another officer and told him the same. The latter had not been initiated in the secret and was startled when he heard that an officer had let this soldier go and had not arrested him. He went to the Major and the latter then ordered the arrest of Passek. The whole regiment was not in action. During the night the report was sent to Oranienbaum. There was great distress among my confederates. They decided before all else to send the second of the Orlov brothers to fetch me to the city; the other two went everywhere spreading the news that I would soon arrive. The Hetman, Volkonsky, and Panin had been initiated in the secret.

At six o'clock on the morning of the 28th, I lay quietly sleeping. It had been a very restless day for me because I knew what was under way. Then Alexei Orlov entered my room and said with great calmness: 'It is time for you to arise; everything is ready to proclaim you.' I asked him for particulars and he said, 'Passek is arrested.' I no longer hesitated; dressing myself as quickly as possible without making a toilette, I entered the carriage that he had brought. Another officer, disguised as a lackey, stood at the door of the coach; another came to meet me a few versts from Peterhof. Five versts distant from the city I met the elder Orlov with the younger Prince Bariatinsky. The latter gave me his place in the carriage, for my horses were exhausted. We drove to the Izmailovsky Regiment and there alighted. There were only twelve men there and a drummer who at once beat the alarm. The soldiers came, embraced me, kissed my feet, my hands, my dress, and called me their saviour. Two of them led forward by the arms a priest with a cross and they began to take the oath of allegiance to me. When that was done I was bidden to step into a coach. The priest with the cross walked ahead. We marched to the Semyonovsky regiment which came to meet us with loud vivas. Then we went on to the Kazan Cathedral where I alighted. The Preobrashensky Regiment arrived with cries of *viva*, and the people said: 'We beg your pardon for being the last to arrive. Our officers held us back, but we have brought four of them with us under arrest as a testimonial of our zeal. We wished the same as our brothers.' Next came the Horse Guard. The people were mad with joy; I have never seen anything like it. They wept and invoked the freedom of the Fatherland.

[71] Princess Dashkov's account of her role in Catherine the Great's *coup d'état*, from *The Memoirs of Princess Dashkov*.

Happiness came at last when I learnt that Her Majesty had arrived at the barracks of the Izmailovski Regiment and had been unanimously proclaimed Sovereign, that she had proceeded thence to the Kazan Cathedral where there was a great concourse of people all eager to swear allegiance to her, and that the other regiments, both Guards and of the line, had done so too.

It was six o'clock in the morning when I ordered my maid to make ready the dress I wore on State occasions, and later hastened to the Winter Palace where I knew she had to appear. I shall never be able to describe how I reached her. All the troops that happened to be in Petersburg had joined the Guards Regiments and now surrounded the Palace, filling the great square and sealing off all avenues of approach.

I therefore left my carriage and was about to cross the Square on foot when I was recognised by some officers and soldiers. Suddenly I felt myself borne aloft over the heads of all sorts and conditions of men and heard myself called by the most flattering names. Blessings and wishes of prosperity accompanied me till finally I was carried into Her Majesty's ante-chamber with one sleeve lost, dishevelled and in the

The Marriage-Fair in the Summer Garden, from
Les Mystères de la Russie, by F. Lacroix, 1845

Constables punish prostitutes by making them
sweep the Nevsky Prospekt at dawn. From *Les
Mystères de la Russie*, by F. Lacroix, 1845

The mock execution of Fyodor Dostoyevsky and
other conspirators from the 'Petrashevtsy' circle,
on Semyonovsky Square, 22 December 1849

The assassination of Tsar Alexander II on the
Ekaterininsky Embankment, 1881. Artist Unknown

The 'Institute for the Education of Well-born
Young Ladies', by the Smolny Monastery.
By I. Ivanov

The palace of Paul I at Pavlovsk, by G. Lory, 1805

The Palace of Peterhof (*'Maison de Plaisance de Sa Majesté Impériale de toutes les Russies'*). By M.I. Makhayev, *c.*1756–60

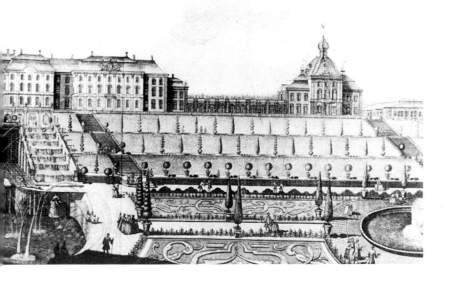

Catherine the Great walking her greyhound in
the gardens of Tsarskoye Selo, by
V. Borovikovsky

Catherine the Great's entry into St Petersburg, accompanied by the Orlov brothers, after the *coup* which made her Empress of all Russias. By P.A. Novelli, *c.*1797

The wedding-feast of Peter the Great's dwarfs,
1710, in Prince Menshikov's house.
By A.F. Zubov

greatest possible disarray. But in my state of excitement I imagined all this to represent a sort of Triumph. Besides, I neither could, not had the time to, put it right and therefore presented myself to the Empress just as I was.

We threw ourselves into each other's arms. 'Thank God', 'Thank Heaven', was all either of us was able to utter.

Her Majesty told me the story of how she had stolen away from Peterhof. My heart beat faster as I listened to her, and I relived in my own emotions all the hopes and fears she must have felt in those critical moments. I too confided in her how anxious I had been during those hours of distress and pain which were decisive for her fate and for the happiness or unhappiness of the Empire. I told her of the annoying mishap which had prevented me going out to meet her. Again we threw ourselves in each other's arms. No happiness could ever have exceeded mine at that moment. It had reached its summit.

Suddenly I noticed that she was still wearing the Order of St Catherine and had not yet put on the blue ribbon of the Cross of St Andrew. (The blue ribbon was not worn by the wife of the Emperor; she was entitled only to the Order of St Catherine which had been founded by Peter I for his own wife. The Emperor Paul was the first to grant the blue ribbon to his wife and the Emperor Alexander followed his example in this respect.) I ran to Mr Panin to borrow his blue ribbon, which I put on the Empress's shoulder. Thereupon she took off her own insignia of the Order of St Catherine and asked me to put them in my pocket.

After a light dinner we proposed to go with the troops to Peterhof. The Empress and I decided to wear the uniform of one of the Guards regiments; she therefore borrowed Captain Talyzin's uniform for the purpose and I that of Lieutenant Pushkin, as these two officers were roughly similar to us in height. These uniforms, by the way, were those the Preobrazhenski Regiment formerly worn from the time of Peter the Great down to the reign of Peter III, who abolished them in favour of Prussian type uniforms. And it is a peculiar thing that no sooner did the Empress arrive in Petersburg, than the soldiers threw off their new Prussian uniforms and donned their old ones which they somehow managed to find.

I went quickly home to change so as to be more useful to the Empress in case of need. When I came back to the Palace, Her Majesty, together with those senators that happened to be in town, was holding a kind of council regarding the manifestoes that should be immediately published, etc. etc. Teplov acted as secretary.

It was more than likely that Peter III had by now been informed of the Empress's flight from Peterhof and of the excitement in town. It therefore occurred to me that he could well have been advised by someone in his entourage to act with courage and determination and to come to Petersburg, if necessary in disguise. This thought struck me so forcibly that I did not want to wait until the sitting of the Council was over. I had no right to force my way into that august assembly, but the two junior officers posted at the door either thought the order they had received not to let anyone in did not apply to me, or else it never occurred to them that I should not go in. In any case, they opened the door for me. I went quickly up to Her Majesty's chair and whispered into her ear what my apprehensions were, adding that if she wanted to take preventive measures she had better take them now without loss of time. Thereupon Her Majesty summoned Mr Teplov to write out an order and relevant instructions in two copies, to be given to two men who were to be posted at the mouth of the two rivers which formed the only possible approaches to the city.

The Empress, who foresaw the embarrassment that my appearance might cause, explained to those venerable old statesmen, who failed to recognise me, who I was and said that my friendship for her, always on the alert to help, had suggested something she had forgotten.

I looked like a boy of fifteen in my uniform, and the appearance of a young and totally unknown Guards officer in the midst of their sanctuary speaking in Her Majesty's ear must have been strange indeed. But no sooner did she mention my name than they all rose from their seats and gravely bowed to me in solemn welcome. I really did behave rather like a small boy and at this mark of respect I blushed and was overcome with confusion.

Soon after the sitting was over and the Empress had given

orders to ensure the safety of the city, we mounted our horses
and reviewed the troops, who numbered twelve thousand
without counting the volunteers who were increasing every
moment.

The troops had been on foot for the past twelve hours and
therefore as soon as we reached Krasny Kabak, just over six
miles away from the city, we made a three-hour halt. We too
were badly in need of rest. I had scarcely slept at all for a
whole fortnight, and although I could not have fallen asleep
at that actual moment, it was the greatest possible bliss to be
able to stretch myself out on a bed and rest my tired limbs.
There was only one bed in that house, which was nothing but
a wretched tavern, and Her Majesty decided that we should
both of us lie on it without undressing. The bed was filthy,
and I covered it with a large cloak which I obtained from
Colonel Karr; but scarcely did we lie down than I noticed a
small door by the Empress's pillow, leading I knew not where.
This worried me, and I asked her permission to get up and
explore the passage. On opening the door I saw that it led
into a dark cubby-hole and thence into the yard outside. I
had two sentries of the Horse Guards Regiment posted there
with strict orders not to move without my permission and not
to let anyone near that door. After this, I went back to bed,
and as we could not sleep, Her Majesty read out to me the
various manifestoes that she intended to publish on our return
to town. We told each other our fears, but henceforth they
were overshadowed by our troops . . .

[72] Peterhof: Martha Wilmot's visit in August 1803,
from *The Russian journals of Martha and Catherine
Wilmot 1803–1808.*

After this ceremony we proceeded, and continuing to drive
thro' a very pretty cultivated Country quite in the English
taste, we at length arrived at the Village of Peterhoff. The
village is pretty, but the Palace and Gardens are the grand
objects.[1] We went into the latter immediately, and I was

---

[1] The Palace of Peterhof was built for the Czar Peter the Great, according to

indeed enchanted with them. Description conveys at best but very imperfect ideas of places and I am a bad describer. But suppose a judicious arrangement of Wood, Lawn, Walks, long Alleys, Magnificent rusticity &c &c &c and then open your minds eye to such a display of Water, Works as indeed I could not have suppos'd it possible for art to produce – Fountain, *Jet d'eaus*, Trees, Pillars, Gladiators with swords of Water! Oh dear! I cou'd not name half the Objects nor half the capricious yet imposing striking fancy that inspir'd the projector in collecting such an assemblage, but the *tout en semble* delighted me . . . One object which interested me more than the rest was a dear little dwelling of Peter the Great in a retir'd part of the Garden and looking on the sea. It consists of but few rooms, and inside his Bed Chamber is a little Kitchen where, t'is say'd, he used often to amuse himself by *dressing his own dinner* . . .

We [walked] about in different directions for two or three hours, meeting such a multitude of well dress'd people (tho' not noblesse, for you must know on a day of this kind the gardens are thrown open for all sorts and kinds of people). There I saw for the first time a proper Merchant's wife. If I describe her dress, you will I fear scarcely believe me that in one of the warmest days that ever came, she was array'd in a Jacket and petticoat of Damask brocaded richly with Gold, stomacher distinct and chiefly compos'd of pearls, a plaited border of pearls as if it was of muslin form'd the front of her cap, while a building scarcely half a yard high compos'd of pearls and diamonds compleated the head dress. On her neck were twenty rows of Pearl, and on her Massy arms hung twelve rows (for I reckon'd them) by the way of bracelets. Thus array'd she walk'd by the side of her bearded Husband, whose dress was likewise the native dress of the country, a Coat of green Velvet with a sort of petticoat Skirt reaching to his heels and embroider'd all round with gold, flat crown'd hat which never quitted his head &c &c. I cannot express to you what pleasure this pair gave me. I am told that in no other part of the world is such a sight to be seen.

the plans of Leblond, in 1715. It was considerably extended by Rastrelli in 1750 and was long used by the imperial family as a summer residence.

After walking for a good while we again return'd to our Wooden House ... We dined, and then Harriet! oh for the pen of puzzlementation to describe our dressing Scene which soon follow'd – men-servants, maid servants, Pomatum, powder, rouge, tea, Coffee, diamonds, pearls, snuff boxes, all hickledy pickledy in the self same little dressing room. Fancy it all I beseech you; and then suppose us like so many butterflys emerging from their Grubs, issuing forth in robes of silver tissue and Diamond Bandeaus – three apiece on two of the heads, long diamond earings and every finery that money could purchase.

We arrived at the Palace at seven o'clock, the rooms of which were all thrown open, and we there met such a crowd of people that we cou'd scarcely advance. At length the Emperor and Empress [Alexander I and Elisaveta Alexeyievna] &c &c appeared and a Polish Dance was begun, the Emperor leading out my beautiful acquaintance M^{dm} Adadoroff and (follow'd by, I dare say, sixty couple) literally walk'd the figure of 8 to music. It was simply a Promenade by which I saw again and again every Grandee who pass'd successively as close to me as they cou'd well do. The Empress look'd charming, and the affable manners which she and all the Imperial family possess are quite delightful. The Empress Mother mov'd thro' the circle and threw us all into extasys by her amiable conduct. I do assure you she bow'd most graciously to me. The two grand Dutchesses, young girls and sisters of the Emperor are very pretty. One of them had a Curricle dress on which was trim'd all round with diamonds – four rows making a Band as broad as a sixpenny ribband, their heads &c adorn'd in proportion. Judge how abundant precious stones must be here, nearly a drug, for they are often more like a jeweller's shop than any adornments selected by good taste. From this you may suppose them cheap. Not at all. I too thought so, and on a slight speculation had some notion of purchasing them to make my Fortune hereafter – but it wou'd not do. My Castle of air vanish'd, for diamonds here bear a value fully equal to what they do in England; and yet the profusion of them is scarcely to be conceiv'd. So leaving them with those who have them we will proceed to the Gardens which by this time began to be illuminated; along every walk were festoons of little sparkling Lamps and the water works now were a perfect blaze of beauty and threw out a diamond spray that sparkled in every direction. The Palaces were illuminated, and in short the entire scene was absolutely like enchantment.

[73] The Marquis de Custine's description of a Court ball at Peterhof to celebrate the Empress Alexandra Feodorovna's name-day, from *Russia, abridged from the French, of the Marquis de Custine.*

July 23, 1839
If Petersburg is a Lapland in stucco, Peterhoff is the palace of Armida under glass. I can scarcely believe in the real existence of so many costly, delicate, and brilliant objects, when I recollect that a few degrees farther north, the year is divided into a day, a night, and two twilights of three months each.

One may ride a league in the imperial park of Peterhoff without passing twice under the same avenue; imagine, then, such a park all on fire. In this icy and gloomy land the illuminations are perfect conflagrations; it might be said that the night was to make amends for the day. The trees disappear under a decoration of diamonds, in each alley there are as many lamps as leaves; it is Asia, not the real modern Asia, but the fabulous Bagdad of the Arabian Nights, or the more fabulous Babylon of Semiramis.

It is said that on the Empress' birthday, six thousand carriages, thirty thousand pedestrians, and an innumerable quantity of boats leave Petersburg to proceed to, and form encampments around, Peterhoff.

It is the only day on which I have seen a real crowd in Russia. A bivouac of citizens in a country altogether military is a rarity. Not that the army was wanting at the fête, for a body of guards and the corps of cadets were both cantoned round the residence of the sovereign. All the multitude of officers, soldiers, tradesmen, serfs, lords, and masters, wandered together among the woods, where night was chased away by two hundred and fifty thousand lamps. Such was the number named to me; and though I do not know whether it was correct or not, I do know that the mass of fire shed an artificial light far exceeding in clearness that of the northern day. In Russia, the Emperor casts the sun into the shade. At this period of the summer, the nights recommence and rapidly increase in length; so that, without the illumination, it would have been dark for several hours under the avenues in the park of Peterhoff.

It is said, also, that in thirty-five minutes all the lamps of the illuminations in the park were lighted by eighteen hundred men. Opposite the front of the palace, and proceeding from it in a straight line towards the sea, is a canal, the surface of whose waters was so covered with the reflection of the lights upon its borders, as to produce a perspective that was magical; it might have been taken for a sheet of fire. Ariosto would perhaps have had imagination brilliant enough to describe all the wonders of this illumination: to the various groups of lamps, which were disposed with much taste and fancy, were given numerous original forms; flowers as large as trees, suns, vases, bowers of vine leaves, obelisks, pillars, walls chased with arabesque work; in short, a world of fantastic imagery passed before the eye, and one gorgeous device succeeded another with inexpressible rapidity.

At the extremity of the canal, on an enormous pyramid of fire (it was, I believe, 70 feet high), stood the figure of the Empress, shining in brilliant white above all the red, blue, and green lights which surrounded it. It was like an aigrette of diamonds circled with gems of all hues. Every thing was on so large a scale that the mind doubted the reality which the eye beheld. Such efforts for an annual festival appeared incredible. There was something as extraordinary in the episodes to which it gave rise, as in the fête itself. During two or three nights, all the around of which I have spoken encamped around the village. Many women slept in their carriages, and the female peasants in their carts. These conveyances, crowded together by hundreds, formed camps which were very amusing to survey, and which presented scenes worthy of the pencil of an artist.

The Russian has a genius for the picturesque; and the cities of a day which he raises for his festal occasions, are more amusing, and have a much more national character than the real cities built in Russia by foreigners. The painful impression I have received since living among the Russians, increases as I discover the true value of this oppressed people. The idea of what they could do if they were free, heightens the anger which I feel in seeing them as they now are . . .

In any other country, so great an assemblage of people would produce overwhelming noise and disturbance. In Russia, every thing passes with gravity, every thing takes the character of a ceremony; to see so many young persons united together for their pleasure, or for that of others, not daring either to laugh, to sing, to quarrel, to play, or to dance, one might imagine them a troop of prisoners about to proceed to their destination. What is wanted in all I see here is not, assuredly, grandeur or magnificence, nor even taste and elegance: it is gaiety. Gaiety cannot be compelled; on the contrary, compulsion makes it fly, just as the line and the level destroy the picturesque in scenery. I see only in Russia that which is symmetrically correct, which carries with it an air of command and regulation; but that which would give a value to this order, variety, from whence springs harmony, is here unknown . . .

On the day of the ball and the illumination, we repaired to the Imperial palace at seven o'clock. The courtiers, the ambassadors, the invited foreigners, and the *soi-disant* populace, entered the state apartment without any prescribed order. All the men, except the moujiks, who wore their national costume, and the citizens who were robed in the cafetan, carried the tabarro, or Venetian mantle above their uniform, which was a strictly enforced regulation, the fête being called a masked ball.

We remained a considerable time, much pressed by the crowd, waiting for the appearance of the Emperor [Nicholas I] and his family. As soon as this sun of the palace began to rise, the space opened before him, and followed by his splendid *cortège*, he proceeded, without being even incommoded by the crowd, through the halls into which, the moment before, you might have supposed another person could not have penetrated. Wherever His Majesty passed, the waves of peasants rolled back, closing instantly behind him like waters in a vessel's track. . . .

A master of the ceremonies had pointed out to me the *ligne* in which I was to ride, but in the disorder of the departure no one kept his place. I could neither find my servant nor my cloak, and, at length, was obliged to mount one of the last of the *lignes*, where I seated myself by the side of a Russian lady who had not been to the ball, but who had come from Petersburg to show the illumination to her daughters . . . If I were not afraid of wearying the reader, I should exhaust all the formulae of admiration in repeating that I have never seen any thing so extraordinary as this illuminated park traversed in solemn silence by the carriages of the court, in the midst of a crowd as dense as was that of the peasants in the saloons of the palace a few minutes before . . .

This ride was unquestionably the most interesting feature in the fête of the Empress. But I again repeat, scenes of magic splendour do not constitute scenes of gaiety. No one laughed, sung, or danced; they all spoke low; they amused themselves with precaution; it seemed as though the Russian subjects were so broken in to politeness as to be respectful even to their pleasures. In short, liberty was wanting at Peterhoff, as it is every where else in Russia.

[74] President Poincaré's naval visit to Tsar Nicholas II, July 1914, at Peterhof, from *An Ambassador's Memoirs 1914–1917* by Maurice Paléologue.

Monday, July 20, 1914.
I left St Petersburg at ten o'clock this morning on the Admiralty yacht, and went to Peterhof. Sazonov, the Minister for Foreign Affairs, Isvolsky, the Russian Ambassador to France, and General de Laguiche, my military attaché, accompanied me. All four of us had been invited to meet the President of the Republic at Cronstadt. The staff of my embassy, the Russian Ministers and Court functionaries will go by rail direct to Peterhof.

The weather was cloudy. Our vessel steamed at high speed between low banks towards the Gulf of Finland. Suddenly a fresh breeze from the open sea brought us a heavy shower, but as suddenly the sun burst forth in his splendour. A few pearl-grey clouds, through which the sun's rays darted, hung here and there in the sky like sashes shot with gold. As far as the eye could reach, in a limpid flood of light the estuary of the Neva spread the immense sheet of its greenish, viscous, changing waters which always remind me of Venice.

At half-past eleven we stopped in the little harbour of Peterhof where the *Alexandria*, the Tsar's favourite yacht, was lying under steam.

Nicholas II, in the uniform of an admiral, arrived at the quay almost at once. We transferred to the *Alexandria*. Luncheon was served immediately. We had at least an hour and three-quarters before us until the arrival of the *France*. But the Tsar likes to linger over his meals. There are always long intervals between the courses in which he chats and smokes cigarettes.

I was on his right, Sazonov on his left and Count Fredericks, Minister of the Court, was opposite us. After a few commonplaces the Tsar told me of his pleasure at receiving the President of the Republic.

'We shall have weighty matters to discuss,' he said. 'I'm sure we shall agree on all points . . . But there's one question which is very much in my mind – our understanding with England. We *must* get her to come into our alliance. It would be such a guarantee of peace!'

'Yes, Sire, the Triple Entente cannot be too strong if it is to keep the peace.'

'I've been told that you yourself are uneasy about Germany's intentions.'

'Uneasy? Yes, Sire, I am uneasy although at the moment I have no particular reason to anticipate a war in the immediate future. But the Emperor William and his Government have let Germany get into a state of mind such that if some dispute arose, in Morocco, the East – any where – they could neither give way nor compromise. A success is essential at any price and to obtain it they'll risk some adventure.'

The Tsar reflected a moment: 'I can't believe the Emperor wants war . . . If you knew him as I do! If you knew how much theatricality there is in his posing! . . .'

'Perhaps I am doing the Emperor William too much honour in thinking him capable of willing, or simply accepting, the consequences of his acts. But if war threatened would he, and could he, prevent it? No, Sire, I don't think so, honestly I don't.'

The Tsar sat silent and puffed at his cigarette. Then he said in a resolute voice: 'It's all the more important for us to be able to count on England in an emergency. Unless she has gone out of her mind altogether Germany will never attack Russia, France and England combined.'

Coffee had just arrived when the French squadron was signalled. The Tsar made me go up on the bridge with him.

It was a magnificent spectacle. In a quivering, silvery light the *France* slowly surged forward over the turquoise and emerald waves, leaving a long white furrow behind her. Then she stopped majestically. The mighty warship which has brought the head of the French state is well worthy of her name. She was indeed France coming to Russia. I felt my heart beating.

For a few minutes there was a prodigious din in the harbour; the guns of the ships and the shore batteries firing, the crews cheering, the *Marseillaise* answering the Russian national anthem, the cheers of thousands of spectators who had come from St Petersburg on pleasure boats and so forth.

At length the President of the Republic stepped on board the *Alexandria*. The Tsar received him at the gangway.

As soon as the presentations were over the imperial yacht steered for Peterhof. Seated in the stern the Tsar and the President immediately entered into conversation, I should perhaps say a discussion, for it was obvious that they were talking business, firing questions at each other and arguing. As was proper it was Poincaré who had the initiative. Before long he was doing all the talking, the Tsar simply nodded acquiescence, but his whole appearance showed his sincere approval. It radiated confidence and sympathy.

Before long we were at Peterhof. Through its magnificent trees and sparkling foundations, Catherine II's favourite residence appeared above a long terrace from which a foaming cascade poured its majestic waters.

Tsarskoye Selo
and the Lycée

---

[75] Catherine, wife of Peter the Great, builds a country house secretly for him at 'Sarskoe', *c.* 1718, from *Original Anecdotes of Peter the Great . . .* by J. V. Stählin-Storckburg.

The Empress wished to make a return to the attention of her husband, and to give him at the same time the pleasure of a surprise, by erecting, without his knowledge, a building in the vicinity of Petersburgh. For this purpose, she pitched upon a very pleasant site, at the distance of about twenty-five wersts southwest of the city, and situated at the end of an immense plain, which afforded the most beautiful prospect to the eye. The only place near it was a village, called Saraskoi Muisa, the Village of Sarah, the name of a noble lady of Ingria, to whom it belonged.

On this spot Catherine built a stone house, and laid out a beautiful garden, with arbours, and an avenue of linden trees. The edifice was raised in so short a time, and with so much secrecy, that the Czar had not the least intimation of the matter. During his two years' absence the works were carried on with such expedition, that it was finished in the third, and fitted up in the most complete and brilliant manner.

In the summer of that year, he came from his army in Poland to Petersburgh, and expressed much satisfaction to the Empress, on seeing the improvements made in his darling city, during his absence.

'I have found,' said she to the Czar, 'a charming situation, salubrious, solitary, and not far distant from hence, where your Majesty, perhaps, would not dislike to build a country house, if you would but take the trouble to go and see it.'

'With all my heart,' replied the Czar, highly pleased to see the Empress so desirous to improve the environs of Petersburgh, 'and I promise to satisfy your wishes, if the place really answers your description.'

'I hope,' replied she, 'it will please you; it is at some wersts distance, on the side of the Moscow road, and commands a most beautiful prospect. If it has remained in a desert state till now, it is because the canton is unfrequented, and but little known.'

Peter the Great, impatient to see so delightful a place, gave his wife his hand, and promised to attend her on the following day.

The Empress immediately gave secret orders to make such preparations at the country house, during the night, as were necessary to give the Czar a suitable reception.

The following day, in the forenoon, they set off for this supposed solitude, attended by a number of sea and land officers, and by a few noblemen high in favour with their Majesties. They were likewise accompanied by a waggon, loaded with provisions and a tent, under which they purposed taking a hasty repast.

At about twelve wersts distance from Petersburgh, they turned aside from the Moscow road, into one which was cut with much care through a wood, and which afforded a view in a straight line as far as the mountain of Duderhof. This attracted the Czar's whole attention. 'The country,' said he with a smile of satisfaction, 'whither my Catherine is conducting us, must be very fine, for the road that leads to it is excellent.'

At the foot of the mountain the road turns to the left, and continues to rise, and descend alternately, with a gentle declivity, so that the place whither they were going did not make its appearance till they reached a particularly elevated spot. Then, all at once, the Czar perceived a very handsome stone building, in a place to which he was a perfect stranger. He was still lost in astonishment, when he was received by the Czarina as mistress of the house. 'This,' said she, 'is the solitude of which I have spoken to your Majesty, and the country house I have built for my sovereign.'

The Czar, on hearing this, embraced her with the utmost tenderness: 'Never,' said he in a transport of joy, 'has my Catherine deceived me, or given me false accounts. The situation is charming, and the pains you have taken to surprise me so agreeably, entitles you to my warmest acknowledgements. I see that you wish to show me, that there are beautiful places about Petersburgh, which though they do not abound in water, are not unworthy such edifices as this.'

The Empress led the Czar through all the apartments, and showed him from the windows, the beauty of the prospect. She then conducted him into a large room, where he found a well-served table.

At dinner the Emperor drank the first glass of wine to the health of his good landlady, and gave much praise to her taste in architecture. The Czarina, in her turn, drank his health, as master of the house; but how great was his surprise when he heard a salute of eleven guns, the instant she put the glass to her lips!

After the repast, which lasted till the evening, he took a walk in the gardens, saw all the buildings belonging to the palace, and on quitting this delightful situation, said he never recollected to have spent so pleasant a day.

Source: M. Forster, the architect who built the palace of Sarskoe, and eyewitness of what is above related.

[76] The Empress Elizabeth's new Palace at Tsarskoye Selo built by Rastrelli; and Catherine the Great's additions; from *Charles Cameron* by Isobel Rae.

When Peter the Great's daughter, the Empress Elizabeth, came to the throne in 1741, she wished to retain Tsarskoe Selo but not the stone villa as a royal residence. She thought

rather in terms of Versailles and employed the Italian architect, Rastrelli, to build a worthy palace for her. This he
certainly did, as the three-storey façade of the palace he
designed for her, nearly 1,200 ft in length, is said to be the
longest in the world, and everything about it was on a similar
stupendous scale. Elizabeth was delighted, and named it the
Catherine Palace, in honour of her mother, Catherine I. The
palace was then even more sumptuous than it is now, since,
to conform with her taste, all the ornaments, pillars and
caryatids were gilded 'with leaf-gold on oil ... the value in
gold amounted to above a million of ducats', and there was
also a gilt balustrade running along the roof adorned with gilt
vases and statues. The opulent effect desired by Elizabeth had
been achieved; the villagers believed that the roof itself was
made of solid gold! When the palace came into Catherine the
Great's hands this decoration had weathered very badly and
she had it repaired and stripped, the caryatids and so on all
being covered in less gaudy paint. Dr Granville, an English
traveller, has stories about these repairs which illustrates the
Empress Catherine's lofty indifference to money:

Some of the contractors offered Her Majesty nearly half a
million of Roubles (silver) to be permitted to collect the
fragments of gold, but the Empress scornfully refused, saying,
'I am not in the habit of selling my old clothes.'

The observant Dr Granville remarked of the façade of the
palace; 'Internally the whole of this stupendous line forms but
one uninterrupted suite of apartments, the projecting portions
of the front serving only to give more capacity to some of the
rooms.' In other words, life in these state rooms, indeed in all
this magnificent palace, was meant to be lived in public, in
ostentation and luxury. This was all very well for the Empress
Elizabeth, but it did not suit the Empress Catherine, who as
early as 1764 had the Hermitage built so that she might enjoy
privacy and relaxation in pleasant surroundings. Yet from the
beginning of her reign she moved her court every summer
from St Petersburg to Tsarskoe Selo.

It is not then surprising that as soon as possible after 1774,
when the Turkish peace treaty permitted her to turn her mind
from war to peace, she decided to modernise the palace. On
13 April 1778, she wrote to Grimm:

There is going to be terrible upheaval in the domestic arrangements at Tsarskoe Selo. The Empress does not intend to live
any longer in two unsuitable rooms; she is going to pull down
the one and only staircase at the end of the house; she wants
to live in the midst of the three gardens; she wants to have the
same view from her windows as from the main balcony. The
grand staircase has been moved to the small wing beside the
entrance on the Gatchina side. She will have ten rooms and
will ransack all the books in her library for designs for their
decoration and her imagination will have free rein – and
everything will be like these two pages, that is to say devoid
of common sense.

This letter rouses speculation. The last sentence suggests that
Catherine's schemes had gone awry, as indeed they may have
done if she had allowed the whole of Rastrelli's main staircase
to be moved without proper architectural supervision. Perhaps this was the cause of the appeal she made to Grimm the
following year, on 6 April 1779, begging him to ask Reiffenstein in Rome to send her two Italian architects:

He will have the kindness to write to the sublime Reiffenstein
telling him to find two good architects, Italians and clever at
their work, whom he will engage for the service of Her
Imperial Majesty of All the Russians by a contract for a
number of years, and he will despatch them from Rome to
Petersburg like a bag of tools. He will not give them millions,
but an honest and sensible salary, and he must choose honest
and sensible men, not men like Falconet, their feet must be on
the ground, not in the clouds. They should be directed to me,
or to Baron Friedrichs, or to Count Bruce, or to M. d'Eck, or
to M. Bezborodko, or to the devil and his grandmother – no
matter, so long as they come, for all my architects have
become too old, or too blind, or too slow, or too lazy, or too
young, or too idle, or too grand, or too rich, or too set in
their ways, or too scatter-brained . . . in a word, anything you
like but not what I require.

Four months later, on 23 August 1779, she wrote the letter
to Grimm telling him that she was now employing 'mister

Cameron'. This is the first mention of Cameron's arrival, and the reason why his biographers put the date as 1779. The hard fact is that no one has succeeded in tracing Cameron's movements from the time the 'Cameron Case' ended in London, culminating in Walter Cameron's committal to the Fleet on 29 August 1776 until the Empress Catherine comments on his work for her in 1779; so, until new evidence can be found, for all intents and purposes the date of Catherine's letter to Grimm on 23 August 1779 must be taken as the beginning of Cameron's working life in Russia. After telling Grimm how she had 'secured mister Cameron', she continued:

> We are designing with him here a terraced garden, with baths below and gallery above; it will be something fine, fine, – to quote Maitre Blaise.

[77] A day in the life of Catherine the Great at Tsarskoye Selo (1768), from *Anecdotes of the Russian Empire* by William Richardson.

Nov 7, 1768: Her Majesty ... rises at five in the morning, and is engaged in business till near ten. She then breakfasts and goes to prayers: dines at two: withdraws to her own apartments soon after dinner: drinks tea at five: sees company, plays at cards, or attends public places, the play, opera, or masquerade, till supper: and goes to sleep at ten. By eleven every thing about the palace is as still as midnight. Whist is her favourite game at cards. She usually plays for five imperials (ten guineas) the rubber; and as she plays with great clearness and attention, she is often successful: she sometimes plays, too, at piquet and cribbage. In the morning between prayers and dinner, she frequently takes an airing, according as the weather admits, in a coach or a sledge. On these occasions, she has sometimes no guards, and very few attendants; and does not chuse to be known or saluted as Empress. It is in this manner that she visits any great works that may be going on in the city, or in the neighbourhood. She is fond of having small parties of eight or ten persons with her at dinner. . . . When she retires to her palaces in the country, especially to Zarskocelo [Tsarskoe Selo] she lays aside all state, and lives with her ladies on the footing of as easy intimacy as possible. Any one of them who rises on her entering or going out of a room, is fined a ruble, and all forfeits of this sort are given to the poor. You will easily perceive, that by her regular and judicious distribution of time, she is able to transact a great deal of business; and that the affability of her manners renders her much beloved.

[78] In the Great Park at Tsarskoye Selo, about 1774, Catherine the Great consoles the Captain's daughter, from *The Captain's Daughter* by Alexander Pushkin.

Marya Ivanovna rose early the next morning and dressed and went quickly to the park. It was a beautiful morning, the sun lighting up the tops of the lime-trees which were already turning yellow beneath the chill breath of autumn. The broad lake lay motionless and gleaming. The swans had just waked up and were solemnly gliding over the water from behind the bushes which shaded the edge of the lake. Marya Ivanovna passed a lovely meadow, in the midst of which a monument had just been erected in honour of the recent victories of Count Pyotr Alexandrovich Rumyantsev. Suddenly a little white dog of English breed ran barking up to her. Marya Ivanovna stood still in alarm. At the same moment she heard a pleasant feminine voice say: 'Don't be afraid, it doesn't bite.' And Marya Ivanovna now saw a lady seated on a bench opposite the monument. Marya Ivanovna sat down at the other end of the bench. The lady gazed at her steadfastly, and Marya Ivanovna, in the course of a few sidelong glances, had surveyed her from top to toe. She wore a white morning gown, a night-cap and a quilted jacket. Marya Ivanovna guessed her to be about forty years old. Her full, highly-coloured countenance expressed dignity and calm, and there was indescribable charm in her blue eyes and slight smile. The strange lady was the first to break the silence.

'You don't live in this neighbourhood, do you?' she asked.
'No, indeed, I only arrived yesterday from the country.'
'Have you come with your family?'

'No, Madam. I came all by myself.' . . .

'I presume that you have come on business of some sort.'

'Yes, Madam. I have come to make a petition to the Empress.'

The lady appeared to be moved. 'Forgive me,' she said in a voice still more kindly, 'if I interfere in your affairs. But I am attached to the Court. Explain your request to me, and I may perhaps be able to render you some assistance.' . . . Marya Ivanovna drew a folded piece of paper from her pocket and handed it to her unknown protector, who perused it in silence.

At first she read with attention and sympathy. But soon a sudden change came over her countenance and Marya Ivanovna, following her every movement with her eyes, was alarmed by the severe expression of the face which, only a few moments before, had been so pleasant and tranquil.

'You are interceding for Grinev?' said the lady coldly. 'The Empress will not be able to forgive him. It was no mere ignorance and levity which made him go over to the Pretender, his desertion was the act of an unprincipled and dangerous scoundrel.'

'Oh, that is not true!' cried Marya Ivanovna.

'Not true?' echoed the lady, flushing up.

'Not true, I swear it is not true! I know all about it. I will tell you all. It was for my sake alone that he bore all that he went through. And if he did not speak up for himself at his trial, it can only have been that he did not wish to involve me.' And she eagerly related the story with which the reader is acquainted.

The lady listened to her attentively. 'Where are you staying?' she asked when Marya Ivanovna had finished, and hearing the name of Anna Vlasyevna, she added, smiling: 'Oh, I know her! Goodbye, do not mention our meeting to anyone. I hope you will not have long to wait for a reply to your letter.'

With these words she rose and entered a covered walk, while Marya Ivanovna returned to Anna Vlasyevna, filled with joyous hope.

Her hostess chided her for taking such an early walk in the autumn, which, she said, was bad for young women. She brought in the samovar and had just embarked, over a cup of tea, on one of her endless tales of the court, when a carriage from the court drew up at the porch, and a footman came into the house with the news that the Empress was graciously pleased to invite Marya Ivanovna to her presence ... The court-chamberlain stated that Empress wished Marya Ivanovna to come by herself, and in the clothes she happened to be in. There was no help for it – Marya Ivanovna seated herself in the carriage and drove to the palace, pursued by the advice and good wishes of Anna Vlasyevna ...

A few minutes later the carriage drew up in front of the palace. Marya Ivanovna ascended the stairs in a state of trepidation. Doors opened wide before her. She traversed a long succession of splendid empty rooms, the chamberlain going before her to show her the way. At last, stopping in front of a closed door, he told her he would go in and announce her ...

The Empress was seated at her toilet-table. There were a few courtiers around her, who respectfully made way for Marya Ivanovna. The Empress addressed her kindly, and Marya Ivanovna recognized the lady with whom she had talked so frankly a short time before. The Empress called her to come near and said, smiling: 'I am so glad to be able to keep my word and fulfil your request. Your business is settled. I am convinced of the innocence of your betrothed. Here is a letter which you will be good enough to take to your future father-in-law.'

[79] English grandees on the Grand Tour visit Tsarskoye Selo in 1792: Catherine's English gardener, Mr Bush, shows them the latest improvements; from *A Tour of Russia, Siberia and the Crimea, 1792–1794* by John Parkinson.

Sir Watkin, Bootle, old Gould and myself made a party today to go and see the palace of Tsarskoe Zelo, Bootle and I in one *kibitki*,[1] Gould and Sir W. in another. ... We saw first the apartments of the Grand Duke and Grand Dutchess, afterwards those of their family the young grand Duke and Grand

[1] Travelling cart.

Dutchesses, and lastly those of the Empress [Catherine the Great]. We asked to see the Favourite's [Zubov] but they would not grant us permission. They open either into the Chinese or the Cupola room. The division of the apartments belonging to the young grand Dutchesses is singular. A Gothic Screen divides the room into two unequal parts; at the back of this the attendants wait. Behind the bed is a Divan where their woman sleeps; and in front of it also is another where another person always sits up. The Curtains enclose the spaces in which this stand as well as the bed; round which white dimitty curtains are drawn; but at the top is open. . . .

The baths consist of two floors, on the super of which there are three apartments, and the lower the baths. In the largest room there is a large bath lined with tin, I believe, into which either hot or cold water can be let in: in the next a large tub with two cisterns (?) above it by means of which the water can be made of any temperature; there is also a Russian Bath. The Empress's dressing room is adjoining the second. The apartment in the middle is of a considerable size, but those at each end rather small. One of these is cased with Jasper and the other with Agate. That which is lined with Jasper is ornamented with columns of agate. I think we were told that this building cost 500,000 roubles: not including the Agate and the Jasper, which comes from the mines of Kolg-wan. When it was finished the Empress walked over it holding Cameron by the Arm and said, It is indeed very handsome 'mais ça coûte'. She frequently dines in the Baths when her party is small. She also sits there a great deal in hot weather on account of their great coolness.

But her usual dining room is in the Gallery. This is a long room encompassed by a broad walk, on one side protected from the South by the building in the middle and on the other from the North. She walks on one side or the other according to the circumstances of the weather. On the Balustrade round this walk she has placed a great number of Bronze busts: and here we saw that of Fox between the busts of Cicero and Demosthenes In order to arrive at the Gallery we descended from the hanging Garden I think by a stair, on which I remarked the statue of Junius Brutus.

After seeing the palace we passed on our return to Mr

Bush's by the *Chambre de matin*, which serves as a repository for all the statues both antique and modern which the Empress has bought. The marble Bust of Fox is here with the rest; but the door being nailed up, we could not gain admittance. All the statues and sculptures are to be placed in a Museum, which she has it (in) contemplation to build.

Bush showed us a superb plan which she had conceived for this Purpose. It would consist of a Colonnade, commencing from the Empress's apartments, making an oblique angle with the end of the palace and leading to the Museum, round which the Colonnade would also run, and the outer apartment of which would be a semi-circle of the dimensions of the Rotunda. The Museum he told me would itself be between two and three thousand feet either long or round, and the whole walk half a mile. It would cost with cream (?) columns a million and a half roubles. At one time the Empress was determined to have all the columns of the Verde antique from Kolgwan. But being calculated that the expense would be £200 each, that idea was dropped. The principal charge arises from the Carriage. Afterwards there was an idea to have them of cast iron. At present the plan is given (back) and Cameron is desired to give another. Is that a modification of this, or something in the way of what Quarenghi showed me? There was to have been a walk on the top of this Colonnade, as well as below.

The garden altogether is six miles in circumference, partly in the French style, as it was laid out at first in the reign of the late Empress, partly in the English. A walk in the latter as I understand runs round the water and is at least four miles in length. Several buildings for different purposes and in honour of several illustrious characters are scattered up and down: for instance the Theatre, the *Chambre de Musique*, the *Chambre de Matin*, the *Amirauté*, the *Temple Turc*, the *Temple Chinois*, the *Arc Chinois*, the *Obelisque de Comte Romanzoff*, the *Colonne de mémoire de comte Frederic Orloff, la colonne Rastrelli, l'Arc Triomphal de Prince Orloff, la Pyramide Egyptienne* (a burial place for dogs), *le pont de marbre, les Bains* and a *Ruine*. Some of these we saw at a distance but as the Ground was covered with snow we did not go up to them. We should I believe have gone to see the

Granite Columns in the Church of Sophia, if old Gould had (not) been impatient to go to dinner.

The Empress passes the months of April, May, June, July and August at Tsarskoe Zelo, except that for about a month of this time in the month of May she goes to Peterhoff. She rises at six; she takes a short walk before breakfast and breakfasts at eight; she then employs about two hours with her Ministers; after which she walks out again and dines at one. After dinner she sits down to cards till five: she then goes out again with the whole royal family to walk. Sometimes they have Music and three times a week a play. She retires to her apartments at eight, never supping. Zuboff leaves her at ten and then gives a great supper to all the generals and courtiers at the Court. He always dines with her, her family very seldom, only indeed on great days. One thing struck me as very remarkable, even when the Grand Duke and Grand Dutchess reside at either of their own country houses, their Children always remain with the Empress. He (Bush) spoke well of Zuboff. He never was known to do any harm to anybody and whenever it is in his power he is glad to do a service. He told me that before Mamonoff and after Landskoi there was a favourite for about two months who was turned off for *incapacity*. He is living now at Moscow.

Besides the hay in the bottom of our Kibitki, we had a featherbed and a wolfskin, so that we lay perfectly soft. Over my velvet boots I put on my *Kirghis*; and over my great coat lined with squirrel skin, my Bearskin Pelisse and Sir Watkin lent me a fur Cap: so that except a little in the face I did not suffer from the cold in the least. The road was so uneven in some places that our Ishworshick was obliged to lean from his seat twice to prevent us from going over.

[80] Pushkin, aged twelve, enters the first class of the Lycée founded by Tsar Alexander I in 1811, from *Pushkin* by David Magarshack.

Pushkin found Petersburg quite unlike Moscow. He was accustomed to Moscow's hills, her scattered suburbs, her multitude of wastelands and her magnificent mansions, with smaller houses clustered round them. But Pushkin now saw a city laid out according to a carefully worked out plan on a completely flat plain. He was struck by the perspective of long, straight streets and avenues, the granite embankments of the Neva and numerous canals, the majestic piles of palaces and the wrought-iron railings of their parks. On August 12 Pushkin passed the entrance examinations to the Lycée, receiving the following marks: Russian grammar, very good; French grammar, good; German, did not study; arithmetic, knowledge elementary; geography and history, knowledge elementary.

The solemn opening of the Lycée, situated in a wing of the Tsarskoye Selo Palace, took place on October 19, 1811, in the presence of Alexander I. The thirty boys of the first year wore their formal, full-dress uniforms, consisting of blue cotton coats, red collars, silver tabs, white trousers, white vests, white cravats, jackboots and tricorn hats. The official proceedings began with a somewhat subdued address by Vasily Malinovsky, the headmaster, and a speech by Alexander Kunitsyn, one of the masters. Pushchin writes that Kunitsyn spoke of 'the duties of the citizen and the warrior', a speech appropriate to the occasion of the approaching war with Napoleon. After the speeches a list of the names of the scholars was read out. The boys came forward, bowed to the Emperor who, Pushkin records, 'bowed very graciously to everyone of us and responded patiently to our awkward bows.' This was the only time the two Alexanders – one an all-powerful emperor surrounded by his courtiers and ministers, and other a puny, penniless, little boy whose fame was to outshine the emperor and his dynasty – stood face to face. Neither of them suspected that they would spend most of their lives hating each other.

In the evening the boys played snowball in front of the illuminated building of the Lycée. Earlier, at tea, the headmaster had told them that because of an order from the Minister of Education, the boys would not be allowed to leave the Lycée and their parents would be allowed to visit them only during the holidays.

The Lycée was to provide an all-round education to future holders of high office, and its founders intended that the students should come from the great Russian noble houses. In fact, the Russian aristocrats refused to send their children away to a boarding school for six years, preferring a domestic education for them. It was the poor noblemen, who could not afford to give their children a good education at home, who availed themselves of the educational facilities of the Lycée. Besides Ivan Pushkin, the students whose names were later to appear in Pushkin's poems included Prince Vladimir Gorchakov, a future Minister of Foreign Affairs, and two future poets: Anton Delvig and Wilhelm Kuechelbecker, the latter an eccentric boy who was soon to become the good-natured butt of his schoolfellows.

Malinovsky, the Lycée's first headmaster, was one of the most liberal pedagogues of the time. His letters, diaries and works disclose that he was a convinced opponent of serfdom and an enthusiastic advocate of 'political changes'. He was a graduate of the philosophy faculty of Moscow University and spent two years as an official of the Russian Embassy in London. His diaries are full of criticisms of the Russian autocracy and the venality of Russian officials. He was in favour of a constitutional monarchy and his views inspired the course of studies at the Lycée. He allowed the scholars complete freedom to discuss political questions and insisted, contrary to the usual practice, that there should be no corporal punishment in the Lycée.

The Lycée was divided into a lower and upper school, each covering three years of studies. The Russian master, Nikolai Koshansky, was little respected by Pushkin. In his poem *To My Aristarchus* (1815), addressed to Koshansky, Pushkin described Koshansky as 'a boring preacher', 'a gloomy censor' and 'a persecutor'. Koshansky's frequent and prolonged absences (according to the Lycée students he suffered from recurrent attacks of *delirium tremens*) caused long interruptions in his lectures, his place being taken by the Alexander Galich, to whom Pushkin addressed two of his epistles.

Pushkin loved to discuss literary subjects with Galich. In his diary Pushkin noted that on March 16, 1834, he was present at a literary meeting where he met Galich 'who a long time ago was my professor and encouraged me to pursue the vocation I have chosen. He made me write my *Recollections of Tsarskoye Selo* for the examination of 1814'.

David de Boudry, the French master, was so extraordinary an historical figure that Pushkin left this extensive note on him in his *Table Talk* (1820–1836):

> Boudry, Professor of French Literature at the Tsarskoye Selo Lycée, was a brother of (Jean Paul) Marat. Catherine II changed his surname at his request, adding the aristocratic *de* which Boudry was very careful to keep. He was a native of Boudry. He highly respected his brother's memory and once in the classroom, talking of Robespierre, said to us, as if it were something very ordinary: 'C'est lui qui sous main travailla l'esprit de Charlotte Corday et fit de cette fille un second Ravaillac'. However, in spite of Boudry's relationship, his democratic ideas, his greasy jacket, and generally, his exterior which reminded one of a Jacobin, he was a very deft courtier on his short little legs. Boudry used to say that his brother was extraordinarily strong in spite of being so thin and so short. He told us many things about his good nature, his love for his relatives, etc etc. As a young man, to prevent his brother from associating with prostitutes, Marat had taken him to a hospital in order to show him the horrors of venereal disease.

Kunitsyn, whose subjects were moral sciences, logic and law, exercised the greatest influence on his pupils. In his poem *19th October (1825)* Pushkin wrote about Kunitsyn:

> He created us, he nurtured our flame,
> He laid the foundation stone for us,
> He lit the pure lamp.

Pushkin mentions Kunitsyn in another poem written in 1836 commemorating the opening of the Lycée:

> Kunitsyn met us
> With a greeting amidst the royal guests.

This is a reference to Kunitsyn's speech in which, taking advantage of the fact that Alexander I was still pursuing his liberal policies, he went so far as to claim that laws 'violated by those who are supposed to uphold them' could not be deemed 'sacred in the eyes of the people'. This speech made Pushkin treat Kunitsyn differently from his other Lycée masters. Pushchin records:

> Pushkin paid much more attention in Kunitsyn's class than in any other classes and that, too, in his own way; he never repeated the lessons, he did not bother to take many notes and refused to copy the professor's lectures (there were no printed textbooks in those days): everything was done *à livre ouvert*.

A curious intruder into Pushkin's Lycée verse is his Lycée valet (each boy had a valet of his own) Konstantin Sazonov, who, during the two years he looked after Pushkin, committed several murders and robberies. In a short poem beginning with the lines: 'In the morning with a penny candle' (1816) Pushkin celebrated his own escape from so 'enterprising' a servant and promised to light a candle before 'the holy ikon' for having remained alive, though constantly 'under the scythe of death: Sazonov was my servant and Peshel – my doctor'. Peshel was the doctor who attended Pushkin in the Lycée sanatorium. . . . Several descriptions of Pushkin were left by his friends and contemporaries but the most striking one was left by himself in a French poem, *Mon Portrait* which he wrote at the Lycée in 1815:

> I am a young scapegrace who is still at school; I am not stupid, I speak with little constraint and no affectation. There never was a chatterbox nor a Doctor of Sorbonne more tiresome and more clamorous than my own person. My figure cannot be compared with those who are tall. My complexion is fresh, my hair fair and wavy. I like society and its noises; I hate solitude; I abhor quarrels and controversies and – study. I love games . . . Yes, that is how God made me and how I want to appear: a veritable demon of mischief, a veritable monkey face, a little too thoughtless. Yes, indeed, such is Pushkin.

Vrai demon pour l'espieglerie,
Vrai singe par sa mine,
Beaucoup et trop d'étourderie.
Ma foi, voilà Pouchkine.

[81] Derzhavin, the patriarch of Russian letters, visits the Lycée to hear the boys, including Pushkin, recite verse, from the Commentary to *Eugene Onegin* by Vladimir Nabokov.

'I saw Derzhavin only once in my life but shall never forget that occasion. It was in 1815 (Jan 8) at a public examination of the Lyceum. When we boys learned that Derzhavin was coming, all of us grew excited. Delvig went out on the stairs to wait for him and kiss his hand, the hand that had written *The Waterfall*. Derzhavin arrived. He entered the vestibule, and Delvig heard him ask the janitor: 'Where is the privy here, my good fellow?' This prosaic question disenchanted Delvig who concealed his intent and returned to the reception hall. Delvig told me the story with wonderful bonhomie and good humour. Derzhavin was very old. He was in uniform and wore velveteen boots. Our examination was very wearisome to him. He sat with his head propped on one hand. His expression was inane, his eyes were dull, his lip hung; the portrait that shows him in housecap and dressing gown is very like him. He dozed until the beginning of the examination in Russian literature. Then he came to life, his eyes sparkled; he was transfigured. It was, of course, his poems that were read, his poems that were analysed, his poems that were praised every minute. He listened with extraordinary animation (*s zhivost'yu neobiknovennoy*). At last I was called. I recited my *Recollections at Tsarkoe Selo* while standing within two yards of Derzhavin. I cannot describe the state of my soul; when I reached the verse where Derzhavin's name is mentioned my adolescent voice vibrated and my heart throbbed with intoxicating rapture ... I do not remember how I finished my recitation [he turned to Derzhavin as he launched upon the last sixteen lines, which were really addressed to Zhukovski, but might be taken to mean Derzhavin]. I do not remember whither I fled. Derzhavin was delighted; he demanded I come, he desired to embrace me . . . There was a search for me, but I was not discovered.'

The Alexander Palace

[82] The Emperor Alexander I's habits at Tsarskoye Selo and at the Alexander Palace, from *The Historical Memoirs of the Emperor Alexander I and the Court of Russia* by the Countess Choiseul-Gouffier.

General O. and his amiable wife obligingly offered to show us the park of Czarsko-Sélo. The emperor had made the greater part of it, or at least enlarged and beautified it. He had it kept with a care and scrupulous cleanliness which I have seen nowhere else. A thousand workmen are employed every day in sweeping the paths and roads, and in cutting, rolling, and raking the grass, which is most beautiful. A few steps from the palace, and even in the presence of the emperor, you can hear the workmen laughing and singing, and the happiness which they seem to enjoy fills your own mind with a feeling of satisfaction . . .

I visited next the apartments of the [Alexander] palace – the grand gilded hall where the empress held her audiences; the apartments of the Emperor Alexander, whose many rooms were both magnificent and tasteful. The walls are covered with lapis lazuli, porphyry, and amber; the floors are incrusted with mother of pearl and precious woods. The grand open gallery which communicates with the apartment of the empress, and where one has a beautiful view of the lake and the ruins and the fields of flowers, is ornamented with bronze busts, mostly of great men of antiquity. They remind one of chapters of Plutarch; one reads them again on the foreheads of these ancient heroes.

At Czarsko-Sélo the Emperor Alexander lived a simple country life. He had no court and in the absence of the grand marshal the emperor himself kept the accounts of the household expenses. He received his ministers only on certain days of the week. Alexander rose generally at five o'clock, made his toilet, wrote, and then went into the park, where he visited his farm and the new buildings which were being constructed, gave audiences to those who had petitions to present, and who often followed him over the whole park, which was always open, night and day. The emperor always walked alone without distrust, and he had sentinels only at the chateau and at the Palace of Alexander. On account of his health he was obliged to observe a strict *régime*. He dined alone in his private apartments, and was accustomed to retire early. At the hour of retiring the band of the guards played under his windows; they usually played plaintive airs, which I could hear from my apartment.

[83] A dinner-party at the Alexander or 'New' Palace (built by Quarenghi), given in honour of the Marquess and Marchioness of Londonderry by the Empress Alexandra Feodorovna, wife of Nicholas I, in September 1836; from *The Russian Journal of Lady Londonderry, 1836-37*

1836, Sunday 25th. We were invited to Tsarkoe Seloe to be presented to the Empress and we were advised to take it on our way to Moscow. The Emperor was absent; he had been overturned in travelling and still suffered from his accident. It is about two hours' drive from St Petersburg. This was our first specimen of Russian posting and strange and wild it was, the four horses abreast to the chariot and a like number to

the britska. A *courier de poste* had been given us by Count
Nesselrode [the Foreign Minister] and he preceded us in a
britska with our cook. We left Seaham [her son], who was
not very well, behind. The dirty, strange coachmen drive their
little wild steeds at a wonderful pace and we soon arrived at
the Palace and with some difficulty discovered the apartments
destined for us. Not being able to understand the servants
whose replies were in Russian, they kindly gave us a negro
who spoke English and we proceeded to establish ourselves
and prepare for dinner which was fixed at four o'clock, but
as we were to be presented we received orders to be ready at
half past three.

The Palace where the Imperial family reside is a little
distance from the great one and was built for the Emperor
Alexander's marriage by the Empress Catherine. Carriages
were sent to fetch us, Lord and Lady Durham, Count and
Countess Nesselrode, etc. We found a very large party assembled and after a short time were conducted into an adjoining
room and Lord L. was presented by Prince Volkonsky and I
by Countess Nesselrode who was accompanied only by her
son and daughter. The former is about eighteen, very tall and
good looking. They say of him '*qu'il est beau et bon comme
l'ange gardierz du ciel*' and I have no difficulty in believing it.
The Empress is a tall graceful figure, her face not very
handsome, but her little head beautifully set and her
expression pleasing and features regular, her hands and arms
beautifully shaped and an air of imperial dignity and grace I
never saw before. Her dress was perfect – simple and of
dazzling whiteness, with a necklace, fringe, drops, etc that I
can still only compare to dark blue glass eggs for never did I
see their like. The eldest daughter was ill, she said, and unable
to appear. The Grand Duchess Olga, her second daughter
who is only fourteen but looks seventeen is very lovely –
slight and fair as a lily, with beautiful blonde hair, singularly
tall for her age and very conversable and agreeable. There is
a peculiar charm about this family. They are gifted by nature
more than the generality: tall, handsome, graceful, well made,
clever, agreeable and different from most royal persons. They
appear conscientiously good and, like the late Emperor Alexander, living to fulfil 'their being's end and aim', to be useful,

to do good and to distribute comfort and improvement on a great scale. The children seem carefully educated, and in the interior appears the domestic comfort, affection and simple privacy of a *ménage* in humble life, and this is singularly set off by the immense power, wealth and great magnificence that surrounds them.

We dined in an immense *salle*, the bay windowed middle of which was partitioned off on each side by open columns, orange trees and plants. (There was) a horse-shoe table and about sixty people. The Empress sat at the top, her son and daughter one on each side. I was next the Grand Duchess Olga whom I found very agreeable. The women were generally plain but remarkably well dressed, and men all in uniform. About twenty or thirty blacks waited. Their appearance in white turbans and scarlet and gold dresses, mingling with the other attendants, was very eastern. The establishment is on an enormous scale. For instance there were four hundred cooks there – forty travel with the Emperor and when the Imperial family move four hundred carriages are required. After dinner two little Grand Dukes came in dressed in the Russian costume – a sort of loose red and gold shirt buttoned up one side without a collar and with a sash. They seemed very happy, quite at their ease rolling on the floor. Their attendants were all English. An old Scotch nurse made acquaintance with me and spoke of the whole family with enthusiastic affection. She had been with them nineteen years, said they were angels as good as they were handsome and the Empress a model to all as a mother and a wife. She concluded by declaring that they all doted on her and could not exist without her; that she kept their money, their jewels, etc. and had charge of everything. This old lady seemed quite a character. After this the Empress came and talked to me, and after enquiring about my children, told me she had her eldest son and three daughters while Grand Duchess but it was not until she ascended the throne that her three other sons were born. She then dismissed us all about six o'clock requesting we would *reposer* and return for the ball at eight o'clock, saying in extenuation of the hour, '*C'est à la campagne et pour les enfants que nous vivons comme des paysans*'.

We returned to our rooms and after an hour's *causerie*

prepared to make a second *toilette* and at the appointed hour returned to the Palace where the great *salle*, the scene of the dinner, had been cleared and prepared for dancing. I had a long conversation with Tchernischev about the Emperor Alexander's death. He died in his arms and might have been saved had he consented to be bled; but no entreaties or prayers could persuade him. The fever rose and the last two days he was delirious. Tchernischev, whose fortune he had made, doted on him and told me his situation forced on him the cruel duty of being present when the body was opened and that he had fainted four or five times. He then related to me a circumstance that with a fatalist like the Emperor Alexander must have had great weight. He was busy in his *cabinet de travail* one beautiful day in August previous to his setting out to the last fatal journey when a dark cloud appeared and increased till darkness forced him to ask for candles. After a time the cloud passed, light returned, and immediately his *valet de chambre* came to take them away. In Russia burning candles *en plein jour* is considered as an omen of death. The Emperor, remembering this, asked his servant if he feared the bad *augure*. The man eagerly denied this and the event passed away, but the poor Emperor on his deathbed recalled it to all their memories. The veneration and almost idolatry that love and gratitude pay to his memory, however deserved and just it may be, is as creditable to the nation as it is honourable to himself.

At eight o'clock, on returning to the Palace, the first objects we saw in our outer room were the two little Grand Dukes going down *les montagnes russes* at a great pace. There was a much larger party in addition to those at dinner and the Empress soon after appeared more beautifully dressed than before. A simple white crape dress laced up each side with diamonds and turquoises, several rows of pearl on her neck and one row she told me belonged to the crown and really were like filberts. She observed the redness of my skin and enquired the cause and I was obliged to tell her the fleas had half devoured me. '*Ah ma chère, quelle honte pour vous.*' She knew Lord L. before her marriage when a girl at her father's the King of Prussia's Court and declared she remembered his perfume and knew it again after twenty years. She recalled scenes of conversations to him. She danced with great grace and dignity. After the ball, supper was served on little round tables that appeared as if by magic and disappeared in the same way. Just before we sat down, the Tsarevich came up to the Empress saying, 'Maman, voilà un courier qui arrive de Papa.' Upon which she sprang up from out of the room followed by all her children. On returning she told us the Emperor would arrive in a few days and that he hoped to see us 'souvent et beaucoup'. After supper she took leave of us, wished us bon voyage, prompt retour, etc and we retired exceedingly fatigued.

A second visit:- ... On Sunday morning, while I was puzzling what I ought or was expected to do, I received a message from the Emperor to inform me la Messe was at eleven and that I should find a door in my room that opened into the chapel. This I understood as a command and therefore got up and commenced dressing, an occupation that certainly took up a good deal of time with everyone during a visit at this Imperial Court. Lord L. accompanied me in uniform. The chapel I have before described having seen it on my former visit to Tsarskoe Seloe. On this occasion it was full. The ladies stood on one side and the gentlemen on the other.

The Imperial family entered and placed themselves near the screen. In the Greek church even the Sovereign does not sit. The singing was very fine, the dresses of the priest extremely rich and the whole ceremony imposing. The ladies appeared entirely absorbed in devotion, crossing themselves, kissing the ground, shedding tears and prostrating themselves with the deepest humiliation, etc. This lasted about an hour and when it was over the Empress spoke to me and I retired to my room to receive visits while the Emperor took Lord L. in his own little calèche to the parade. The day was deplorable – rain and snow, and it was impossible for me to stir out had I been so inclined. At four o'clock we were dressed for dinner, and as usual the Imperial carriages were sent for us. We found a large party assembled and the Empress, who the night before was dressed in muslin and bands of gold like a Greek statue without a jewel on her classically shaped head or her graceful figure now appeared clothed with Eastern splendour – a

Turkish dress of gold stripes with green and red velvet, a necklace fringe, strings and drops of enormous emeralds and diamonds. The dinner was very magnificent – above a hundred people. The Grand Duchess Hélène, wife to the Grand Duke Michael, a very pretty person, Prince Dimitri Golitsin, the Governor of Moscow, the French Ambassador, Monsieur de Barante, his wife and daughter, Prince Menshikov, the head of the navy, Count Tchernischev, the head of the army, and the latter introduced his wife to me, a pleasing person who had just returned from a visit to England for her health. The dinner passed as usual, the ladies going to dinner first, the Emperor and the other gentlemen following. I sat next the Grand Duchess Olga who talked a great deal to me and spoke most perfect English. At half past six o'clock we were dismissed and desired to return to the *spectacle* at seven.

The time was short; nevertheless all contrived to change their *toilette* and the Empress reappeared in a still more lovely one than the last – the richest blonde over the palest pink, trimmed with large opals and diamonds and strings of pearl down to her feet.

The French actors performed two little *vaudevilles* in a *salle* fitted up as a theatre and afterwards we returned to the *grand apartement* and the dancing began. Soon after eleven supper was brought in, and the same magic wand cleared the whole away, and the dancing was resumed.

[84] At the Alexander Palace the French Ambassador discusses with Tsar Nicholas II the prospects for the Franco–Russian alliance in the 1914 War, from *An Ambassador's Memoirs 1914–1917* by Maurice Paléologue.

November 21, 1914.
Although my audience was a private one I had to put on my full-dress uniform, as is fitting for a meeting with the Tsar, Autocrat of all the Russians. The Director of Ceremonies, Evreinov, went with me. He also was a symphony in gold braid.

From Tsarskoie-Selo station to Alexander Palace is a short

distance, less than a verst. In the open space before one reaches the park, a little church, mediaeval in style, raises its pretty cupola above the snow; it is the 'Feodorovsky Sobor', one of the Empress's favourite resorts for private devotion.

Alexander Palace showed me its most intimate side, for ceremonial was reduced to a minimum. My escort consisted only of Evreinov, a household officer in undress uniform and a footman in his picturesque (Tsaritsa Elizabeth) dress with the hat adorned with long red, black and yellow plumes. I was taken through the audience rooms, then the Empress's private drawing-room, down a long corridor leading to the private apartments of the sovereigns in which I passed a servant in very plain livery who was carrying a tea tray. Further on was the foot of a little private staircase leading to the rooms of the imperial children. A lady's maid flitted away from the landing above. The last room at the end of the corridor is occupied by Prince Mestschersky, personal aide-de-camp. I waited there barely a minute. The gaily and weirdly bedecked Ethiopian who mounted guard outside His Majesty's study opened the door almost at once.

The Emperor received me with that gracious and somewhat shy kindness which is all his own.

The room in which he received me is small and has only one window. The furniture is plain and comfortable; there are plain leather chairs, a sofa covered with a Persian rug, a bureau and shelves arranged with meticulous care, a table spread with maps and a low book case with photographs, busts and family souvenirs on the top shelf.

As usual the Emperor hesitated over his preliminary remarks, which are kind personal enquiries and attentions, but soon he became more at his ease: 'Let's make ourselves at home and be comfortable first, as I shall keep you some time. Have this chair. . . . We'll put this little table between us; that's better. Here are the cigarettes: Turkish. I've no business to smoke them as they were given to me by a fresh enemy, the Sultan. But they're extremely nice and, anyhow, I haven't any others. . . . Let me have my maps. . . . And now we can talk.'

He lit his cigarette, offered me a light and went straight to the heart of the subject: 'Great things have happened in the three months since I saw you last. The splendid French army and my dear army have already given such proof of valour that victory can't fail us now. . . . Don't think I'm under any illusion as to the trials and sacrifices the war still has in store for us; but so far we have a right, and even a duty, to consider together what we should have to do if Austria or Germany sued for peace. You must observe that it would unquestionably be in Germany's interest to treat for peace while her military power is still formidable. But isn't Austria very exhausted already? Well, what should we do if Germany or Austria asked for peace?'

'The first question,' I said, 'is to consider whether peace can be *negotiated* if we are not forced to *dictate* it to our enemies. . . . However moderate we may be, we shall obviously have to insist on guarantees and reparations from the Central Powers, demands they will not accept before they are at our mercy.'

'That's my own view. We must *dictate* the peace and I am determined to continue the war until the Central Powers are destroyed. But I regard it as essential that the terms of the peace should be discussed by us three, France, England and Russia – and by us three alone. No Congress or mediation for me! So when the time comes we shall impose our will upon Germany and Austria.'

Pavlovsk

[85] The work of Cameron, Brenna and others in building Pavlovsk, from *Charles Cameron* by Georges Loukomski.

The Park, at first in the Dutch style and later in the French, was remodelled by Cameron according to English taste, which became the universal fashion towards the end of the eighteenth century. Catherine wrote to Voltaire on June 25th, 1772: 'I love to distraction these gardens in the English style – their curving lines, the gentle slopes, the ponds like lakes. My Anglomania predominates over my plutomania . . .' But if English taste predominated in the treatment of the garden, it was found mingled with Greek and Roman forms in architectural detail. The influence of Palladio and of the other great Italian masters upon Inigo Jones and Sir William Chambers, that special phase of Classicism which may be seen in London, was transmitted to Russia by Cameron, and this is his special distinction.

Cameron, as already mentioned, also built at Tsarskoe the Cathedral Church of St Sophia (1782–1787). The silver tool which served for the foundation stone bears the inscription in English: Charles Cameron Architect, 1782 . . .

Cameron worked not only for the Empress; she also found him a post with her son and heir, the Grand Duke Paul, and his Consort, the Grand Duchess Marie Feodorovna (an intimate friend of the unfortunate, Marie Antoinette), who were both great admirers of his work. The palace he built for them, called Pavlovsk (1781–1796), is a square building, with a cupola almost copied from the Pantheon, though resting on a circular colonnade and with semi-circular wing-colonnades on each side of the central structure, reminiscent of Palladian villas (Rotonda, Badoer, etc).

However, Cameron did not have a free hand here, and must have had considerable difficulties in his relations with Kuechelbecker, the 'Director' of the building operations, a rather pedantic and tiresome German. The Grand Duchess also liked to give her advice, insisted on modifications while work was already in progress, and suspected Cameron to be slow and extravagant in his taste. Moreover, he was sometimes surrounded by unscrupulous and jealous contractors as well as envious assistants such as Brenna, an Italian architect whom he had met in Rome and invited to join him. Cameron, nevertheless, remained adamant. His Scottish pride and pertinacity did not permit of any compromise. In order to break his resistance, the Grand Duchess pretended to negotiate with Quarenghi and possibly dealt with Brenna direct without Cameron's knowledge. Cameron wanted decoration similar to that at Tsarskoe, with arabesques and vivid colours, but Marie and Paul were in favour of something 'simpler and noble'. As a result of this circumstance, it is sometimes difficult to trace exactly which part is Cameron's and which Brenna's (e.g. the Hall of War and the Hall of Peace).

In the centre of the Corps de Logis is the Italian Hall. It is circular, with a cupola, lighted from above, and has deep niches all round. It is decorated with reliefs brought from Italy and placed on mauve and white artificial marble walls. A frieze decorated with eagles and garlands is surmounted by a gallery of which the windows and the oriels are separated by coriatides supporting the dome. Clerisseau congratu-

lated Cameron on it. On one side of the Italian Hall is the
Graecian Hall, on the other – the Staircase and the Vestibule.

The Graecian Hall has Corinthian columns in verde
antico, statues in the antique style placed in niches and
decorative vases of porphyry and alabaster. There are, on
the same ground floor, the salons, the studies and the
ballrooms.

Cameron also completed the first floor and a few rooms on
the second, before he was superseded by Brenna. A fire in
1803 damaged many rooms, including some of Cameron's,
and although all was reconstructed, no doubt under the
control of Brenna and the supervision of Quarenghi and
Voronikhin, this was not done exactly according to Cameron's original drawings. For instance, two projects of the
round hall, one by Brenna and another according to a rough
sketch of Cameron's, permit one, on comparing them, to
draw a careful distinction in attributing parts to one or the
other . . .

In the park of Pavlovsk, Cameron built a number of
specially interesting works . . . Fortunately, all the drawings,
some of them signed and dated, have been preserved in the
archives of Pavlovsk Town, and later transferred to the Palace
Museum. They can be divided into three groups: (1) signed
projects, (2) unsigned projects, yet which can be attributed to
Cameron, and (3) projects executed by assistants and pupils
in his workshops. Of buildings by Cameron, other than those
connected with Tsarskoe and Pavlovsk, nothing has been
known even in Russia until 1910, let alone in England. The
drawings for the decoration of the Pavlovsk Palace, exhibited
in Moscow in 1913, and particularly the album of original
designs at the Institute of Engineering, St Petersburg, date
from 1764, when Cameron was still in Rome, and show the
wide range of his imagination, whether in antique detail, or
candelabra, or furniture design, and prove how Cameron was
always anxious to bring the whole into perfect accord. This
album of 115 drawings, bound in leather, bears the inscription 'Drawings'.

All Cameron's drawings are easily distinguishable from
those by other contemporary architects, such as Quarenghi.
Their manner is delicate and veiled, the line is very often

broken, full of fancy and brio, all is dictated by temperament, rather feminine, and displays impatient emotion bordering on ecstasy. The colours, a mixture of blue and brown, yet very warm, render them almost irreproduceable. He seems to have cared little for accuracy, for he visualised architecture in space, in nature, and not on paper. His drawings were thus not easily understood, and this may account for some of the many misunderstandings between him and the Grand Duchess Marie, and for his frequent quarrels with his assistants. However, the somewhat negligent manner of Cameron's drawings did not imply any lack of attention to technical detail, of which he always took great care. All that he built was solid, though expensive to a degree, which sometimes irritated even Catherine, his only patron, who realised his true qualities and gave him commissions on a scale worthy of his genius.

The work of Charles Cameron proves a missing link in the chain of the history of architecture in Russia. Uniting as it did the Eighteenth Century Baroque with the Empire style of the beginning of the Nineteenth Century, and although English in taste, it was based on the principles of Roman Classical Art and introduced certain sobriety and simplicity of design in the evolution of Russian decorative art. It has, as it were, cured it of the Baroque tendency under Cameron's healthy lead, and given it an entirely new direction.

[86] The martial manias of Paul I, from *Mémoires Secrets sur la Russia, particulièrement sur la fin du règne de Catherine II et le commencement de celui de Paul I* by C.P. Masson.

With the exception of the Kalmouks and the Kirguis, Paul is the ugliest man of his Empire; he does not stamp his own face on his currency as he himself finds it so frightful. Here are a few signs of Paul's character through his actions which prove that his behaviour as Grand Duke was not to change when he became Emperor.

Near his Pavlowsky palace, there was a terrace from which he could observe all the sentries he had enjoyed placing wherever there was room for a sentry box. On this covered terrace, he spent most of his day: armed with a telescope, he would watch all that was happening. Often he sent a footman to tell such and such a sentry to button or unbutton his uniform by one button, and to shoulder arms higher or lower, or to vary his paces round the box. He often went himself to deliver these important orders as far as a quarter of a mile away, and would beat the soldier, or, if he were pleased, put a rouble into his uniform jacket.

Pavlowsky was unguarded but all comers and goers had to explain their mission or their journey to the Guard. Every evening, each house was searched to ascertain if there were any strangers. If a man led a dog or wore a round hat, he was arrested. Soon, in spite of its beauty, Pavlowsky became deserted: one avoided it and fled if one saw Paul, even at a distance. This infuriated him, and he often had those that shunned his presence pursued and arrested so as to interrogate them.

All the officers of his Battalion were arrested one day because he had not been saluted properly when they filed past him after drilling. He got them to march in front of him for a week, sending them back every day to the guard-house until he had been satisfied by their salute.

Once exercising his regiment of heavy mounted cavalry, an officer's horse fell down. Paul ran up, furious: 'Get up, you wretch.' 'I cannot, Your Highness, my leg is broken.' Paul, cursing, spat on him as he walked away.

Furtively and unexpectedly, he once came across one of his 'bodyguards'. The officer, never having seen him, did not turn out the guard. Paul walked back, buffeted the man, disarmed him and had him put under arrest. Once he was going from Tsarskoe-Selo to Gatschina. The road went through a swampy forest. All of a sudden Paul remembered something and ordered the coachman to turn back. The coachman: 'As soon as possible, Your Highness; the road is too narrow.' Paul: 'What, rascal? Won't you turn instantly?' The coachman, instead of answering, hurried to a spot where he could do so: at once Paul flies through the carriage door, calls his equerry and orders him to arrest and punish the rebel coachman. The equerry promises a turn in a minute. Paul foaming with rage, yells at the equerry: 'You are a scum like him,' he screamed, 'let him turn over and break my neck, but he must obey as I order him instantly.'

During this rage, the coachman did turn, but Paul had him flogged there and then.

Once riding along his horse shied: he ordered his equerry, Markov, to let him die of hunger. On the eighth day, Markow reported the horse's death. Paul said, 'Good' (*C'est bon* – French original). Once, since his Coronation, riding in a St Petersburg street, another horse shied under him. He dismounted at once and ordered his equerrys to hold a kind of council about it: the horse was condemned to be lashed fifty times. This was done in front of the passersby, Paul himself counting the strokes and saying (in French), '*C'est pour avoir manqué à l'Empereur.*'

Once a poor soldier, flogged to the bone on Paul's orders for a small drilling mistake, screamed out in his despair: 'Oh miserable bald head, oh cursed bald head.' The indignant Autocrat at once ordered the man to be knouted to death and as well had it published that he forbade anyone to talk of baldness in mentioning a head, or snub-nosedness when speaking of a nose, under threat of death also by the knout. Having read the story of a prophet ordering forty-two children to be eaten by a bear for being similarly insulted, he no doubt thought his head was worth that of an Elijah.

[87] Lord Hertford and Garter King at Arms present the Garter to Alexander I at Pavlovsk, from *Original Letters from Russia, 1825–1828*, edited by Charlotte Disbrowe.

Know then that contrary to all established etiquette, the charming Empress Mother invited me to dine at Paulofsky, with the Marquis and suite, Mr Disbrowe and John. At first when I expressed a wish to go to Sarkoselo to see the ceremony of the Investiture of the Garter, I was told it was out of the question, and Sposo said it would not do for me to go as badeau when he was invited officially. Judge then

my surprise at one o'clock on Saturday to receive an
express invite from His Imperial Majesty. Such a scouring
of mantua makers and milliners, a fête day besides, so there
were very few shops open. However, my amiable Mme.
Turin did wonders for me, and half-past seven on Sunday
morning four new gowns were brought home, for as usual
there was great uncertainty about trains or no trains, but
both must be ready. The embassy was present at Czarkoselo
in great state, but neither the Emperor nor Empress dined at
Paulofsky. The latter is not allowed to encounter the least
fatigue, and the former did not *choose* to come, so that
there were only three of the Imperial Family at dinner, the
Empress Mother and Grand Duke and Duchess Hélène. One
hundred and twenty sat down, and there was a very beautiful display of demoiselles d'honneur. Our countrymen were
very much struck. The dinner was very plainly served, and
the table ornamented with a quantity of corn flowers, which
looked extremely pretty. Everything was supposed to be in
country style. Lord Hertford sat opposite the Empress, and
Garter King at Arms next to him, nodding and grinning at
a great rate, not comprehending a syllable of what was said,
not even when the Grand Duchess spoke in English. We
were dismissed early after dinner, with an invite to meet
Her Majesty at the Pavillion des Roses, and spend the evening with her, which we did. I played at her table at mou-
che, and she gave lessons to Lord Hertford in the game
with the greatest good humour and affability. You remember the Pavillion des Roses. The young people played aux
petite jeux and amused themselves famously. They were
very romping games, and the Empress was highly diverted
with the peals of laughter that could not be repressed every
now and then. Little Francis Seymour and young Midship-
man Murray amused her particularly. Our young men say
they never saw young ladies romp with so much propriety.
The Empress did not sit down to supper, but walked about
talking to her guests and doing the honours like a private
person. We returned about halfpast eleven, all delighted
with our day's amusement, but I fear poor Lord Hertford
suffered from fatigue and gout very much. The doors of the
Pavillion were left open, and the populace allowed to be

spectators and to stand some way in the room. They were very orderly, and required no guards to keep them in bounds.

Next day, as soon as I was up, I received the reigning Empress's commands to go and see her privately. She received me on a balcony, and gave me strawberries and cream, and was kind and amiable as possible. The dear little Grande Duchess Alexandra, at whose christening you attended, came in and was very gracious to me and made me cry. She was just what Albinia was when I left her. At one o'clock the investiture of the Garter took place, so privately that the public saw nothing but the actors in it get out of the gilt carriages and walk across the colonade. Even the Empresses were not admitted; but a curtain was placed before a doorway, and they and the children peeped through it. The Empress told me that to her dismay she found that towards the end of the ceremony the little Olga had contrived to thrust her whole head through a hole in the curtain. Mr Disbrowe saw the pretty face come through and was so enchanted and amused that he nearly forgot to bow in the right part of the ceremony. Lord Hertford was splendidly dressed, indeed all the costumes were much admired. The Marquis and Sir G. Naylor, Garter King at Arms headed the procession; next Lord Marcus Hill, with the George on a cushion, Lord Seymour with the sword, Capt Meynell the hat for the Emperor, Capt Seymour the mantle, Windsor Herald and attendants with the seals and admonition, and then the two pages, Francis Seymour and young Murray with Lord Hertford's hat and King Garter's crown. The day was lovely, and the crowd round the palace gaily dressed, so that it was altogether a very pretty sight. The Emperor would not put on the proper costume; indeed he curtailed the whole ceremony very much, to the utter despair of King Garter.

I stood under a window to which all the Imperial Family came, and they were all most gracious to me.

The Embassy and the Mission dined with the Ministre de la Maison, Prince Pierre Volkonsky. I was with the Modènes, and just as we were thinking of getting into the carriage to return to St Petersburg the Empress sent to beg me to come and take tea with her at the Sauvagerie, which of course I did, nothing loath; and she stuffed me with bread and *buther*, as she called it, showed me the place, and then sent me home charmed and as proud as needs be.

LIFE, CUSTOMS AND MORALS IN ST PETERSBURG

Previous page:
'Two o'clock on the Nevsky Prospekt': *c.* 1830,
artist unknown

[88] Peter the Great's amusements and eating habits, from *Memoirs of Peter the Great* by Sir John Barrow.

Petersburg now [1715] began to assume the consequence as well as the appearance of a great capital; and vast numbers flocked thither from Moscow, and other interior towns, seeing that the seat of commerce would eventually be established there. The Tzar had now become almost universally popular. Desirous of assimilating the manners of his subjects, as he had already done their dress, to those of other European nations, he encouraged frequent social assemblies: he even ordered his senators and his generals alternately to open their houses twice a week for these assemblies, at which conversation, cards, and dancing might be resorted to; they were to commence at eight and end at eleven o'clock; they were open to all of the rank of gentlemen, foreigners as well as natives, and equally so for their wives and daughters. This was a great step gained in civilisation; and the ladies gladly profited by the indulgence, and rapidly improved in their manners, conversation, and dress.

The balls and entertainments of the Tzar had hitherto always been given at Prince Menzikoff's palace, but his own summer and winter palaces being finished in the course of the year 1715, he now entertained his guests at one or other of these; except on grand festivals, and extraordinary occasions, when the entertainments were held at the senate-house. At these public dinners, several tables were laid out, appropriated to the several classes of persons, as senators, clergymen, officers of the army and navy, merchants, ship-builders and others; the Tzarina and the ladies at a separate table, and generally above stairs. These entertainments commonly ended with hard drinking. After dinner the Tzar used to go from one room and table to another, conversing with every set according to their different professions or employments, more particularly with the masters of foreign trading vessels, making minute inquiries into the several branches of their traffic, and marking down in his pocket-book, as usual, whatever occurred to him as worthy of notice. 'At these dinners', says Bruce, 'I have seen the Dutch skippers treat him with much familiarity, calling him *Skipper Peter*, with which he seemed to be highly delighted.'[1]

But the most extraordinary account of the manner in which the Tzar entertained is given in a manuscript, in the handwriting of Dr Birch, among the Sloane Papers in the British Museum:-

There are twenty-four cooks belonging to the kitchen of the Russian court, who are all Russians; and, as people of that nation use a great deal of onion, garlic, and train oyl, in dressing their meat, and employ linseed and walnut oyl for their provisions, there is such an intolerable stink in their kitchen, that no stranger is able to bear it, especially the cooks being such nasty fellows that the very sight of them is enough to turn one's stomach. These are the men who, in great festivals, dress about 70 or 80 or more dishes. But the fowls which are the Czar's own eating are very often dressed by his grand *Marskal* Alseffiof, who is running up and down with his apron before him among the other cooks till it is time to take up dinner, when he puts on his fine clothes, and his fullbottomed wig, and helps to serve up the dishes.

The number of the persons invited is commonly two or three hundred, though there is room for no more than about an hundred, at four or five tables. But as there is no place assigned to any body, and none of the Russians are willing to go home with an empty stomach, every body is obliged to seize his chair and hold it with all his force, if he will not have it snatched from him.

The Czar being come in, and having chosen a place for himself, there is such scuffling and fighting for chairs, that nothing more scandalous can be seen in any country. Though the Czar does not mind in the least, nor take care for putting a stop to such disorder, pretending that a ceremony, and the formal regulations of a *Marskal* make company eat uneasy, and spoil the pleasure of conversation. Several foreign ministers have complained of this to the Czar, and refused to dine any more at court. But all the answer they got was, that it was not the Czar's business to turn master of the ceremonies

[1] Memoir of P. H. Bruce, Esq.

and please foreigners, nor was it his intention to abolish the freedom once introduced. This obliged strangers for the future to follow the Russian fashion, in defending the possession of their chairs by cuffing and boxing their opposer.

The company thus sitting down to table without any manner of grace, they all sit so crowded together that they have much ado to lift their hands to their mouths. And if a stranger happens to sit between two Russians, which is commonly the case, he is sure of losing his stomach, though he should have happened to have ate nothing for two days before. Carpenters and shipwrights sit next to the Czar, but senators, ministers, generals, priests, sailors, buffoons of all kinds, sit pellmell without any distinction.

The first course consists of nothing but cold meats, among which are hams, dried tongues, and the like, which not being liable to such tricks, as shall be mentioned hereafter, strangers ordinarily make their whole meal of them, without tasting anything else, though, generally speaking, every one takes his dinner beforehand at home.

Soups and roasted meats make the second course, and pastry the third.

As soon as one sits down, one is obliged to drink a cup of brandy; after which they ply you with great glasses full of adulterated *tookay*, and other vitiated wines, and between whiles a bumper of the strongest English beer, by which mixture of liquors every one of the guests is fuddled before the soup is served up.

The company being in this condition make such a noise, racket and helloing, that it is impossible to hear one another, or even to hear the musick which is playing in the next room, consisting of a sort of trumpets and *corpets*, (for the Czar hates violins), and with this revelling noise and uproar the Czar is extremely diverted, particularly if the guests fall to boxing and get bloody noses.

Fortunately the company had no napkins given them: but instead of it they had a piece of very coarse linen given them by a servant, who brought in the whole piece under his arm, and cut off half an ell for every person, which they were at liberty to carry home with them: for it had been observed that these pilfering guests used constantly to pocket the napkins.

But at present two or three Russians must make shift with but one napkin, which they pull and haul for, like hungry dogs for a bone.

Each person of the company has but one plate during dinner; so if some Russian does not care to mix the sauces of the different dishes together, he pours the soup that is left in his plate, either into the dish, or into his neighbour's plate, or even under the table; after which he licks his plate clean with his finger, and last of all wipes it with the table cloth.

The tables are each 30 or 40 feet long, and but two and a half broad. Three or four *messes* of one and the same course are served up to each table. The dessert consists of divers sorts of pastry and fruits, but the Czarina's table is furnished with sweetmeats. However, it is also observed, that these sweet-meats are only set out on great festivals, for a show, and that the Russians of the best fashion have nothing for their dessert but the produce of the kitchen garden (as peas, beans, &c,) all raw.

At great entertainments it frequently happens that nobody is allowed to go out of the room from noon till midnight. Hence it is easy to imagine what pickle a room must be in, that is full of people who drink like beasts, and none of them escape being dead drunk.

They often tie eight or ten young mice on a string, and hide them under green peas, or in such soups as the Russians have the greatest appetites to; which sets them a *kecking* and vomiting in a most beastly manner, when they come to the bottom and discover the trick. They often bake cats, wolves, ravens and the like in their pastries, and when the company have eat them up, they tell them what stuff they have in their guts.

The present butler is one of the Czar's buffoons, to whom he has given the name of *Wiaschi*, with this privilege, that if any body else calls him by that name, he has leave to drub them with his wooden sword. If therefore any body, upon the Czar's setting them on, calls out *Wiaschi*, as the fellow does not know exactly who it was, he falls a beating them all round, beginning with Prince Mentzicoff, and ending with the last of the company, without excepting even the ladies, whom he strips of their head clothes, as he does the old

Russians with their wigs, which he tramples upon. On which occasion it is pleasant enough to see the variety of their bald pates.

Besides this employment at entertainments the said *Wiaschi* is also surveyor of the *ice*, and executioner for torturing people; on which occasion he gives them the knout himself, and his dexterity in this business has already procured him about thirty thousand thalers, the sixth part of the confiscated estates of the sufferers being his perquisite.

At what time these extraordinary scenes occurred, there are no means of ascertaining, as the paper is without date; but the mention of the Tzarina's name points to a period subsequent to the marriage of Catherine. It is well known that Peter, simple and abstemious in his diet as he became towards the latter part of his life, as well as in the use of wine and strong liquors, never ceased to take pleasure in seeing his guests enjoy themselves, and encouraging them to drink frequently, even until they became intoxicated, and was amused with their noise and revels. When alone with his Tzarina, he was equally moderate in his eating and drinking. When only his own family was present his usual dinner hour was twelve o'clock. His table was frugal, and he ate only of plain dishes, – such as soup with vegetables in it, water gruel, cold roast meat, ham, and cheese; a little aniseed-water before dinner, and a cup of *quass* or Russian beer, or in lieu of this, a glass of wine. One dish only was served up at a time, and, in order to have it hot, the dining-room was contiguous to the kitchen, from whence the dish was received from the cook through a small window. At one, he was accustomed to lie down and sleep for about an hour; the rest of the afternoon and the evening were spent in some amusement or other, till ten o'clock, when he went to bed, and he always got up at four in the morning, summer and winter. Between this hour and twelve he transacted all his business with his ministers. Although he never supped, he generally sat down with the Empress and his daughters at table; and, though now grown sober and serious, he still preserved in company the gaiety of his disposition, his familiarity with his inferiors, and his dislike of ceremony. Peter never restrained himself through life in putting to practice, whenever he thought it necessary, any of his oddities and eccentricities, most of which, absurd and puerile as they might appear to be, had each of them an aim at some particular end; each of them had its place on the surface of his sphere of action; and all of them converged to one central point, and that point was Russia.

Besides the coarse and boisterous parties that have been described, he had others of a more rational nature. He had a garden in Petersburg laid out on an island, in which was built a large banqueting-room. When an entertainment was to be given in this garden, it was necessary that the company should come in boats; and, in order to accommodate the different ranks of his guests, he presented them accordingly with yachts, small sailing vessels, barges of ten or twelve oars, and smaller boats; and these means of conveyance were given to them on this condition – that each should keep his vessel in repair, and when worn out, build another at his own expense. Nor were these vessels to be kept up for pleasure alone, or suffered to remain useless, for, on a given signal being made for sailing or rowing, the proprietors, with their respective crews, were obliged to attend, whether to row on the broad Neva, or sail down to Cronstadt. In the latter case, all the manoeuvres of a fleet were put in practice by signals, such as making or shorterning sail, forming the line, furling sails, &c., by which the young nobles and gentry acquired a taste for the naval service, while they were enjoying the trip as an amusement.

[89] The wedding party of dwarfs arranged for Peter the Great's amusement, from *Mémoires pour Servir à l'Histoire de l'Empire Russien sous le Règne de Pierre le Grand* by F. C. Weber.

In 1701 the Czar, wanting to improve the ceremonies of his niece Anne's marriage to the late Duke of Courland (Frederic William), organised as an entertainment the wedding feast of Dwarfs; I think this farce deserves its place in my account of the Russian Court, although it happened before my arrival in that country.

On November 11th, the Princess' marriage was solemnised and the date of November 13th (new style) of the same month was chosen for that of the Dwarfs. To invite the guests, two richly dressed and good looking dwarfs went about, drawn in a three-wheeled chaise by a handsome beribboned horse. Equally well dressed in Russian style, two servants rode in front of them.

The wedding took place on the date arranged in the Fortress Church according to the Russian rite. As master of ceremonies, a very small dwarf conducted the procession, carrying a wand decorated with ribbons, the badge of his office. He was followed by the betrothed very cleanly turned out.

The Czar followed accompanied by his Ministers, Princes, Boyars and officers.

All the male and female Dwarfs followed, a total of seventy-two, some in the service of the Czar, of the Dowager Czarina, of Prince and Princess Menzicoff, and other persons of quality; as well, many had been brought from the furthest corners of Russia.

The rear of the procession was brought up by many spectators. Having reached the church, the betrothed were placed in the middle of the assembly. The Priest, having asked the bridegroom if he would take this girl to be his wife, he answered in a loud voice, addressing his mistress, 'Yes, you and no other.' The girl having been asked if she had not promised marriage to someone else, she answered, '*Cela seroit vraiment bien joli!*' But when it came to the point and she was asked whether she would take this man to be her husband, she answered, 'Yes', but in such a low voice one could hardly hear her, which caused the company greatly to laugh.

According to the custom of the Russian Church and as a great compliment, the Czar himself held the crown over the bride's head.

The ceremony over, everyone went by boat to the Palace of Prince Menzicoff. The banquet was prepared in the very Hall where two days before, the Czar had entertained all the guests invited to the Duke's marriage. In the middle of the hall, a number of small tables were placed for the newly weds as well as for the other dwarfs all elaborately dressed *à l'allemande*. The bride and the groom sat at two separate tables under two little silken thrones. The head of the bride as well as that of the two dwarfs assisting her were adorned with three laurel wreaths. The groom too had one over his head.

Between the two assistants, there was a groom by the name of Tranchant to whom the married gave a favour to thank him for the trouble he had taken, and he gave a kiss to the bride and groom to thank them for the favour.

This small gathering was served by a marshal, eight deputy marshals, all dwarfs, each wearing a lace and ribbon bow on the right shoulder to show off their temporary duties which they did with such competence and grace they greatly pleased their masters.

The Czar sat on one side with the Duke of Courland, the Russian Ministers, foreigners and Generals: on the other the Duchess of Courland, her sisters, the Princesses, and the principal ladies of the court. The Princes, Boyars, Russian and German officers followed. They sat at narrow tables all along the four walls of the hall so as to watch the Dwarfs sitting in the middle.

The small marshal with his eight deputies gave the first toast in front of the Czar's table, their wands of office in one hand and in the other their glasses. After a deep bow to the ground, they knocked them back to the sound of music played in an adjacent room.

Behind the house had been placed small canons that were to be fired at each toast. However, because the younger son of Prince Menzicoff was dying (and did die before the end of the day), this order was countermanded.

The Dwarfs started dancing *à la Russe* after dinner – this lasted till eleven o'clock that night. It is easy to imagine the pleasure taken by the Czar and the company in viewing the comical somersaults and strange grimaces and ridiculous postures of this medley of pygmies whose very faces made one laugh. One had a protuberance on his buttocks and the shortest legs; another was noticeable on account of his monstrous belly, a third swayed about as if he were a badger, on tiny crooked legs; others had twisted mouths, longish ears, and piggy eyes.

When the entertainment was over, the newly weds were brought to the Czar's palace, where they were bedded down in His Majesty's own room.

[90] The Empress Anne's passion for hunting, from *Palmyra of the North* by Christopher Marsden.

In one of the indoor gardens or conservatories was a large aviary where the birds were sometimes let loose for the Empress to shoot at with gun or bow and arrow. She was passionately fond of shooting. All over the palaces loaded guns lay ready to hand and she and her ladies would fire out of the windows at passing birds, filling the rooms with smoke and noise. Hunting and riding she loved also, and had nearly forty hunters in her stables. It was forbidden, under pain of terrible punishment, for any private person to hunt within a distance of twenty miles of the outskirts of the capital. For the court hunts, bears, wolves, boars, stags, and foxes were collected from all over Russia and Moscow would send six hundred live hares at a time to St Petersburg for the chase. The list of game killed by the Empress with her own hand between June and August one year included nine stags, sixteen roe-deer, four boars, a wolf, three hundred and seventy-four hares, sixty-eight wild duck and sixteen assorted sea-fowl. Knowing her love for this sport her courtiers, when abroad, would send her gifts for the palace kennels: Prince Cantemir once bought thirty-four pairs of basset hounds for the Empress in Paris for £275, while Prince Scherbatov, an old-fashioned nobleman who frowned on luxury, obtained for her sixty-three pairs of sporting dogs, beagles and terriers, in London. . . .

Though freedom from vermin was not an outstanding feature of eighteenth-century Europe, foreign travellers found Russian society exceptionally abundant in this respect. When ladies went to pay a call they always left their fur pelisses – of blue or black fox, of ermine and sable – with their lackeys, who were in the habit of lying down and going to sleep on them while they waited for their mistresses in the servants' quarters. When their precious furs were put on again the ladies found them teeming with life. At a whist party a lovely woman would pull out a rich gold snuff-box, as if to take a pinch, at the same time scratching her temples vigorously; and then, delicately nipping a little beast between her fingers, place it on the enamelled lid of the box and crack it with her nail. Even more common was it to see officers or other people of rank and fashion rid themselves of lice in company and drop them on the floor without even bothering to stop talking.

[91] The lunatic 'house' and Venereal Hospital in 1801, from *Picture of Petersburg* by H. Storch.

The house for lunatics consists of four and forty chambers in two opposite rows; one of which is appropriated to the men and the other to the women visited with this dreadful malady. Here likewise the utmost attention is paid to cleanliness; by which means and by the gentle treatment of the patients numbers are restored to the community. The raving are not chained, but held by thongs to their bed, and in general only lenient methods are tried, a strict diet, &c. The proportion of Russians here to foreigners is but small; and the number of men is about one fourth greater than that of the female sex; grief, love and pride are here, as every where else, the ordinary sources of frenzy, but in this place drunkenness is the most prolific. Of 229 patients admitted into this house in three years, 161 recovered, eleven were sent to the poor-house as incurable, and forty-seven died. The city hospital is under the control of the college for general provision.

Not less general in its tendency is the VENEREAL HOSPITAL, which has thirty beds for men and just the same number for women; and all that apply are gratuitously admitted, but not discharged until they are completely cured. It is not permitted to ask the name of any person that applies for admission, who at the time of reception receives

a cleanly dress with a cap, on which is inscribed the word
SECRESY.

[92] Details of the population of St Petersburg in
1801, showing the extraordinary disparity between the
numbers of men and women, and the preponderance of
Germans among foreign residents, from *Picture of
Petersburg* by H. Storch.

According to the calculations and inferences of the academi-
cian Krafft, in the space of time from 1764 to 1780, the
average of all the living amounted to 164,000. The last five
years, from 1775 to 1780, taken alone, allows us to estimate
the number of people at 174,778. According to the last cen-
sus it amounted in the year 1784 to 192,846, and in the year
1789 to 217,948, namely:

	Men	Women	Together
Guards, artillery, &c	30,635	5792	36,427
Fleet	10.160	3717	13,877
Military in general	40,795	9509	50,304
Other registered inhabitants	107,725	59,919	167,644

The amount of the foreigners settled here for a time or in
perpetuity . . . composes the 'seventh part' of the population,
and accordingly are in number 32,000. Accurately to deter-
mine the relative proportion of the several nations, is impossible; nevertheless it is manifest from the slightest survey, that
the GERMANS are beyond all comparison the most numerous; and that, next to them, the FRENCH and SWEDES have
the largest share in the exotic population. In order, however,
to come at a clearer knowledge of this proportion, so interesting to the foreign reader, I have, by the church-lists of the
communions not of the Greek religion, multiplied the mean
total of the baptisms by 31 as the general proportion of the
fertility of the place. The results are of this calculation are as
follows. There are living at St Petersburg

17,660　Germans
3,720　Finns
2,290　French
1,860　Swedes
　930　English
　50　Dutch, and
2,490　Catholics, who are neither French nor Germans,
　　　　and therefore Poles, Italians, Spaniards, Portuguese,
　　　　&c

———

29,000

[93] The Russian baths, from *The Russian Journals of Martha and Catherine Wilmot 1803–1808*.

I don't think I have yet mention'd the Russian Baths. I bathed yesterday Evening, and have the power of doing so twice a week if I chuse. To give you at once a just idea of it, 'tis neither more or less than the ditto of those we visited at Bath for five shillings a plunge; but the true Russian Bath admits a Vapour which I cou'd not Support half a minute, and in the midst of that Vapour they remain for half an hour or more. Warm water [is] pour'd over the Victims from time to time till every pore is wide open. The High and Mighty then go into a Bed prepared in another little room well heated. The humbler folks frequently plunge from that state of heat into the snow. Our Bath is as we chuse, Vapour or Water. I always prefer the latter which is introduced by two conductors, one of hot the other of cold water, into a large bathing tub. You know Bathing is a religious ceremony here; and tho' Slander with a thousand tongues proclaims the absence of cleanliness, I freely own as far as I have seen the lower orders are superior to our country folks and the higher ones pretty equal (admitting exceptions to every general rule). But there are various striking resemblances. First a Russ Peasant infallibly scratches his head speaking to a Noble, as Paddy does when he says 'Praise your honour's honour'. Secondly, speaking of heads, the Sundays' amusement at the Cabin doors is well known and often practised.

And thirdly the Music is almost the same. You know the perfection of a true Irish tune is to hold the last note as long as possible, and then fling the voice on the same note an octave higher. Here 'tis also the proof of Excellence, and the tunes are plaintive to a degree – even Melancholy.

[94] The 'Butter Week' festivities, including the *Gulanie* or promenade, from *Russia: 1842* by J. G. Kohl.

Easter, itself, commences in the middle of the night before Easter Sunday, and the festivities are kept up for eight days. This actual centre of the festival is preceded by a preparatory fast of seven weeks, and this fast again is preceded by eight days' feasting and rejoicing, as a preparation for the fast. We may, therefore, most conveniently consider this connected series of spring festivities under the three following heads:

Firstly, the eight days' feasting and stuffing, called by the Russians *Masslanitza*, Butter-week.

Secondly, the seven weeks' fast, called, to distinguish it from other fasts occurring at different times, *Welikoi posd*, the great fast; and

Thirdly, the feast of Easter itself, with its tail.

In the fashionable world of Petersburg, the approach of the great fast is indicated so early as the beginning of February, nay, even in January, by an increased bustle and activity, that is to say, by more frequent balls, and more and more brilliant carnival diversions. But, for the generality of the people, the indulgences and amusements with which they take leave of the good things of life are concentrated in that one week which is called *Masslanitza*, and which commonly falls about the middle or the end of February.

The seven days of the Butter-week may be said to contain the quintessence of all the Russian festivites for the whole year; and, with the exception of Easter week, there is no week in the year that affords a Petersburger so much earthly pleasure as this. First and foremost, it affords, as its name implies, butter, whereas the succeeding fast-weeks allow nothing but oil – a circumstance characteristic of the abundance that prevails during the *Masslanitza*.

*

In front of the nut-cracking, tea-drinking, swinging, and gliding concourse of pedestrians, which is in continual motion
about the tables of bonbons and raisins before those theatres,
there is left a fine wide area. This is destined for the people
of quality, who come about noon in their carriages to survey
the joyous assemblage, and to furnish themselves not the
worst part of the spectacle. In no country is it so customary
as in Russia for the wealthy to appear on all occasions in
their rich equipages to make what is called a *gulanie* (a
promenade).

Such *gulanies* take place not only in the Butter-week at
the *Katscheli*, but also in the Easter-week, and throughout
all Russia on the 1st of May. On their estates the Russians
likewise make such *gulanies* with their visitors, mustering for
the purpose every thing that deserves the name of horse and
carriage – droschkas, caleches, chaises, landaus, vehicles of
all kinds, drawn by four, three, two horses, and by one
horse. All the inmates of the house fill the carriages, which
drive about the country in one long train.

With the prodigious multitude of equipages kept in the
Russian cities, where nobody, from a tailor of any repute
upwards, goes on foot, the great public *gulanies* are always
highly animated, and present one of the grandest and most
amusing spectacles in their kind that can be desired. But one
is not so much astonished at the grandeur of the *gulanies* in
Moscow and Petersburg, as at that exhibited in many a
provincial town, where on such occasions you see more
splendid carriages drawn by four and slx horses than you
meet with in many a large capital of Western Europe. In the
Russian provincial towns there is proportionately a much
greater display in equipages, because there is no ordinance
limiting the number of horses to be used there, so that every
one may drive as many as he pleases; because, moreover,
they have not yet adopted in the provinces the tone of the
capitals, where in the highest circles it is a point of etiquette
on certain occasions to drive but two horses, whereas in the
country nobody would think of visiting a neighbour but in a
carriage and six. At such public *gulanies*, however, it is, of
course, the fashion for each to appear with as many horses
as befit his rank. It might be supposed that, in this case,

none but splendid equipages and state carriages would make their appearance. Nothing of the sort; on the contrary, every one has a right to join the procession with his humble vehicle, of whatever class it may be; and amidst the carriages and four of the grandees are to be seen those of the tradesman and artisan drawn by two only.

[95] The Masquerade: Nicholas I's conduct, from *Russia: 1812* by J. G. Kohl.

Measuring, cutting, sewing, they presently converted the stage into a handsome Turkish tent, which was open in front. At the back of the tent arose with the like rapidity a gallery for the musicians, and on either side benches for the spectators. Meanwhile, the magicians had completed the floor over the pit, made steps to ascend to the imperial box, and, by removing the fronts, seats, and doors, of the side boxes on that tier, turned them into mere passages.

The clock had in quick time struck ten, a quarter, half past, but in equally quick time the workmen got through the different parts of their job; and by three-quarters the din of hammers and saws had ceased. The new creation was finished; the clouds of dust had dispersed, the labourers retired, and now from the opening heavens burst the brilliant sun of the chandelier, descending through the regions of space, and flinging its beams from the centre over this new-made world. At the same moment, thousands of wax candles seemed to light themselves up, like stars, along the fronts of the different tiers of boxes. A servant now appeared on the floor with a censer, filling the air with perfume, as though he had been the first inhabitant of the infant world paying his homage to the sun. Rapidly as this creation had been produced, so rapidly was it peopled. About eleven o'clock the children of men poured into it from all quarters. There came also frogs, and birds, and all the different characters usually seen on such occasions. At half-past eleven the emperor entered, and the music suddenly struck up in thundering tones. It was a chorus accompanied by the whole orchestra. It is usual in Russia to open public balls that have any tincture of national importance with such an air; in general it is the Russian national hymn: 'For the Emperor and sacred Russia,' &c.

The moment the emperor entered, all my reveries about chaos and creation were dispelled. My whole attention was engrossed by this representative, of a power which has not its equal on earth, and which, in his personal presence, must electrify every imagination with irresistible force: indeed I cannot conceive it possible for any reflecting and rational mind to think and feel otherwise than I did. Such seemed also to be the impression of the public generally, for, wherever the emperor paused for a moment, there the spectators ranged themselves, as if acted upon by some invisible power, as iron filings by a strong magnet. But the emperor mingled with them as much as he could, going continually up stairs and down stairs. The young ladies in dominoes were eager to approach him. He courteously gave them his arm, and walked about in the rooms joking with them. Many who have not access to him at other times go to this masquerade merely to have the satisfaction of walking for once arm in arm with the emperor. He took every thing goodhumouredly, and was never at a loss for an answer. Once, as I was passing him, the fair mask with whom he was walking, said, '*Ah! comme tu es beau!*' – '*Oh! oui!*' replied the emperor, '*ah! et si tu aurais vu comme je l'étais autrefois!*' Another mask said to him, '*Il y a peu de dames aujourd'hui.*' – '*Oui. Mais quant à mod, je suis content; je te prends pour cent.*' One mask, however, seemed to teaze him with her importunateness, when, spying one of his great courtiers, he transferred her to his arm with the words, '*Voilà T . . . une jolie petite dame pour toi.*' This gentleman led her about for some time, till he found an opportunity to get rid of her; and I could not help inwardly congratulating her that she was so closely masked.

At this masquerade, at which there were, besides the emperor, several German princes and many Russian grandees, chance sometimes brought together extraordinary contrasts, for instance, the heir to a German kingdom and the heir-presumptive to a retail shop in the Perspective; the Emperor of all the Russians and a French governess; the minister of the finances of an empire containing sixty million inhabitants and a merchant's clerk in the costume of a frog . . .

[96] Russian eating-habits, from *Russia: 1842* by J. G. Kohl.

Perhaps the climate of Russia, where the summer is always excessively hot, as the winter always excessively cold, is the cause of the decided and strictly maintained distinctions between the summer and the winter cuisine. Every season has its own soup, its own poultry, its own pastry. To many, a positive date for their enjoyment may be given. Fruit comes in on the 8th of August, ice on Easter Sunday. Religion, which has much to do with the Russian table, prohibits the eating of certain articles of food before a certain day. Saturday's dishes differ throughout the whole country from Sunday's; Friday and Wednesday, as fastdays, have other food prescribed than Monday and Thursday. It is all one, in Germany, what food is set before the guests at a funeral; in Russia, it must be a kind of rice-soup, with plums and raisins. The cake broken over the head of the newly-born child, is of a particular kind. Weddings, betrothments, &c, have all their appointed dishes, and it must not be forgotten that these household regulations hold good for not less than 300,000 German square miles, and forty millions of people.

Meat is almost always eaten by the Russians (we speak of the great bulk of the people) either boiled, pickled, or salted; they seldom smoke meat, not even their hams and bacon; roasting is almost unknown to them. It is incredible how bad the bread is, considering the goodness of the corn; it is [all] more or less sour, and why this is so, is not easy to discover. Another fault is that it is never sufficiently baked, but that is characteristic of a people who choose to eat more unripe than ripe fruit. It were easy to leave their fruit a little longer on the tree, their bread a little longer in the oven, but that is never done. Pasties of all kinds (pirogas) are in great favour with the Russian; things so little known in Germany that we have not even a word for them. The Russians pack every thing that can be chopped up, into pies; vegetables, fruit, mushrooms, flesh and fish; the paste is generally detestable . . .

Of liquids, the most national and most general is kwas, which occupies the same place as a beverage, that shtshee does as a dish. The Russian of the lower class can no more live without kwas, than fish without water. It is not only his constant drink, but the foundation of all his soups and sauces, which are rarely made with simple water, but almost always with kwas. Kwas is the basis of all his food, solid and liquid; in kwas all things dissolve and swim; even on the tables of the wealthiest, among the wines and liqueurs, instead of decanters of water appear decanters of kwas. Fortunately it is a light and wholesome beverage. It is prepared in the following manner: A pailful of water is put into an earthen vessel, into which are shaken two pounds of barley-meal, half-a-pound of salt, and a pound-and-a-half of honey. This mixture is put in the evening into a kind of oven, with a moderate fire, and constantly stirred; in the morning it is left for a time to settle, and then the clear liquid is poured off. The kwas is then ready, and may be drunk in a few days; in a week it is at its highest perfection. As kwas is thought good only when prepared in small quantities, and in small vessels, every household brews for itself.

[97] Etiquette in St Petersburg in the mid-1870s, from *Handbook for Travellers in Russia, Poland and Finland*, published by John Murray.

13. – SOCIETY.

Winter is the season for gaieties in Russia. Travellers with letters of introduction will find the *salons* of St Petersburg as brilliant as those of Paris, but they are unfortunately not many. There is no dancing during the forty days that precede Easter. Christmas and the Carnival are the gayest periods. Two or three court balls are then given, and 'distinguished strangers' who have been presented at home will sometimes receive invitations after having been presented to H.I.M. through their own Embassy or Legation.

It is necessary to wear a uniform at court. French is the

language spoken in society, but English is generally understood. Strangers are expected to make the first call, which is
returned either in person or by card. In leaving cards on
persons who are not at home, one of the edges of the card
should be turned up. It is necessary to leave a card next day
on any person to whom the stranger may have been introduced at a party. Those who are introduced *to* the stranger
will observe the same politeness. Great punctuality is exacted
at St Petersburg in the matter of leaving cards and entertainments and introductions. Visiting on New Year's Day may
be avoided by giving a small contribution to the charitable
institutions of the city, which will be duly acknowledged in
the newspapers.

No presents are given to servants, except at New Year
and Easter, when the porters of much-frequented houses will
offer their congratulations in anticipation of a donation of 1
to 5 rubles, according to the number of visits paid. The
hours for calling are 3 to 5 P.M.; dinner parties are generally
convened for 6 or 6.30 P.M.; and receptions commence at
about 10 P.M., and last very late. Guests are expected to be
punctual where members of the Imperial Family are invited.
Ladies wishing to pass a 'season' at St Petersburg should
recollect that Russian ladies dress very richly and in great
taste. The charges of dressmakers at St Petersburg being
exorbitant, it is advisable to come provided with all the
necessary *toilettes*. At balls, the only dance in which the
stranger will not at first be able to join is the Mazurka, a
kind of *cotillon* imported from Poland. It is also necessary to
observe the partners are not engaged for the whole of a waltz
or polka, but only for a turn.

In summer there are generally two or three *salons* out of
many open for evening receptions. Ladies can in summer
wear *robes montants*, and gentlemen light trousers and white
waistcoats, with dress coats. The same costume is worn at
dinner parties in summer.

Travellers should not forget that a Russian invariably
takes off his hat whenever he enters an apartment, however
humble, or a shop; and an omission to pay this respect to
the holy image suspended in the corner of every room will
immediately be noticed and will hurt the feelings of the host

or hostess. Topcoats must always be removed on entering Russian houses, as a point of etiquette and politeness. It is scarcely necessary to add that galoshes should likewise be removed on entering a house.

[98] A Petersburg Russian, from *An Unpleasant Predicament* by Fyodor Dostoyevsky.

A couple of words about Akim Petrovitch. He was a man of the old school, as meek as a hen, reared from infancy to obsequious servility, and at the same time a goodnatured and even honourable man. He was a Petersburg Russian; that is, his father and his father's father were born, grew up and served in Petersburg and had never once left Petersburg. That is quite a special type of Russian. They have hardly any idea of Russia, though that does not trouble them at all. Their whole interest is confined to Petersburg and chiefly the place in which they serve. All their thoughts are concentrated on preference for farthing points, on the shop, and their month's salary. They don't know a single Russian custom, a single Russian song except *Lutchinushka*, and that only because it is played on the barrel organs. However, there are two fundamental and invariable signs by which you can at once distinguish a Petersburg Russian from a real Russian. The first sign is the fact that Petersburg Russians, all without exception, speak of the newspaper as the *Academic News* and never call it the *Petersburg News*. The second and equally trustworthy sign is that Petersburg Russians never make use of the word 'breakfast', but always call it *Frühstück* with especial emphasis on the first syllable. By these radical and distinguishing signs you can tell them apart; in short, this is a humble type which has been formed during the last thirty-five years.

[99] The effect of the Petersburg weather in November on Mr Golyadkin, from *The Double: A Petersburg Poem*, by Fyodor Dostoyevsky.

It was striking midnight from all the clock towers in Petersburg when Mr Golyadkin, beside himself, ran out on the Fontanka Quay, close to the Ismailovsky Bridge, fleeing from his foes, from persecution, from a hailstorm of nips and pinches aimed at him, from the shrieks of excited old ladies, from the Ohs and Ahs of women and from the murderous eyes of Andrey Filippovitch. Mr Golyadkin was killed – killed entirely, in the full sense of the word, and if he still preserved the power of running, it was simply through some sort of miracle, a miracle in which at last he refused himself to believe. It was an awful November night – wet, foggy, rainy, snowy, teeming with colds in the head, fevers, swollen faces, quinseys, inflammations of all kinds and descriptions – teeming, in fact, with all the gifts of a Petersburg November. The wind howled in the deserted streets, lifting up the black water of the canal above the rings on the bank, and irritably brushing against the lean lamp-posts which chimed in with its howling in a thin, shrill creak, keeping up the endless squeaky, jangling concert with which every inhabitant of Petersburg is so familiar. Snow and rain were falling both at once. Lashed by the wind, the streams of rainwater spurted almost horizontally, as though from a fireman's hose, pricking and stinging the face of the luckless Mr Golyadkin like a thousand pins and needles. In the stillness of the night, broken only by the distant rumbling of carriages, the howl of the wind and the creaking of the lamp-posts, there was the dismal sound of the splash and gurgle of water, rushing from every roof, every porch, every pipe and every cornice, on to the granite of the pavement. There was not a soul, near or far, and, indeed, it seemed there could not be at such an hour and in such weather. And so only Mr Golyadkin, alone with his despair, was fleeing in terror along the pavement of Fontanka, with his usual rapid little step, in haste to get home as soon as possible to his flat on the fourth storey in Shestilavotchny Street.

[100] Count Vronsky entertains a foreign Prince on a visit to St Petersburg, from *Anna Karenina* by Leo Tolstoy.

In the middle of winter Vronsky spent a very dull week. He was attached to a foreign prince who was paying a visit to Petersburg and he had to show him the sights of the city. Vronsky himself had a distinguished appearance and, in addition, he possessed the art of carrying himself with respectful dignity and was used to the company of such exalted personages. And so he was appointed to attend on the prince. But his duties seemed a little too strenuous to him. The prince did not wish to miss anything about which he might be asked at home whether he had seen it in Russia and, besides, he wanted to enjoy as many Russian amusements as possible. Vronsky had to act as his guide in both. In the mornings they went sightseeing and in the evenings they took part in the national amusements. The prince enjoyed unusually good health even among princes; both by gymnastic exercises and by taking good care of his body he had brought himself to such a state of physical fitness that in spite of the excesses he indulged in when enjoying himself, he looked as fresh as a big shiny green Dutch cucumber. The prince had traveled a great deal, and he found that one of the chief advantages of the facilities of modern communications was that they made national amusements so easily accessible. He had been in Spain, where he had serenaded and became on intimate terms with a Spanish woman who played the mandolin. In Switzerland he had shot a chamois. In England he had taken fences in a pink coat and shot two hundred pheasants for a bet. In Turkey he had been in a harem, in India he had ridden an elephant, and now in Russia he wished to sample all the typically Russian amusements.

Vronsky, who was, as it were, his chief master of ceremonies, found it rather hard to apportion all the Russian amusements offered to the prince by different people, such as trotting races, pancakes, bear hunts, troikas, gypsies, and orgies with smashing of crockery in the Russian fashion. And the prince assimilated the Russian national spirit with quite extraordinary facility, smashed trays of crockery, sat with a gypsy girl on his lap, and seemed to be always asking, 'What next? Surely that's not all the Russian national spirit consists of?'

As a matter of fact, of all the Russian amusements the prince preferred French actresses, a ballet dance, and white-seal champagne. Vronsky was used to princes, but whether it was that he had himself lately changed or whether he had been in too close a proximity to this particular prince, that week seemed to him terribly wearisome. All the week he felt like a man who had been put in charge of a dangerous lunatic, was afraid of that lunatic, and at the same time, being in such close proximity to him, afraid for his own reason too. Vronsky always felt that he must never for a moment relax his tone of strict official respectfulness so as not to be insulted. The prince's manner of behaving toward those very persons who, to Vronsky's astonishment, were ready to spare no efforts to provide him with Russian amusements, was contemptuous. His views of Russian women, whom he wanted to study, more than once made Vronsky flush with indignation.

[101] The feverish pre-war atmosphere in St Petersburg in 1914, from *The Road to Calvary* by Alexei Tolstoy.

An extraneous observer from some tree-lined provincial sidestreet, if chance brought him to Petersburg, would in moments of concentration experience a complicated feeling of intellectual stimulation and emotional depression.

Wandering along the straight and foggy streets, past gloomy houses with darkened windows and with sleepy doorkeepers at the gates; looking long at the sullen water-waste of the Neva, at the bluish lines of the bridges with their rows of lanterns lit even in daylight, at the colonnades of uncomfortable and joyless palaces, at the un Russian pile of the Cathedral of St Peter and Paul, at the miserable little boats bobbing up and down on the dark water, at the innumerable barges loaded with green wood moored along the granite embankments; peering into the pale and worried faces of passersby whose eyes were as foggy as their city – seeing and noting all this, the extraneous observer, if well-intentioned, would draw his head closer into the collar of his coat, and if disaffected would begin to think that it would be a good thing to hit out and smash all this petrified enchantment to smithereens.

Long ago, in the far-off days of Peter the Great, the verger of Holy Trinity – a church still standing near Holy Trinity Bridge – was coming down from the belfry in the twilight when he saw a banshee – a bareheaded, gaunt woman; he was very frightened and afterwards shouted at the inn: 'A desert will be in the place of Petersburg' – for which he was seized, tortured in the Secret Chancery and afterwards mercilessly knouted.

It has been the custom ever since to think that something was wrong with Petersburg. One day eye-witnesses saw the devil himself riding in a droshky on Vassilov Island. Then again, one midnight, when a gale was blowing and the river was in spate, the bronze Emperor leaped from his granite rock and galloped over the pavement stones. On another occasion a Privy Councillor riding his coach was accosted by a dead man, a dead government clerk who pressed his face to the coach window and would not let go. Many such stories were current in the city. . . .

Two centuries had passed like a dream: Petersburg, standing on the edge of the earth in swamp and wilderness, had daydreamed of boundless might and glory; palace revolts, assassinations of emperors, triumphs and bloody executions had flitted past like the visions of a delirium; feeble women had wielded semi-divine power; the fate of nations had been decided in hot and tumbled beds; vigorous strapping young fellows with hands black from tilling the soil had walked boldly up the steps of the throne to share the power, the bed and the Byzantine luxury of queens.

The neighbours looked with horror at these frantic ravings and the Russian people listened in fear and sorrow to the delirium of their capital city. The country nurtured these Petersburg wraiths with its blood but could never sate them.

Petersburg lived a restless, cold, satiated, semi-nocturnal life. Phosphorescent, crazy, voluptuous summer nights; sleepless winter nights; green tables and the clink of gold; music, whirling couples behind windows, galloping troikas, gipsies, duels at daybreak, ceremonial military parades to the whis-

tling of icy winds and the squealing of fifes, before the terri-
fying gaze of the Byzantine eyes of an Emperor – such was
the life of the city.

In the last ten years huge enterprises had sprung into being
with unbelievable rapidity. Fortunes of millions of roubles
appeared as if out of thin air. Banks, music-halls, skating
rinks, gorgeous public-houses of concrete and glass were
built, and in them people doped themselves with music, with
the reflections of many mirrors, with half-naked women,
with light, with champagne. Gambling clubs, houses of assig-
nation, theatres, picture houses, amusement parks cropped
up like mushrooms. Architects and business men were hard
at work on plans for a new capital city of unheard-of luxury,
to be built on an uninhabited island near Petersburg.

An epidemic of suicides spread through the city. The
courts were crowded with hysterical women listening eagerly
to details of bloody and prurient crimes. Everything was
accessible: the women no less than the riches. Vice was
everywhere – the imperial Palace was stricken with it as with
a plague.

Petersburg, like every other city, had a life of its own,
tense and intent. But the central force that governed its
movements was not merged with the thing that might be
called the spirit of the city. The central force strove to create
peace, order and expediency, while the spirit of the city
strove to destroy them. The spirit of destruction was everywhere; it soaked everything with its deadly poison, from the
stock exchange machinations of the notorious Sashka Sakel-
man and the sullen fury of the workmen in the steel foun-
dries to the contorted dreams of some fashionable poetress
sitting at 5 a.m. in the Bohemian basement café 'Red Jingle'.
Even those who would have fought against all this destruction merely increased it and rendered it more acute without
knowing it.

It was a time when love and all kindly and healthy feelings
were considered in bad taste and out of date. No one loved;
but all were thirsty and snatched like men poisoned at everything sharp that would rend their bowels.

Young girls were ashamed of their innocence and married
couples of their fidelity to each other. Destruction was con-

sidered in good taste and neurosis a sign of subtlety. This was the gospel taught by fashionable authors suddenly emerging from nowhere in the course of a single season. People invented vices and perversions for themselves merely to be in the swim.

Such was Petersburg in 1914. Tormented by sleepless nights, deadening its misery with wine, gold and loveless love, the shrill and feebly emotional strains of tangos for its funeral dirge, the city lived as if in expectation of a fatal and terrible day of wrath. There were auguries in plenty, and new and incomprehensible things were emerging from every cranny.

[102] *Memories of St Petersburg* by William Gerhardie, from a talk broadcast by the BBC in 1953.

When I chance to meet someone who has lived in Petersburg in the old days we touch off like this:

'And do you remember the Summer Garden?'

'Yes, yes, of course I do, and the Islands in the early autumn. That scent . . .' (associated, you perhaps reflect, with your first, and, as you then thought, your only love).

'And the white nights of Petersburg?'

'And the Palace Quay,' you interrupt, 'that long pink-granite walk beloved of Pushkin, and that quite incredibly broad Nevski Prospekt on a cold winter afternoon, and the ice in early spring moving on the river, and the quay-side private palaces jostling each other in the dusk. Blocks of ice piling on one another; above, a small fugitive red sun.'

'Oh yes, oh yes! What memories it all brings back!' . . .

But how can I speak of something, to me particular, that sounds like nothing in particular: a drive one of many to the Islands, where private carriages congregated on a Sunday afternoon in the late spring or early autumn (whereas driving up and down the full length of the Palace Quay, roughly between the Winter Palace and the British Embassy, was more of a winter pleasure). I still retain the feeling, as I alighted from my parents' carriage and stood and looked out to the Finnish Bay glowing in the evening sunlight, the feeling of bulging into open space; and, coloured by the setting sun and by a tragic sense of being fifteen and hopelessly in love with a girl of seventeen, it brings back to me the living breath of Petersburg. But how impart its essence? . . .

'And do you remember our Petersburg sunsets?' asks a Russian refugee.

'Oh, don't I!' says the other.

'The sky ashen and pink; the water a rosy mirror; the trees' silhouettes as if each cut out separately. The dark etching of the Kazan Cathedral against a pearly background . . .'

'Oh, don't speak of it! Don't. But when they light the lamps on the Troitski Bridge, what . . .?'

'And that bit of canal there by the Spasskaya . . .'

'And the heavy arch with the clock at the end of the Morskaya . . .'

'Don't!' . . .

It is a common sign of stupidity to identify one's personal nostalgia with the idea that the past must have been better than the present. Better for whom? Not necessarily even better for oneself, since nostalgia is largely independent of one's personal fortunes. 'Emotion recollected in tranquillity' is a definition of poetry, not a vindication of the past. There is a sediment of poetry in all of us, deposited without our knowing by the stream of time. It has little or nothing to do with the merits of the general social scene considered sociologically. But when the sediment is disturbed by memories it feeds our nostalgia. In dead sober mood, it must be owned that Petersburg was not without its spate of plain or ugly, vulgar, and sometimes really hideous, buildings, particularly in the meaner quarters . . .

But something of the un-Russian character of that north- ern citadel, today barely two and a half centuries old, can be gleaned from the general picture. At first it was a town of prim Hanseatic type of architecture with a few Byzantine churches with gold, onion-shaped domes thrown in for good measure. But when the female line came to the throne it took on a southern Italian magnificence. Peter's daughter, the Empress Elizabeth, for example, dissatisfied with a native architect, called in an Italian, Bartolomeo Rastrelli, and informed him that she required a number of palaces for the purpose of impressing foreign dignitaries. He set to work and produced outsize palaces and outsize churches in baroque. There was nothing Russian about them, except that parts of the interiors were executed by Russian masters who excelled in the carving of wood, stone, and ivory. Though the architect was Italian, the builder was a Russian – by name, Kvasov. Together they built the Summer Palace, the Anitschkin Palace, the Winter Palace, the Vorontsov Palace, the Smolni Monastery, and, on the outskirts, the Palace of Tsarskoye Syelo, which received Rastrelli's special attention on his receipt of the Empress Elizabeth's command: 'Transform Tsarskoye Syelo into a Russian Versailles.'

Since Elizabeth insisted that her mother's original mansion should form the nucleus of the transformation, and the grand staircase be shifted about according to her latest whim, several generations of architects at later epochs had had a go at making a decent job of this Russian Versailles, including the English architect Charles Cameron. They did their cumulative best ... But one thing, in that cold, wide, sprung, elegantly poised St Petersburg, was Russian, and Russian to the core: the harness, the style of driving. The accent was on speed. Horses snorting, reins held taut, the coachmen with their enormous cushioned and pleated bottoms built up – no less – to fill, indeed to form a single unit with, the box: the more ample the posterior, the more dashing the general turn-out. The best streets were not, like the others, cobbled. You drove over hexagonal blocks of wood fitting into a pattern, and I recall the differences in sound when, after thundering over the cobblestones, the horses plop-plopped over the wooden blocks. Again, it comes back to me, the speed of sleighs, a net fastened in front to catch the lumps of snow flying from the horses' hooves.

Select Bibliography

ADAMS, JOHN QUINCY, *The Memoirs of John Quincy Adams, comprising portions of his diary from 1795–1848*, ed. Charles Francis Adams, Philadelphia, 1874–1877.

ANSIFEROV, P., *Dusha Petersburga*, Leningrad, 1922.

BADDELEY, J.F., *Russia in the Eighties*, London, 1921.

BARRATT, GLYN, *The Rebel on the Bridge*, London, 1975.

BARROW, SIR JOHN, *Memoirs of Peter the Great*, London, 1836.

BATER, JAMES, H., *St Petersburg: Industrialisation and Change*, London, 1976.

BELY, ANDREI, *Petersburg*, transl., annotated and introduced by R. A. Maguire and John Malmstad, Sussex, 1978.

BROWN, CLARENCE, *Mandelstam*, Cambridge, 1973.

BYRON, ROBERT, *First Russia, then Tibet*, London, 1933.

CASANOVA DE SEINGALT, GIOVANNI JACOPO, *Memoirs of Jacques Casanova de Seingalt in London and Moscow*, transl. from the Italian by Arthur Machen, New York, n.d.

CATHERINE THE GREAT, *Memoirs*, transl. by Katherine Anthony, New York and London, 1927.

CHOISEUL-GOUFFIER, COUNTESS SOPHIE (DE TISENHAUS), *Historical Memoirs of the Emperor Alexander I and the Court of Russia*, transl. from the French by Mary B. Patterson, London, 1904.

CONWAY, SIR WILLIAM MARTIN, *Art Treasures in Soviet Russia*, London, 1925.

COXE, WILLIAM, *Travels into Poland, Russia, Sweden and Denmark, interspersed with historical relations and political inquiries*, Dublin, 1784.

CUSTINE, MARQUIS ASTOLPHE LOUIS LEONARD DE, *Russia, abridged from the French*, London, 1854–5.

DASHKOV, PRINCESS, E.R., *The Memoirs of Princess Dashkov*, transl. by Kyril Fitzlyon, London, 1958.

DESCARGUES, PIERRE, *The Hermitage*, transl. by K. Delavenay, London, 1961.

DISBROWE, CHARLOTTE, (ed) *Original Letters from Russia, 1825–28*, London, 1878.

— *Old Days in Diplomacy*, London, 1903.

DOSTOYEVSKY, FYODOR, *Crime and Punishment*, transl. by Constance Garnett, New York, 1963.

— *An Unpleasant Predicament*, transl. by Constance Garnett, London, 1919.

— *The Double: a Petersburg poem*, transl. by Constance Garnett, London, 1917.

GERHARDIE, WILLIAM, *Memories of St Petersburg*, radio talk reprinted in *The Listener*, 1953.

GONCHAROV, IVAN, *Oblomov*, transl. by David Magarshack, London, 1954.

GOGOL, N., *Tales of Good and Evil*, transl. by David Magarshack, London, 1949.

HAMILTON, LORD FREDERIC, *Vanished Pomps of Yesterday*, London, 1943.

— *Handbook for Travellers in Russia, Poland and Finland*, published by John Murray, London, 1875.

HERZEN, ALEXANDER, *Memoirs of the Empress Catherine II written by herself*, London, 1859.

— *My Past and Thoughts: the Memoirs of Alexander Herzen*, transl. by Constance Garnett and Humphrey Higgens, London, 1968.

HINGLEY, RONALD, *Dostoyevsky: his life and work*, London, 1978.

HOARE, SIR SAMUEL JOHN GURNEY, LLD, MP, *The Fourth Seal: the end of a Russian Chapter*, London, 1930.

JERRMANN, EDWARD, *Pictures of St Petersburg*, transl. from the German by Frederick Hardmann, London, 1852.

JOHNSTON, SIR CHARLES, *Eugene Onegin by Alexander Pushkin, a translation*, London, 1977.

KARSAVINA, TAMARA, *Theatre Street*, London, 1930.

KELLY, LAURENCE, *Lermontov: tragedy in the Caucasus*, London, 1977.

KOHL, JOHANN GEORGE, *Russia. St Petersburg, Moscow, Kharkoff, Riga, Odessa, the German provinces on the Baltic, the Steppes, the Crimea, and the interior of the Empire*, London, 1842.

KROPOTKIN, PRINCE P., *Memoirs of a Revolutionist*, London, 1899.

LEE, ROBERT, *The Last Days of Alexander and the First Days of Nicholas*, London, 1854.

LONDONDERRY, THE MARCHIONESS OF, *The Russian Journal of Lady Londonderry 1836-7*, ed by W. A. L. Seaman and J. R. Sewell, London, 1973.

LONGWORTH, PHILIP, *The Three Empresses*, London, 1972.

LOUKOMSKI, GEORGES, *Charles Cameron*, London, 1943.

MAGARSHACK, DAVID, *Pushkin*, London, 1967.

MARSDEN, CHRISTOPHER, *Palmyra of the North*, London, 1932.

MASSON, CHARLES FRANÇOIS PHILIBERT, *Mémoires Secrets sur la Russie, particulièrement sur la fin du règne de Catherine II et le commencement de celui de Paul I*, Amsterdam, 1800-3. Transl. by Marie Noële Kelly.

MAZOUR, ANATOLE, *The First Russian Revolution, 1825*, Stanford USA, 1961.

NABOKOV, VLADIMIR, *Eugene Onegin: A novel in verse by Aleksandr Pushkin*, transl. from the Russian with a Commentary by Vladimir Nabokov, London, 1975.

NIKITENKO, ALEXANDER, *The Diary of a Russian Censor*, transl. and ed by Helen Jacobson, Amherst USA, 1975.

OUDARD, G., (ed) *Lettres d'Amour de Catherine II à Potemkin*, Paris 1934. Transl. from the French by Marie Noële Kelly.

PALÉOLOGUE, MAURICE, *An Ambassador's Memoirs 1914-1917*, transl. by F. A. Holt, London, 1924-25.

PARKINSON, JOHN, *A tour of Russia, Siberia and the Crimea, 1792-1794*, ed by William Collier, London, 1971.

PUSHKIN, ALEXANDER, *The Bronze Horseman: A Tale of St*

Petersburg, a poem from *Selected Works* of Pushkin in 2 vols, transl. by Irina Zheleznova, Moscow, 1974.

—— *The Captain's Daughter*, anon translation, Moscow, 1974.

RAE, ISOBEL, *Charles Cameron*, London, 1971.

REED, JOHN, *Ten Days that Shook the World*, London, 1932.

RICHARDSON, WILLIAM, *Anecdotes of the Russian Empire. In a series of letters written a few years ago from St Petersburg*, London, 1784.

SCHERER, EDMOND, *Melchior Grimm*, ed. Calmann Lévy, Paris, 1887. Transl. by Marie Noële Kelly.

SÉGUR, COMTE LOUIS PHILIPPE DE, *1753–1832; Mémoires, ou Souvenirs et anecdotes*, Paris, 1824–26. Transl. by Marie Noële Kelly.

SITWELL, SIR SACHEVERELL, *Valse des Fleurs*, London, 1941.

STÄHLIN-STORCKBURG, J. V., *Original anecdotes of Peter the Great, collected from the conversations of several persons of distinction at Petersburg and Moscow*, London, 1788. Transl. by L. J. Richou.

STORCH, H., *Picture of Petersburg*, London, 1801.

TOLSTOY, ALEXEI, *The Road to Calvary*, transl. by Edith Bone, London, 1945.

TOLSTOY, LEO, *Anna Karenina*, transl. by David Magarshack, New York, 1961.

—— *Hadji Murad*, from *Master and Man, and other Stories*, transl. by Paul Foote, London, 1977.

VOGÜE, EUGÈNE MELCHIOR DE, *Voyageurs en Russie*, Vevey, 1947. Transl. by Laurence Kelly.

WALISZEWSKI, K., *Peter the Great*, transl. from the French by Lady Mary Lloyd, London, 1898.

WEBER, FRIEDRICH CHRISTIAN, *Mémoires pour Servir à l'Histoire de l'Empire Russien sous le Règne de Pierre le Grand*, la Haye, 1725. Transl. by Marie Noële Kelly.

WILMOT, MARTHA and CATHERINE, *The Russian Journals of Martha and Catherine Wilmot. Being an account of two Irish ladies of their adventures in Russia as guests of the celebrated Princess Daschkaw, containing vivid descriptions of contemporary court life and society, and lively anecdotes of many interesting historical characters, 1803–1808*, ed the Marchioness of Londonderry and H. M. Hyde, London, 1934.

Index